NULL SUBJECTS

The null subject has always been central to linguistic theory, because it tells us a great deal about the underlying structure of language in the human brain, and about the interface between syntax and semantics. Null subjects exist in languages such as Italian, Chinese, Russian, and Greek where the subject of a sentence can be tacitly implied, and is understood from the context. In this systematic overview of null subjects, José A. Camacho reviews the key notions of null subject analyses over the past 30 years and encompasses the most recent findings and developments. He examines a balance of data on a range of languages with null subjects and also explores how adults and children acquire the properties of null subjects. This book provides an accessible and original account of null subject phenomena, ideal for graduate students and academic researchers interested in syntax, semantics, and language typology.

JOSÉ A. CAMACHO is an Associate Professor of Linguistics at Rutgers University, New Jersey.

CAMBRIDGE STUDIES IN LINGUISTICS

General Editors: P. AUSTIN, J. BRESNAN, B. COMRIE,
S. CRAIN, W. DRESSLER, C. J. EWEN, R. LASS,
D. LIGHTFOOT, K. RICE, I. ROBERTS, S. ROMAINE,
N. V. SMITH

Null Subjects

In this series

106 SHARON INKELAS AND CHERYL ZOLL: *Reduplication: doubling in morphology*
107 SUSAN EDWARDS: *Fluent aphasia*
108 BARBARA DANCYGIER AND EVE SWEETSER: *Mental spaces in grammar: conditional constructions*
109 HEW BAERMAN, DUNSTAN BROWN AND GREVILLE G. CORBETT: *The syntax–morphology interface: a study of syncretism*
110 MARCUS TOMALIN: *Linguistics and the formal sciences: the origins of generative grammar*
111 SAMUEL D. EPSTEIN AND T. DANIEL SEELY: *Derivations in minimalism*
112 PAUL DE LACY: *Markedness: reduction and preservation in phonology*
113 YEHUDA N. FALK: *Subjects and their properties*
114 P. H. MATTHEWS: *Syntactic relations: a critical survey*
115 MARK C. BAKER: *The syntax of agreement and concord*
116 GILLIAN CATRIONA RAMCHAND: *Verb meaning and the lexicon: a first phase syntax*
117 PIETER MUYSKEN: *Functional categories*
118 JUAN URIAGEREKA: *Syntactic anchors: on semantic structuring*
119 D. ROBERT LADD: *Intonational phonology, second edition*
120 LEONARD H. BABBY: *The syntax of argument structure*
121 B. ELAN DRESHER: *The contrastive hierarchy in phonology*
122 DAVID ADGER, DANIEL HARBOUR AND LAUREL J. WATKINS: *Mirrors and microparameters: phrase structure beyond free word order*
123 NIINA NING ZHANG: *Coordination in syntax*
124 NEIL SMITH: *Acquiring phonology*
125 NINA TOPINTZI: *Onsets: suprasegmental and prosodic behaviour*
126 CEDRIC BOECKX, NORBERT HORNSTEIN AND JAIRO NUNES: *Control as movement*
127 MICHAEL ISRAEL: *The grammar of polarity: pragmatics, sensitivity, and the logic of scales*
128 M. RITA MANZINI AND LEONARDO M. SAVOIA: *Grammatical categories: variation in romance languages*
129 BARBARA CITKO: *Symmetry in syntax: merge, move and labels*
130 RACHEL WALKER: *Vowel patterns in language*
131 MARY DALRYMPLE AND IRINA NIKOLAEVA: *Objects and information structure*
132 JERROLD M. SADOCK: *The modular architecture of grammar*
133 DUNSTAN BROWN AND ANDREW HIPPISLEY: *Network morphology: a defaults-based theory of word structure*
134 BETTELOU LOS, CORRIEN BLOM, GEERT BOOIJ, MARION ELENBAAS AND ANS VAN KEMENADE: *Morphosyntactic change: a comparative study of particles and prefixes*
135 STEPHEN CRAIN: *The emergence of meaning*
136 HUBERT HAIDER: *Symmetry breaking in syntax*
137 JOSÉ A. CAMACHO: *Null subjects*

Earlier issues not listed are also available

NULL SUBJECTS

JOSÉ A. CAMACHO
Rutgers University, New Jersey

CAMBRIDGE
UNIVERSITY PRESS

CAMBRIDGE UNIVERSITY PRESS
Cambridge, New York, Melbourne, Madrid, Cape Town, Singapore,
São Paulo, Delhi, Mexico City

Cambridge University Press
The Edinburgh Building, Cambridge CB2 8RU, UK

Published in the United States of America by Cambridge University Press, New York

www.cambridge.org
Information on this title: www.cambridge.org/9781107034105

© José A. Camacho 2013

This publication is in copyright. Subject to statutory exception
and to the provisions of relevant collective licensing agreements,
no reproduction of any part may take place without the written
permission of Cambridge University Press.

First published 2013

Printed and bound in the United Kingdom by the MPG Books Group

A catalogue record for this publication is available from the British Library

Library of Congress Cataloging-in-Publication Data

Camacho, José.
  Null subjects / José A. Camacho, Rutgers University, New Jersey.
      pages cm
  Includes bibliographical references and index.
  ISBN 978-1-107-03410-5 (Hardback)
  1. Grammar, Comparative and general–Null subject. 2. Principles and parameters (Linguistics) I. Title.
  P299.N85C36 2013
  415–dc23
                                                                      2013006187

ISBN 978-1-107-03410-5 Hardback

Cambridge University Press has no responsibility for the persistence or
accuracy of URLs for external or third-party internet websites referred to in
this publication, and does not guarantee that any content on such websites is,
or will remain, accurate or appropriate.

This book is dedicated to Lucía, Yésica and Liliana

Contents

	Acknowledgements	*page* xi
	List of abbreviations	xii
1	**Introduction**	**1**
1.1	Variation and invariance in Generative Grammar	1
1.2	The Null Subject Parameter	2
1.3	Variation in the Minimalist Program	5
1.4	Macro- and micro-parameters	6
1.5	Organization of the book	8
	PART I WHAT IS THE NULL SUBJECT PARAMETER? A LITTLE HISTORY	11
2	**The Null Subject Parameter: introduction**	**13**
2.1	Syntactic properties associated with the Null Subject Parameter	13
2.2	Interpretive differences between null and overt subjects	26
2.3	Typology of Null Subject Languages	31
2.4	Chapter summary	38
3	**The core content of the Null Subject Parameter**	**39**
3.1	Introduction	39
3.2	Null thematic subjects and no null expletives	41
3.3	Subject inversion and no null expletives	50
3.4	*That*-trace effects and overt expletives	51
3.5	Free subject inversion and *that*-trace effect violations	52
3.6	Variation in logophoricity	62
3.7	Chapter summary	65
4	**The nature of the Extended Projection Principle and the Null Subject Parameter**	**67**
4.1	*Pro*	68

ix

4.2	The pronominal agreement hypothesis	76
4.3	Deletion	86
4.4	Is the Extended Projection Principle universal?	93
4.5	The revised Null Subject Parameter	105
4.6	Chapter summary	106

PART II ON IDENTIFICATION 107

5 Identification and morphology — 109
5.1	The minimal morphological threshold (MMT)	112
5.2	The structure of ϕ-features	115
5.3	Agree	120
5.4	Deriving null subjects in sample languages	124
5.5	Identification and locality	138

6 Discourse identification — 146
6.1	Topics and *pro*	146
6.2	Typology of topics	149
6.3	Topic identification in an inflection-rich null subject language	151
6.4	Subject identification in discourse null subject languages	164
6.5	Chapter summary	173

7 Null/overt subject contrasts — 174
7.1	*Pro* as a weak pronoun	175
7.2	On the difference between null and overt pronouns	177
7.3	Deriving expletives	186
7.4	Chapter summary	189

8 The status of preverbal subjects in null subject languages — 190
8.1	Preverbal subjects as CLLD phrases	192
8.2	Against PS-as-CLLD	202
8.3	The status of preverbal subjects	208
8.4	Chapter summary	208

9 Parametrization, learnability and acquisition — 210
9.1	L1 acquisition and the unmarked value of the Null Subject Parameter	211
9.2	Null subjects in early bilinguals and in L2 acquisition	220
9.3	Development of null subjects	225
9.4	General conclusions	227

References	229
Index	245

Acknowledgements

Several people have generously contributed to this book in many ways. First, I would like to thank Ursula Atkinson for help with Bavarian data, Pilar Barbosa for discussion of Portuguese data, Veneeta Dayal for Hindi data and discussion, Audrey Li for clarification on issues related to Chinese, Paco Ordóñez for discussion of Catalan data, Andrés Saab for illuminating discussion on null subjects, Vieri Samek-Lodovici for judgements and discussion of Italian data, Liliana Sánchez for help and discussion of the Quechua and Spanish data, Ur Shlonsky for discussion and comments on partial null subject languages, Luis Silva-Villar for discussion on expletives in Western Iberian dialects and Jacqueline Toribio for a generous supply of Dominican Spanish data and discussion of their meaning. Additionally, José Elías-Ulloa was instrumental in obtaining judgements to confirm patterns in Shipibo. I am very grateful to three anonymous reviewers, who provided useful feedback, and to Neil Smith, who carefully read the manuscript and suggested very insightful additions and changes to it. On the technical side, the Ling-Tex user group has been a vital source of wisdom to make things look they way I wanted them to look, in particular Alexis Dimitriadis and Alan Munn, who frequently and quickly responded to queries about LaTeX. Two of Alexis' macros have made the layout of this book much easier.

This book is the result of a general project on null subjects, parts of which have been presented at the University of Geneva, Romania Nova 2010 (Campos do Jordão), the University of Campinas, the University of Rio de Janeiro, Brazil. I wish to thank Paco Ordóñez and Mary Kato for the wonderful opportunity to present at Romania Nova and Campinas, and Maria Eugênia Duarte and Marcus Maia, for the unforgettable invitation to visit and present at UFRJ.

Abbreviations

1	first person or class 1
2	second person or class 2
3	third person or class 3
ABS	absolutive case
ACC	accusative case
ADD	additive
ADDR	addressee
AGR	agreement
ASP	aspect
AUX	auxiliary
BP	Brazilian Portuguese
C	complementizer agreement
CAUS	causative
CCS	Central Colombian Spanish
CL	clitic
COND	conditional
CONTR	contrastive
COP	copula
CP	complementizer phrase
DAT	dative case
DEF	definite
DESID	desiderative
DIR	directional case
DS	Dominican Spanish
DSEC	Dominican Spanish from El Cibao
EP	European Portuguese
ERG	ergative
EXCL	exclusive
EXP	expletive
EVID	evidential
FEM	feminine
FOC	focus
FORM	formal
FUT	future tense
FV	final vowel

GEN	genitive
HON	honorific
HRSAY	hearsay
IMP	imperfect tense
IMPER	imperative
IMPERF	imperfective aspect
INAN	inanimate
INC	incompletive aspect
INCL	inclusive
INE	inessive case
INTEN	intensifier
INTIM	intimate
IRR	irrealis mood
MAS	masculine
MIN	minimal
MOD	modal
NEG	negation
NEUT	neuter
NOM	nominative case
NON-FORM	non-formal
NSL	null subject language
OBJ	object
ONOM	onomatopoeia
OP	operator
OPC	Overt Pronoun Constraint
OPT	optative
P	person
PART	participant
PASS	passive
PERF	perfective aspect
ϕP	ϕ-feature phrase
PL	plural
PRED	predicative
PRES	present tense
PRIOR	prior
PROG	progressive aspect
PROPOS	propositive
Q	question marker
REFLEX	reflexive
RI	root infinitive
S	subject agreement
SG	singular
SPECIF	specific
SPKR	speaker
SS	same subject

SUBJ	subject
TEP	totally empty position
TNS	tense
TOP	topic
TR	transitive
ZG	Zurich German

1 *Introduction*

1.1 Variation and invariance in Generative Grammar

Perhaps one of the most revolutionary tenets that Generative Grammar assumed from its outset was the idea that all languages share common underlying grammatical features, a belief that helped address the puzzling way in which children learn languages. In particular, as Chomsky has repeatedly observed (see Chomsky, 1975, 1988, for example), children learn grammatical rules and patterns for which they have little, confusing and sometimes contradictory evidence (the so-called poverty of stimulus or Plato's problem). Furthermore, they do not assume certain grammatical rules that could be generalized from the available data.[1] Chomsky has concluded from these observations that much of the grammatical knowledge we have must be innate, and that the grammars of languages are much closer to each other than it would seem at first sight. Both of these conclusions together suggest an explanation for why the acquisition process seems so effortless and on target: if children come with an innate predisposition for languages that contains fairly specific and delimited principles, then they can simply make sense of the linguistic input around them, guided by such innate principles. The tenet that languages are underlyingly close has led to important discoveries about similarities in apparently very different patterns across languages.

While languages may show surprisingly similar abstract patterns, we also observe obvious surface variation. For example, aspect plays a comparatively small role in the verbal morphology of English compared to the elaborate aspectual distinctions of the Russian paradigm. This tension between underlying similarity and surface variation has been formalized in many different ways over the years. In the 1980s framework of Generative Grammar, principles represented the invariant component of languages and parameters the variation dimension.

---

[1] Needless to say, the poverty-of-stimulus argument remains a controversial issue in the broader cognitive-science community.

2   *Introduction*

To take a particular example of this approach, English or Spanish speakers usually ask questions by displacing the question-word to the beginning of the clause, whereas Chinese speakers leave those questions words in the same position as in a declarative, as we see in (1)–(2).

(1) ¿A quién piensa Pedro que viste?   (Spanish)
     to whom thinks Pedro that saw.2SG
     'Who does Pedro think that you saw?'

(2) Zhangsan yiwei Lisi mai-le **shinwe**   (Chinese)
     Zhangsan thinks Lisi bought what?
     'What does Zhangsan think Lisi bought?'

Closer examination of these languages suggested that both types have similar properties, and that the difference may be related to the stages of the derivation (see Huang, 1982): English and Spanish displace the question-word before the question is overtly pronounced, whereas Chinese does so after it is overtly pronounced, at the level of Logical Form (LF). Thus, an invariant principle (question-words must take scope over the clause) can be expressed in two ways: through overt or covert movement.[2] While the validity of the generalization proposed by Huang has subsequently been challenged, it exemplifies well the overall research strategy within the generative paradigm, as well as a specific formulation of how a common underlying principle can yield superficial variation through a parameter.

As noted, having a common underlying principle with a limited range of variation facilitates the process of L1 acquisition: if the child's knowledge includes the notion that question-words must take scope over the rest of the clause, determining whether they move overtly or covertly becomes a matter of processing the available input.

Within the Principles and Parameters version of the 1980s, the Null Subject Parameter (NSP) was one of the most studied and formalized instances of invariance~variation. This parameter tried to account for the fact that subjects are obligatorily overt in some languages but not in others.

1.2 The Null Subject Parameter

The NSP attempts to provide a unified analysis for the observation that clauses require obligatorily overt subjects in some languages like French and English but not in others (Spanish, Irish, Italian, Chinese), as illustrated in (3)–(4).

---

[2] In more recent theoretical approaches, the difference can be cast in terms of where the copy of the question-word surfaces overtly.

(3) a. We left.
  b. * Left

(4) a. Chuirfeadh Eoghan isteach ar an phost sin. (Irish)
    put.COND. Owen in   on that job
    'Owen would apply for that job.'
                (from McCloskey and Hale, 1984, 490, ex. 4)
  b. Chuirfidís   isteach ar an phost sin. (Irish)
    put.3.PL.COND in   on that job
    'They would put in on that job.'

One could simply propose a typological description of this difference along the lines of (5). While this is a reasonable statement of the facts, it raises some questions, such as why speakers interpret *chuirfeadh* 'would put' in (3b) as having the same type of subject (agent, theme) as in (3a), regardless of whether the actual subject is present or absent.

(5) Languages of the world vary among those that have obligatory subjects and those that have optional subjects.

An alternative approach is to assume that clauses in all languages have subjects and the variation comes from whether the overt expression of that subject is obligatory or not. The explicit formalization of this proposal was initially formulated as the **Projection Principle** (Chomsky, 1981, 38), a principle that suggests that the lexical properties of the words determine the shape of a clause throughout its derivation. For example, a transitive verb like *eat* is marked in the lexicon as assigning two theta roles, so it will require two syntactic arguments (subject and object) to realize those theta roles and those arguments must be realized at all times. In other words, if a given head is lexically specified as assigning a theta role, that role must be assigned to a syntactically realized constituent, and this constituent must be present at all levels of representation.

The Projection Principle makes thematic subjects obligatory in all clauses in all languages because a verb like *chuirfeadh* 'would put' in (4) assigns a theta role, hence it must have a syntactic argument to bear that role, regardless of whether it is overt or null, otherwise the Projection Principle will be violated.[3]

This formulation does not account for why syntactic subjects seem to be obligatory in languages like English even when the subject is semantically vacuous, as in (6)–(7). Since *seem* in (6a) does not assign an interpretation

---

[3] The Projection Principle does not directly derive the requirement that the subject appear in Spec, IP. In the Principles and Parameters framework, this is a by-product of the fact that nominative case was assigned in Spec, IP.

(i.e. a theta role) to its subject, the Projection Principle does not require an overt argument; however, the absence of the expletive *it* renders the example ungrammatical, as seen in (6b).

(6) a. It seems to be raining.
     b. * Seems to be raining.

The situation is slightly different for the expletive in (7a): the verb *surprise* does assign two theta roles, one of them to the indirect object *me*, the other to the clause *that you couldn't finish your meal*, but the expletive in the preverbal subject position arguably does not receive a separate theta role. In fact, when the clausal subject appears initially, as in (7b), the expletive is no longer possible. This suggests that the clause is the thematic subject both in (7a) and (7b), and that the expletive is somehow doubling that subject in (7a). Likewise, it shows that the presence of the expletive in (7a) is not related to the Projection Principle, since the subject theta role is assigned to the clause.

(7) a. It surprised me [that you couldn't finish your meal].
     b. [That you couldn't finish your meal] surprised me.

The facts just described regarding expletives led to the principle in (8), which essentially captures the fact that even non-theta-assigning verbs require an overt expletive subject in English and other languages. The qualification that the subject must be in Spec, IP is meant to derive the difference between (7a) and (7b). In the first case, the clausal subject is not in Spec, IP, therefore an expletive is required.

(8) All clauses must have a subject (in Spec, IP).

The Projection Principle (the requirement that thematic arguments be present throughout the derivation) and the requirement that clauses have subjects constitute the **Extended Projection Principle** (EPP) (see Chomsky, 1986, 116 and Svenonius, 2002, 9 for a summary), although EPP is frequently used with the more restricted meaning that clauses require subjects.

Once one assumes a principle like the EPP, it follows that languages are much more similar than what (5) would suggest, and it also follows that clauses don't really ever lack a subject, they simply have ones that are syntactically present but not overtly realized. In this way, the examples in (4a–b) and (3a) above have similar underlying representations, perhaps along the lines of (9). In (9a), *pro* represents a null subject in Irish, and it appears in the position where overt subjects usually appear in that language.

(9) a. chuirfidís *pro*.
     b. We left.

Once one assumes some invariant principle like the EPP, the research questions shift in a completely different direction: given that English-like and Irish-like languages are substantially identical at the level of semantic representation, what is it that allows Irish to have a null subject? As we will see below, many answers have been given to this question, but one traditional and influential intuition was that the inflectional information on the verb identifies the null subject in the Irish example but not in the English ones. Irish is particularly suggestive in this respect, because it has two types of tenses, those that have distinctive person and number morphology and those that do not. Null subjects are only possible with those that have distinctive morphology (see McCloskey and Hale, 1984).

1.3   Variation in the Minimalist Program

With the advent of the Minimalist Program (MP) in the early 1990s (Chomsky, 1993 and much subsequent work), much of the theoretical machinery that made it possible to express parametric variation was eliminated. Given the stated goal of simplifying the overall theoretical model, parameters no longer have an independent place in accounting for variation across grammars. Rules or principles that only apply at certain levels of representation are also avoided. As a result, the analysis of overt/covert wh-movement suggested in previous sections would need to be retooled because it relies on different levels of representation. Rather, the MP restricts variation to two perhaps related sources: differences in specifications of lexical items and where copies of items surface. For example, in early minimalist formulations, the difference between verb movement in French and English was related to the strength of a lexical feature of inflection, which resulted in attracting the verb in French but not in English. Feature strength is a property of individual lexical entries (in this case inflection). In the case of wh-movement in English vs. Chinese, the difference is not whether the wh-word moves earlier or later: it moves in both languages at the same time, but in English the lower copy of that movement is deleted, whereas in Chinese, the lower copy remains.

Over the past several years, other theoretical constructs have changed radically. The notion of agreement has become central in articulating syntactic relationships between constituents, but unlike in earlier versions, agreement is disconnected from movement in recent proposals (see Hornstein, 2009 and most specifically Linares, 2012), so that two elements can agree at a distance. As a result, the triggers for constituent movement are now even less obvious than before, and in general they have been subsumed under the notion of EPP features, a shorthand term for describing that a constituent has moved.

All of these changes have forced researchers to undertake a radical revision of the NSP within minimalist ideas: from proposals that eliminate *pro* as an independent theoretical construct to revisions and parametrization of the EPP (Alexiadou and Anagnostopoulou, 1998; Tomioka, 1999; Ordóñez and Treviño, 1999; Manzini and Savoia, 2002; Holmberg, 2005; Saab, 2009; Barbosa, 2009; Biberauer *et al.*, 2010; Sigurðsson, 2011 among many others). Extending empirical coverage of the null subject phenomenon outside of the better-known cases has been less of a concern, with some important exceptions. One of them relates to the evolution of NS varieties into overt-subject grammars in cases such as European and Brazilian Portuguese (Kato, 1999, 2000; Duarte, 2000; Kato and Negrão, 2000; Modesto, 2000, 2008; Barbosa *et al.*, 2005; Camacho, 2008, 2010a), and Caribbean and non-Caribbean Spanish (Cabrera, 2007; Camacho, 2008, 2010a), as well as other languages or constructions (Cole, 2000, 2009; Nicolis, 2008; Holmberg *et al.*, 2009; Shlonsky, 2009; Camacho and Elías-Ulloa, 2010; Roberts, 2010b; Camacho, 2011).

1.4 Macro- and micro-parameters

The original formulation of the NSP illustrates a very broad parameter that narrows down the possibilities offered by Universal Grammar. In some sense, one can view these macro-parameters as dividing languages from the top down, and having consequences over large sets of grammars. For example, as Baker (2008a) suggests, there might be a single parameter that will distinguish between head-initial vs. head-final languages, or another one that will separate non-configurational polysynthetic languages from configurational, isolating ones. Furthermore, macro-parameters provide a natural framework to explain the process of first language acquisition, because they allow for a 'cascade effect' (see Smith and Law, 2007): once a macro-parameter is set, many others may follow without further input. For example, if a language is head-initial, the child will only need to learn that parameter once, and not individually for each category.

The original view of macro-parameters has faced the inexorable results of research over the past few decades. In the words of Pica (2001, v–vi): "Twenty years of intensive descriptive and theoretical research has shown, in our opinion, that such meta-parameters [e.g. the Null-Subject Parameter, or the Polysynthesis Parameter] do not exist, or, if they do exist, should be seen as artifacts of the 'conspiracy' of several micro-parameters." In this view, parameters determine variation in a small scale, and even when it seems that they apply to large-scale differences, that is only because of the cumulative effect of several micro-parameters. This perspective, which Baker (2008b, 156) calls the Borer–Chomsky conjecture, is instantiated in the idea "that all parameters of variation are attributable to differences in the features of particular items (e.g. the functional heads) in the lexicon."

Baker (2008a) points out that if only macro-parameters existed, languages should cluster around a positive or negative value of the parameter, with nothing in between, and with no mixed cases. However, this is obviously not the case for any of the proposed macro-parameters. For example, very few if any languages are consistently head-initial or head-final in all possible instances, as one would expect from a macro-parametric setting. Rather, they vary with respect to directionality depending on the type of category, or depending on a subset of items within a category (for example unergative vs. unaccusative verbs).

Another argument against the macro-parametric view comes from the idea that they can be reduced to a generalized set of micro-parameters. For example, Kayne (2005, 7) suggests that "the systematic obligatoriness of pronominal agreement morphemes in Mohawk is just an extreme example of what is found to a lesser extent in (some) Romance."

However, Baker (2008a) points out that if all variation is micro-parametric, we should find a full range of variation depending on how widely the micro-parameter extends across categories. As a result, we should have languages that generalize the micro-parameter to all possible categories (like polysynthesis in Mohawk) on one extreme, and languages where we only find it in a few constructions, at the other extreme, with all different possibilities in the middle. What we shouldn't find in principle is languages that cluster along one or another point in the continuum. Thus, there is no particular reason why a language should show head-initial features on all prepositions, or on N–Adjective combinations, since these outcomes would simply be the result of a collection of potentially independent micro-parameters. This observation leads Baker to argue both for macro- and micro-parameters: macro-parameters determine clusters of identical patterns and micro-parameters show some degree of variation at the edges of those clusters.

The position we will develop in this book is that the cluster of properties initially correlated with the NSP do not form a macro-parameter in the above sense. Rather, the essential correlation we will sustain is that inflectional richness (defined in terms of morphological structure) will determine whether a language has or lacks NSs. In some sense this is a macro-parameter, although, as we will see, it is not of the yes/no variety, but rather a scale along which languages define the possibility of having NSs. This second sense (the point in the scale at which individual languages define the possibility of having NSs) can be seen as a micro-parameter. As we will see, this view also includes languages like Chinese, which have null subjects but no inflection to identify them.

1.5 Organization of the book

Baker (2008a) notes that "History has not been kind to the Pro-drop Parameter as originally stated." However, from a certain point of view, the evolution of the NSP presents an ideal illustration of how theory can change in a dynamically developing discipline such as linguistics, and of how theory can trigger a wealth of empirical discoveries that, in turn, force changes in the initial proposals. From this point of view, examining the evolution of the NSP can be an important lesson in the challenges and achievements of theoretically driven linguistic research. With this perspective in mind, the first part of this book introduces the core properties of the NSP. Chapter 2 presents the syntactic and interpretive properties originally associated with the parameter, as well as the general typology of null subject languages. Chapter 3 reviews what some of the leading proposals on NSs predict regarding the association of those core properties. As we will see, not all of those properties ended up correlating with the availability of NSs. Chapter 4 introduces existing proposals on how the EPP is satisfied in null-subject languages (NSLs). Specifically, I will review approaches that endorse the independent availability of a null pronoun *pro*, those that assume that *pro* does not exist, but rather that subject-properties are encoded in verbal inflection (the pronominal agreement hypothesis), and those that suggest that *pro* is the product of ellipsis.

By the end of the first part, I hope to have a clear picture of the essential properties of the NSP, the minimal syntactic primitives required to account for them, and also an illustration of the rapidly evolving, sometimes contradictory nature of theory-construction within generative grammar.

In Part II, I address the issue of how NSs are identified. Chapter 5 discusses NSs identification in connection with overt morphological inflection, and Chapter 6 looks at discourse identification when morphology fails. Chapter 7 considers a number of instances where the null/overt contrast determines the distribution of subjects, and Chapter 8 examines the parallelism between overt subjects and dislocated elements. Finally, Chapter 9 introduces research related to acquisition of NSs and how the theory presented in the rest of the book interacts with those findings.

This book presupposes a basic understanding of linguistic theory although I have tried to explain all concepts as clearly as possible. Some background in generative linguistics is helpful but not absolutely required.

PART I
What is the Null Subject Parameter? A little history

2 *The Null Subject Parameter: introduction*

2.1 Syntactic properties associated with the Null Subject Parameter

As I mentioned in the introductory chapter, the NSP derives from the idea that clauses in all languages have subjects (the EPP in (8), Section 1.2). Languages that apparently lack subjects actually have null versions of them (both thematic and expletive), and this parametric setting correlates with a cluster of syntactic properties. The six properties initially related to the NSP included (a) having null subjects, (b) having null resumptive pronouns, (c) having free inversion in simple sentences, (d) availability of 'long wh-movement' of subjects, (e) availability of empty resumptive pronouns in embedded clauses and (f) presence of overt complementizers in *that*-trace contexts (Perlmutter, 1971; Chomsky and Lasnik, 1977; Kayne, 1980; Taraldsen, 1980; Jaeggli, 1982; Rizzi, 1982; Safir, 1985; Jaeggli and Safir, 1989). In addition, null and overt subjects are interpreted differently in NSLs (see Montalbetti, 1984, among others). In this section, we will review and exemplify the different properties associated with the NSP.

2.1.1 Null subjects

As expected, NSLs have null subjects. In languages like Chamorro and Irish, subjects must be null when the verb shows person subject agreement. Thus, in the Chamorro example in (1a), the pronoun *gui'* cannot appear because the verb agrees with the subject in person and number, whereas in (1b), the verb agrees in number but not in person, so the subject can be overt or null (see Chung, 1998, 30–31). In other languages like Spanish or Quechua, overt pronouns are not constrained by inflectional morphology in the way they are in Chamorro. For example, in (2), the pronoun *nosotros* can be present or absent, depending on certain discourse conditions. Likewise, the Quechua examples in (3) show that the subject *Huwan* can be overt or null, although (3c) with an overt pronoun would require a very specific context for the overt pronoun to be pragmatically appropriate.[1]

(1)   a. Ha-fahan *pro*/*gui' i   lepblu.
             AGR-buy   he   the book
             'He bought the book'

        b. Täi-mamahlao   (hao)!   (Chamorro)
             AGR.not.have-shame you
             'You're shameless.'   (from Chung, 1998, 30–31 ex. 19b–20b)

(2)   a. Salimos.   (Spanish)
             left
             'We left.'

        b. Nosotros salimos.
             we   left
             'We left.'

(3)   a. Huwan-mi   papa-ta   mikhu-n.   (Quechua)
             Huwan-FOC/EVID potato-ACC eat-3.SG
             'Huwan eats potatoes (attested).'

        b. Papa-ta   mikhu-n-mi.
             potato-ACC eat-3.SG-FOC/EVID
             'S/he eats potatoes.'   (from Sánchez, 2010, 24)

        c. Pay-mi   papa-ta   mikhu-n.
             3.SG-FOC/EVID potato-ACC eat-3.SG
             'S/he eats potatoes.'

Subjects can be thematic or expletive, and some languages allow both types of subjects to be null, or just one of them. Thus, in principle we find four possible combinations of null/overt and expletive/thematic, although languages with null thematic subjects and overt expletives are rare. Whether this scarcity is accidental or reflects some deeper property of grammars remains to be seen.

(a)   Null thematic subjects/null expletive subjects

Spanish, Chamorro and Quechua have both null thematic subjects (illustrated above) and null expletives, seen in (4)–(6). These examples also illustrate an asymmetry between expletive and thematic subjects: whereas thematic subjects can be null or overt in Spanish, there are no overt expletives

---

[1] Each example in (3) has a different assertion structure: in the first one, *Huwan* is focused, in the second one, the whole clause has wide focus.

2.1 Syntactic properties associated with the Null Subject Parameter

corresponding to English *it* (cf. (4a) vs. (4b)).² As with Spanish (4a), the Chamorro example in (5) illustrates a use of a weather-verb like *uchan* 'rain' without any overt expletive. Finally, example (6) illustrates the same point for Quechua: No overt pronoun or deictic can appear with a weather verb.

(4)   a. *pro* nieva.   (Spanish)
           snows
           'It is snowing.'

      b. * Ello nieva.
           it   snows
           'It is snowing.'

(5)   Kao [put fin] um-uchan?   (Chamorro)
      Q   by   end AGR-rain
      'Did it rain in the end?'   (from Chung, 1998, 337)

(6)   a. *pro* para-chka-n-mi.   (Quechua)
           pro rain-PROG-3.SG-FOC/EVID
           'It is raining.'

      b. * Pay/*Kay para-chka-n-mi.
           (s)he/this rain-PROG-3.SG-FOC/EVID
           'It is raining.'   (from Sánchez, 2010, 24)

(b)   Overt thematic subjects/null expletive subjects

In Cape York Creole, thematic subjects are overt but expletives are null, as shown in (7) and (8). The first example illustrates a verb that assigns a theta role to its subject, and has an overt subject *mi* 'I'. The second example shows a verb that does not assign a theta role to its subject, but can appear without an overt subject.³

(7)   Mi ran.   (Cape York Creole)
      I   run
      'I am running.'   (from Crowley and Rigsby, 1979, 187)

(8)   (I) rein.   (Cape York Creole)
      3   rain
      'It is raining.'   (from Crowley and Rigsby, 1979, 187)

---

² Example (4b) is grammatical in El Cibao varieties of Dominican Spanish, see Section 3.2.1.
³ According to Crowley and Rigsby (1979), *i* is a 3rd p. agreement marker, which is almost obligatory for some speakers in all 3rd p. contexts. The 3rd p. pronoun is *im*.

(c)   Null thematic subjects/overt expletives

In Finnish, thematic subjects can be null whereas some expletives are obligatorily overt. Thus, the subject *minä* 'I' is optional in (9), but the overt expletive *sitä* is obligatory in (10).[4]

(9)   (Minä) puhun   englantia.   (Finnish)
        (I)   speak.PL English
        'I speak English.'   (from Holmberg, 2005, 539-540)

(10)   a. * Leikkii lapsia   kadulla.   (Finnish)
           play   children in-street
           'There are children playing in the street.'

        b. Sitä leikkii lapsia   kadulla.
           EXP play   children in-street
           'There are children playing in the street.'
                                        (from Holmberg and Nikkane, 2002, 71–72)

(d)   Overt thematic subjects/overt expletive subjects

This last possibility is illustrated by English or French, which require overt subjects in both types of clauses (pronominal *elle* and expletive *il* respectively in French), although in diary register certain subjects can be dropped (see Haegeman, 1990 and Section 9.1 below):

(11)   a. Elle arrive demain.   (French)
           she arrives tomorrow
           'She's arriving tomorrow.'

        b. * Arrive demain.
             arrives tomorrow
             'She/He's arriving tomorrow.'

(12)   a. Il   pleut beaucoup içi.   (French)
           EXP rains a lot   here
           'It rains a lot here.'

        b. * Pleut beaucoup içi.
             rains a lot   here
             'It rains a lot here.'

Thus, in principle all combinations of null/overt and thematic/expletive are possible. However, there are further distinctions in the typology of both expletive and thematic subjects, which I will explore in turn.

---

[4] I will return to additional complications in the full distribution of expletives in Finnish in Section 4.2.4. For illustrative purposes, these examples should suffice for now.

2.1.2 Typology of null expletive subjects

The paradigm given in the previous section is more complicated than its presentation suggests. Svenonius (2002, 5–7) notes that some expletives may be quasi-referential, so that the full taxonomy can be divided into two major classes: expletives that have some kind of referential capability, and those that are completely referentially empty. Among the first type, he quotes weather-verb and extraposition expletives, illustrated in (13)–(14) respectively. The second type includes presentational/impersonal expletives, illustrated in (15)–(16).

(13) Aquí *pro* siempre llueve.   Quasi-referential expl. (Spanish)
      here *pro* always rains
      'Here it always rains.'

(14) It surprised me [that Santos won]   Extraposition expl. (English)

(15) *pro* parece que sabe   la verdad.   Raising expl. (Spanish)
      pro seems that knows the truth
      'It seems that s/he knows the truth.'

(16) *pro* hay unos visitantes en la puerta.   Existential expl. (Spanish)
      pro are some visitors   in the door
      'There are some visitors at the door.'

Chomsky (1981, 323–325) argues that weather-verb expletives like *it* are quasi-argumental because they can control an infinitival subject, as illustrated in (17). In the English example, the argument goes, the subject of the first clause determines the 'content' of the second subject. In the second example from Hungarian, the null subject of 'clouded' also determines the content of the 'causing an early twilight.'

(17) a. It often clears up here right after snowing heavily.
                                              (from Svenonius, 2002, 6, ex. 5a)
      b. Korai szürkületet okozva befelhösödött.   (Hungarian)
         early twilight.ACC causing clouded
         'It clouded, causing early twilight.' (from Kiss, 2002, 119, ex. 39a)

These two examples contrast with an expletive like *there*, which cannot control a subject, as seen in (18a). Furthermore, the difference between *it* and *there* is independent of the construction they appear in, since control is possible with *this* in a similar context, as seen in (18b). This contrast between (18a) and (18b) suggests that the referential properties of the expletive determine control, not necessarily the type of expletive construction.

18 *The Null Subject Parameter: introduction*

(18) a. * There is often a party here right before being a wake.
(from Svenonius, 2002, 6, ex. 5b)
b. This is often a gathering place before being a hiring place.

I don't think the examples in (17) show that the expletive has referential content, or that a theta role is assigned to the expletive, in particular because it is not clear what that content or theta role would be. Although the snowing event and the event of clearing up are intuitively connected in some sense in (17a), it is less clear that the subject of *clearing up* controls (i.e. has the same reference as) the subject of *snowing heavily*. The same objection holds for the relationship between *clouding* and *causing early twilight* in (17b).

In addition to the distinction between quasi-referential and non-thematic expletives, languages show different expletives depending on the construction, as pointed out by Nicolis (2005, 2008) and Sheehan (2007, ch. 5). Romance-based creoles are especially interesting, as seen in the table in (19), from Sheehan (2007, 240) (adapted from Nicolis, 2005).[5]

(19) Null expletives in Romance-based Creoles.

	Quasi-ref.	Extraposition	Raising	Exist.
Kriyol	overt	overt?	optional	overt
Haitian	optional	overt	null	null
Mauritian	DP	optional?	overt	overt
Cape Verdean	null	null	null	null
Papiamentu	null	null	null	null

Finnish is somewhat similar to Haitian Creole, since expletives are optional with weather verbs and extraposed subjects and possibly existential ones as well. Specifically, Holmberg and Nikkane (2002) note that Finnish has examples like (20), where the verb is clause-initial and no expletive is required. These examples contrast with (10a) above, where the expletive is obligatory (if nothing else appears in first position).

---

[5] Question marks indicate that data are inconclusive. Sheehan does not explain what a quasi-referential DP is in Mauritian, but Nicolis (2008, 278) suggests Mauritian has null expletive subjects.

(20) a. On ilmennyt ongelmia. (Finnish)
  have appeared problems
  'Problems have appeared.'

 b. Sattui onnettomuus.
  occurred (an) accident
  'An accident occurred.'

 c. Tuli kiire.
  came haste
  'We/they are in a hurry.'

 d. Oli hauskaa että tulit käymään.
  was nice that came-2.SG visiting
  'It was nice that you came by.'

(from Holmberg and Nikkane, 2002, ex. 19)

Holmberg and Nikkane (2002) account for this difference by making the EPP feature optional (i.e. the feature that triggers overt movement of a constituent to the clause-initial position). If this feature is optional, the structures of the examples in (20) will not require overt movement of any constituent to clause-initial position. This movement, in turn, is related to the focus structure of the clause, in particular, it licenses constituents that are marked as [-focus]. Thus, in (10a) above, movement is obligatory (because the EPP feature is present) and it licenses the [-focus] nature of the moved constituent. In their analysis, Finnish is a topic-oriented language, which triggers the need to have an overt constituent preceding the verb in most circumstances.

German presents a slightly more complicated picture, as Sheehan (2007, 239–240) notes: expletives are required with meteorological verbs but not with existentials. Thus, the weather-verb *regnen* 'to rain' obligatorily appears with the expletive *es*, as seen in the contrast between (21a)–(21b). On the other hand, an existential clause can appear with the expletive *es*, as in (22a) or without it (cf. (22b)). In the latter case, the adverbial *vor der Tür* 'in front of the tower' fulfills the constraint against having the verb in first position.

(21) a. Gestern regnete es. (German)
  yesterday rained EXP
  'Yesterday it rained'

 b. * Gestern regnete.
  yesterday rained
  'Yesterday it rained.' (from Sheehan, 2007, 239–240)

(22)   a. Es   steht ein Mann vor   der Tür.   (German)
         there stood a   man   in-front-of the tower
         'There stood a man in front of the tower.'

       b. Vor   der Tür   steht (*es) ein Mann.
          in-front-of the tower stood EXP a   man
          'There stood a man in front of the tower.'

(from Sheehan, 2007, 239–240)

From these data, we can conclude that the connection between null argument subjects and null expletives is not direct, and that the availability of null argumental subjects is neither a necessary nor a sufficient condition for null expletives: Finnish has null argumental subjects in certain circumstances, but overt expletives are obligatory in certain cases.

2.1.3   Free Subject Inversion

Languages like Spanish or Italian have a default, unmarked word order SVO that is most compatible with discourse contexts where no part of the clause is focused. However, these languages also display an alternative VS word order in declarative sentences, that may be associated with distinct assertion structures (see Zubizarreta, 1998). This alternative word order is illustrated in (23), where the verb appears in first position.

(23)   a. Habló Marta.   (Spanish)
          spoke Marta
          'Marta spoke.'

       b. Mangia Gianni.   (Italian)
          eats   Gianni
          'Gianni eats.'

The availability of an alternative word order has been claimed to be the defining property of the NSP (see Chomsky, 1981; 253–255; Rizzi, 1982; Burzio, 1986, ch. 2.2). According to Rizzi, the three other properties to be discussed below follow from the fact that NSL like Italian or Spanish have an available postverbal subject position, which is precisely the one occupied by the subject in (23).

2.1.4   Null resumptive pronouns

Examples like (24) illustrate another property that distinguishes NSLs from overt subject languages. This example involves a DP with a relative clause, and the antecedent (*la mujer* 'the woman') of the relative clause is interpreted

2.1 Syntactic properties associated with the Null Subject Parameter

as the subject of the most embedded clause *que no venga* 'that not come'. The long-distance link between the antecedent and the null position inside the embedded clause, illustrated in (24b), crosses a wh-island (headed by *quién* 'who'), and under normal circumstances, this wh-island should prevent such a long-distance link. In fact, the English counterpart of (24a) is ungrammatical, as seen in (25).

(24)   a. Esta es la mujer que me pregunto [quién cree [que no venga]]
            this is the woman who CL wonder who thinks that not come
            'This is the woman that I wonder who believes might not come.'
     b. la mujer [$_{CP}$ OP$_i$ [$_{IP}$ I+V [$_{CP}$ quién cree [$_{CP}$ que [$_{IP}$ t_i no venga]]]]]

(25)   * This is the woman that I wonder who believes might come.

On the other hand, if the subject of *venga* 'come' is a null resumptive subject, as shown in (26a), there would be no violation of the wh-island extraction constraint because there would be no extraction. In that sense, the null resumptive parallels the overt subject we find in English in (26b). Since English lacks null resumptive pronouns, the non-movement strategy is not available in (25).[6]

(26)   a. Esta es la mujer [OP que me pregunto [quién cree [que *pro* no venga.]]
     b. This is the woman that I wonder who she believes might come.

2.1.5   Violation of the that-trace filter

The *that*-trace filter attempts to formalize asymmetries in subject and object questions in English, specifically when the question-word is extracted across more than one clause (i.e. long-distance wh-movement). This context is illustrated in (27a), where the wh-word *who* relates to the embedded verb *meet*. In this context, whenever the complementizer is overt (i.e. *that*), questions about objects are possible (as in (27a)), but questions about subjects are not, as seen in (27b) (see van Riemsdijk and Williams, 1986, 161–163).

(27)   a. Who do you think that he will meet?
     b. * Who do you think that will meet Jim?

If the complementizer is deleted, both subjects and objects can be extracted, as observed in (28). Chomsky and Lasnik (1977) formalized this contrast as the

---

[6] Although this presentation doesn't directly link the availability of a null subject with the availability of a postverbal position, such an analysis is feasible.

***that*-trace filter** (cf. (29)), a filter that bans configurations such as (27b) with a wh-trace in COMP and an overt complementizer *that*.[7]

(28)   a. Who do you think will meet Jim?
           b. Who do you think he will meet?

(29)   *That*-trace filter
        *[S_i that [$_{NP}e$] ...],
        unless S_i (or its trace) is in the context [$_{NP}$ _ NP ...]

Cowart (1997) has confirmed the existence of *that*-trace effects experimentally. Specifically, in one of his studies, he found that speakers judged sentences with object extraction much more acceptable than those with subject extraction when *that* was overt.[8] In another study, he found that acceptability varies across embedding verbs (for example *suppose* vs. *hear*).

NSLs do not show *that*-trace asymmetries, as Perlmutter (1971) discovered. Thus, (30a) is grammatical, and in fact, the complementizer cannot be deleted, as seen in (30b).

(30)   a. ¿Quién piensa-s   que vendrá?   (Spanish)
            who   think-2.SG that will come
            'Who do you think that will come?'
        b. * ¿Quién piensa-s   vendrá?
            who   think-2.SG will come
            'Who do you think that will come?'

The *that*-trace asymmetry between English and Italian/Spanish was linked to the idea that NSs in NSLs are generated in postverbal position. For example, Jaeggli (1980, 261) argues that the grammaticality of (30a) follows from the fact that Spanish has postverbal subjects, hence extraction takes place from the postverbal subject position, a position where the trace is governed.

Rizzi (1982) argues that the Northern Italian dialects Trentino and Fiorentino support this idea, because subject wh-movement can be shown to take place from a postverbal position (see Rizzi, 1986a; Giupponi, 1988; Brandi and Cordin, 1989; Poletto, 1993; Barbosa, 1995, 31–33). In Fiorentino, a subject clitic obligatorily agrees with a non wh-subject when it is preverbal, as shown by the grammaticality of feminine *l'* in (31a) agreeing with (*la Maria*) vs. the ungrammaticality of masculine/default *gl'* in (31b).

---

[7] The clause about the context [$_{NP}$ _ NP ...] in (29) is intended to cover cases of extraposed relative clauses; see van Riemsdijk and Williams (1986).

[8] Additionally, sentences with *that* were much more acceptable overall than those without *that*.

However, when the subject is postverbal, the clitic can take the default, 3.SG.MAS form *gli*, as shown in (31c).

(31) a. La Maria l'   è venut-a.   (Fiorentino)
         the Maria 3.SG.FEM is come-FEM
         'Maria has come.'   (from Barbosa, 1995, ex. 53a)

     b. *La Maria gli a telefonà.
        the Maria 3.SG has telephoned.
        'Mary has telephoned.'   (from Barbosa, 1995, ex. 53b)

     c. Gl' è   venut-o   la Maria.
        3.SG is.3.SG come.MAS the Maria
        'Maria has come.'   (from Brandi and Cordin, 1989, ex. 14)

This agreement pattern provides a marker for subject position: if the clitic agrees, the subject must be preverbal, and if it does not, the subject is postverbal, as schematized in (32).

(32) a.   S   CL   V+I
           ↑_____↑

     b.   CL   V+I   S
              ↑__╫__↑

In this context, we can test the position from which a wh-subject is extracted, based on whether the clitic has or lacks agreement.[9] As the examples in (33) show, the clitic does not agree, suggesting that they originate in a postverbal position and move the beginning of the clause. As such, example (33a), with a fully agreeing clitic (3.PL.FEM clitic *le*) is ungrammatical, whereas (33b), with a non-agreeing, default clitic (3.SG.MAS *gli*), is grammatical. If we assume the corresponding initial structures in (32) for each of those examples, then extraction must obligatorily take place from the postverbal subject position depicted in (32b), as in (34). In addition, Brandi and Cordin (1989, 125) show that the same holds for subject extraction from embedded clauses.

(33) a. *Quante   ragazze le   sono venute?   (Fiorentino)
         how many girls   3.PL.FEM are come
                                         (from Brandi and Cordin, 1989, ex. 39a)

     b. Quante   ragazze gli   è venuto con te?
        how many girls   3.SG.MAS is come with you
        'How many girls came with you?'
                                         (from Brandi and Cordin, 1989, ex. 37a)

---

[9] Note that because wh-subjects are moved to the beginning of the clause, they appear to always be preverbal, but what determines clitic agreement is the initial position from which the subject is extracted.

(34)   wh-S   CL   V+I   wh-S

Note, however, that with the generalization of the VP-internal subject hypothesis, which assumes that all subjects are generated inside the VP (see Zagona, 1982; Koopman and Sportiche, 1991), and the adoption of the Copy theory of movement (see Chomsky, 1993 in its minimalist reincarnation), one can no longer explain these asymmetries based on the availability of a postverbal subject position for NSLs, because both English and Italian/Spanish are now assumed to have a VP-internal (i.e. postverbal) position for subjects from which they move to the higher preverbal one, leaving deleted copies in preverbal position, as depicted in (35). The primary difference between both languages involves whether the verb also has been deleted from the lower position or not (or, in older terms, whether the verb has moved or not).

(35)   a. English: [$_{IP}$ DP [$_I$ [$_{vP}$ ~~DP~~ V]]]
       b. Italian: [$_{IP}$ DP [$_I$ V [$_{vP}$ ~~DP V~~]]]

Thus, under current minimalist assumptions, the account of the subject–object long-distance wh-extraction differences between English and Spanish/Italian cannot be based on the availability of the postverbal subject position in Spanish/Italian (see Pesetsky and Torrego, 2001 for an alternative analysis of *that*-trace effects).[10]

A separate but important question is the following: in its original formulation, the *that*-trace filter eliminated configurations with an overt complementizer in subject extractions, but as Barbosa *et al.* (2005, fn. 7) point out, what seems to be more relevant is "the fact that subjects are extracted from postverbal position." This conception raises a few practical issues: how do we know what counts as a *that*-trace filter violation in any given language? Second, how do we know whether extraction has happened from a postverbal position? Is it just a matter of whether the language has alternative SV/VS word orders? I will return to these issues in Chapter 3.

---

[10] Szczegielniak (1999) attempts to derive *that*-trace effects within a minimalist theory of phases, and specifically argues that the connection between lack of *that*-trace effects and NSs arises because NSLs do not project a Spec, TP, hence the A-subject remains in situ, whereas English/French does project Spec, TP (and the subject must move obligatorily, one must assume). It also follows that in NSLs, the preverbal subject is not in Spec, TP. This approach is highly compatible with the pronominal agreement analysis that I will present in Section 4.2.

2.1 Syntactic properties associated with the Null Subject Parameter 25

2.1.6 Long wh-extraction

Long wh-extraction entails movement of a wh-word across a clausal boundary in contexts where another wh-operator occupies potential intermediate landing sites. In the relative clause example in (36a), the relative pronoun *che* 'that' (or a null relative operator) is linked to its argumental position as a subject of *abbia visto* 'has seen', and this link should normally be blocked by the wh-word *chi* 'who(m),' as schematized in (36b).

(36)   a. L'uomo che mi domando chi abbia visto.   (Italian)
             the-man that CL wonder who has seen
             'The man who I wonder who he has seen.'   (from Chomsky, 1981, 240)

         b. L'uomo che mi domando [chi *t* abbia visto]

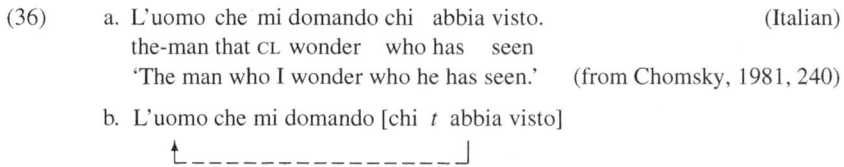

The example in (37a), from Suñer (1994, 354), shows a similar situation in Spanish with a question word (*quién* 'who') linked to its argumental position as a subject of *había prestado* 'had lost' bypassing the indirect object wh-word (*a quiénes* 'to whom'), as schematized in (37b).[11]

(37)   a. ¿Quién$_2$ dijiste (tú) a quiénes$_3$ (no) les había t_2 prestado un montón de
             who said you to whom not CL had lent a lot of
             dinero t_3?   (Spanish)
             money
             'Who did you say to whom had (not) lent a lot of money?'

         b. ¿Quién dijiste [a quiénes no les había *t* prestado ...?]

2.1.7 Section summary

To summarize this section, I have presented the culster of six original properties proposed for the NSP (null subjects, null expletives, free subject inversion, null resumptive pronouns, long wh-extraction and absence of *that*-trace effects). Four of them were tied to the availability of a postverbal subject

---

[11] I find ungrammatical both (37a) and the Spanish translation of (36) in (i). This suggests that Spanish and Italian may have subtle differences in the potential positions of null subjects.

     (i)   *El hombre que me pregunto a quién haya visto/vio.   (Spanish)
             the man that CL ask to whom had seen/saw
             'The man who I wonder whom (he) saw.'

position, which, in turn, was connected with the existence of *pro* in preverbal position. NSs were possible because of the rich-agreement properties of the NSLs. The existence of null expletives was also indirectly connected: subjects can be postverbal in these languages because null expletives satisfy the EPP, although if the EPP were not a universal principle, the reason to postulate null expletives would disappear, as we will see.

We have also seen potential objections to some of these analyses, in particular given changes in theoretical assumptions, the availability of the postverbal subject position only in NS languages becomes problematic.

2.2 Interpretive differences between null and overt subjects

One fundamental asymmetry between overt and null-subject languages is that NSLs may potentially contrast null vs. overt pronouns in subject position, a contrast that can be used to convey several interpretive differences. Put in a different way, null subjects are not simply the null counterpart of overt pronouns (but see Section 4.3). In this section, I present some of the interpretive distinctions that correlate with the null/overt distinction.

2.2.1 Arbitrary and generic interpretations

Holmberg and Sheehan (2010, 129) point out the importance of distinguishing between arbitrary and generic null subject pronouns. Arbitrary ones denote people in general, but exclude the speaker and the addressee, like *they* in *they like spicy food in Peru*, whereas generic ones denote people in general including the speaker and the addressee, much like English *one*. Consistent NSLs have arbitrary null subjects, but resort to a distinct strategy to express a generic statement. For example, the 2nd person is productively used in generic contexts in many varieties of Spanish (as in English), although the subject can be overt or null, as in (38). This speaker is comparing the impossibility of making copies of videogames with the impossibility of copying a movie shown in a movie-theater (as opposed to copying a book for personal use). In this example, the use of the 2nd person does not directly refer to the addressee, but is rather intended as a generic statement (see Hernanz, 1990).

(38) Es como en el cine   ... tu   puedes mirar la pelicula por la que has
      is like   in the movies   you can   watch the movie   for the that have
      pagado pero no te la puedes llebar. [*sic*]   (Spanish)
      paid   but not CL CL can   take
      'It's like the movies, you can watch a movie you have paid to see, but you can't take it.'   (from www.x360sos.com/archive/ index.php/t-3433.html)

2.2 Interpretive differences between null and overt subjects

An overt pronominal's reference cannot be arbitrary in Spanish and in many other languages (cf. Suñer, 1983; Jaeggli, 1986). Because of this restriction, (39a) cannot mean 'someone or other said that they had come', whereas (39b) can. This interpretive restriction is intuitively connected to the null/overt pronoun alternation, so that if null subjects are somehow the default option in these languages, overt ones must specialize in some way, and will be more restricted in distribution (cf. the Avoid Pronoun Constraint originally proposed by Chomsky, 1981, 65).

(39)   a. Ellos dijeron que habían venido.   (Spanish)
               they said   that had   come
               'They (specific only) said that they had come.'
    b. Dijeron que habían venido.
               said   that had   come
               'They (specific or arbitrary) said that they had come.'

A similar example of this interpretive effect can be illustrated in Shipibo. This language has obligatory 1st and 2nd person subjects and optionally null 3rd person ones (see Camacho and Elías-Ulloa, 2010). According to Valenzuela (2003b, 409), if a clause with a 3rd person subject appears with the plural *-kan* morpheme on the verb and is interpreted as impersonal, the subject must be obligatorily null. In those cases, however, the interpretation need not be plural, but rather indefinite or arbitrary, as in (40).

(40)   Shee   a-rá-kan-ai   yapa.   (Shipibo)
           ONOM:frying do.AUX-EVID-PL-INC fish.ABS
           'Fish is being fried / Someone is frying fish.'

Native speakers seem to obtain an arbitrary reading for examples like (40) and for (41a), where the 3rd person subject pronoun is absent. If an overt 3rd person pronoun appears (cf. *tsoabaon* in (41b)), the arbitrary reading is dispreferred at least for some of them. Once again, this is in line with the idea that whenever null subjects are available, overt pronouns tend to have a more restricted and specialized distribution.[12]

(41)   a. Ea-ra   tee-kan-ke.
               1.SG-EVID work-3.PL-TNS
               'Someone worked for me.'

---

[12] Thanks to J. Elías-Ulloa for help eliciting these data. As he points out (p.c.), some speakers do allow an overt pronoun, and in such case there are two possible interpretations: a partitive reading (some of them) and an arbitrary reading (someone or other).

b. Tsoabaon-ra xeke be-kan-ke.
   3.PL-EVID   corn bring-TNS
   'Some of them brought corn.'

In a related matter, Holmberg and Sheehan (2010, 129) point out that Brazilian Portuguese contrasts with European Portuguese (and Spanish as well) in allowing a generic interpretation for (42), which in EP/Spanish must be interpreted referentially (i.e. 'that's how he/she makes the dessert'). To obtain a generic interpretation in that context, EP/Spanish must add a clitic *se*, as (42b)–(42c) illustrates.[13]

(42) a. É assim que faz   a   doce.   (Brazilian Portuguese)
         is thus that makes the sweet
         'This is how one makes the dessert.'
      b. É assim que se faz   a   doce.   (European Portuguese)
         is thus   that CL makes the sweet
         'This is how one makes the dessert.'
      c. Es así que se hace el dulce.   (Spanish)
         is thus that CL makes the sweet
         'This is how one makes the dessert.'

The examples in (39) and (42c) seem to show opposite effects. In the first set, the null subject has a wider array of possible interpretations, whereas in the second case, the null subject cannot be interpreted generically. However, note that (42c) the contrast is not between a null and overt subject, but rather between a null subject with and without a generic clitic. One might argue that the fact that generic interpretations are available in (42a) but not in (42c) is independent of the availability of null subjects, since, after all, the first example has a null subject even if Brazilian Portuguese increasingly uses overt subjects across the board. However, it may also be the case that the loss of clitics in BP is directly connected to the loss of null subjects.

2.2.2   *Reference to clauses*

Iatridou and Embick (1997) point out that a null thematic pronoun cannot be used to refer back to a full clause in languages like Greek, as illustrated in (43). The same effects can be seen in Catalan (see Iatridou and Embick, 1997, 61–62) and in Spanish. For example, (44b) cannot be used to recover the

---

[13] *Se* can also be a reflexive or reciprocal clitic. In the reflexive interpretation (42c) would mean 'That's how he/she makes him/herself the dessert.'

statement in (44a) because the subject is null. By contrast, the demonstrative *eso* 'that' (or in some varieties *ello* 'that') can, as seen in (44c).

(43) a. O Kostas ine panda argoporimenos. (Greek)
the Kostas is always delayed
'Kostas is always delayed.'

b. Pragmatika. ke *pro epise ton patera tu na tu agorasi aftokinito.
indeed and pro convinced the father his MOD him buy car
'Indeed, and he convinced his father to buy him a car.'
(from Iatridou and Embick, 1997, ex. 2)

(44) a. [Gabriel siempre está retrasado]_i (Spanish)
Gabriel always is late
'Gabriel is always late.'

b. * Claro, y pro_i ha convencido a su padre de que compre un carro.
of course and has convinced to his father of that buy a car
'Of course, and that has convinced his father to buy him a car.'

c. Claro, y eso_i ha convencido a su padre de que compre un carro.
of course and that has convinced to his father of that buy a car
'Of course, and that has convinced his father to buy him a car.'

Iatridou and Embick (1997) note that a null pronominal expletive can point to a clause in some cases like in (45). However, the null category is arguably an expletive in these examples, because the clause is extraposed. We can see this in (45b), where the null category precedes the clause it points to (just as in *it_i is a shame [that the bird hit the glass window]_i*. In the examples in (43), on the other hand, the relevant clause is not extraposed (Iatridou and Embick, 1997, 61). Spanish shows the same effect (cf. (46)). The assumption, then, is that this expletive pronoun does not directly refer to the clause in the sense that the demonstrative does.

(45) a. An o Kostas argisi *pro* tha ine dropi. (Greek)
if the Kostas is late FUT be shame
'If Kostas arrives late, it will be a shame.'

b. *pro* ine dropi pu o Kostas tha figi.
be shame that the Kostas FUT leave
'It is a shame that Kostas will leave.'
(from Iatridou and Embick, 1997, ex. 6)

(46) a. Si Gabriel se retrasa, *pro* será una lástima. (Spanish)
if Gabriel CL is late, *pro* will be a shame
'If Gabriel is late, it will be a shame.'

b. Es una lástima que Gabriel se retrase.
   is a   shame   that Gabriel CL is late
   'It is a shame that Gabriel is late.'

Iatridou and Embick (1997) argue that the phenomenon observed in (43) is syntactic in nature, that is, *pro* cannot be coindexed with the category IP/CP due to a ϕ-feature mismatch: IP/CP lacks number, gender and possibly person, whereas thematic *pro* requires all three of them.

2.2.3 Quantifier binding

The second interpretive difference was first formalized by Montalbetti (1984, 95) as the **Overt Pronoun Constraint** in (47). This constraint suggests that whenever a language has overt and null pronouns, the overt one cannot be bound as a variable. In other words, (48a) can be interpreted as meaning that each student thinks that that same student is intelligent, but this bound variable reading is not possible in (48b), which can only be interpreted, according to Montalbetti, as meaning that each student thinks that some salient person in the discourse is intelligent.

(47)   **Overt Pronoun Constraint (OPC)**
        Overt pronouns cannot link to formal variables iff the alternation overt/ empty obtains.

(48)   a. Todo estudiante$_i$ cree   que *pro*$_i$ es inteligente.   (Spanish)
           every student   thinks that   is intelligent
           'Every student$_i$ thinks that he$_i$ is intelligent.'
        b. Todo estudiante$_i$ cree   que él$_{*i/j}$ es inteligente.
           every student   thinks that he   is intelligent
           'Every student$_i$ thinks that he$_j$ is intelligent.'

The OPC has been attested in several unrelated languages, among them Chinese, Japanese, Korean (see Kanno, 1997; Yamada, 2005) and Tarifit (Ouhalla, 1988). However, in work on the acquisition of Spanish as an L2, Comínguez (2011) has not found a clear pattern for the native control group. To further confound the situation if the overt pronominal is focused the bound reading becomes possible (see Sánchez, 1994; Lozano, 2002), as illustrated in (49).

(49)   Todo atleta cree que ÉL va   a ganar la competición, no otro
        every athlete thinks that he is going to win the competition not another
        atleta.
        athlete
        'Every athlete thinks that HE is going to win the competition, not another athlete.'

2.3 Typology of Null Subject Languages

A primary typological distinction among NSLs is whether the verbal paradigm displays overt person/number morphology or not. Thus, languages like Spanish, Italian or Quechua encode grammatical person and number in most of the verbal paradigm (cf. (50)), whereas others like Japanese have morphemes that do not encode person/number (cf. (51), provided by Hiroshi Aoyagi, p.c.), and others like Chinese have no inflectional morphology whatsoever (cf. (52)).

(50) Quechua morphological paradigm

    a. Tiya-ni   live-1.SG   'I live'
    b. Tiya-nki   live-2.SG   'you live'
    c. Pay tiya-n   live-3.SG   'he/she lives'
    d. Tiya-nchik   live-1.PL.INCL   'we (inclusive) live'
    e. Tiya-yku   live-1.PL.EXCL   'we (exclusive) live'
    f. Tiya-nkichik   live-2.PL   'You (pl) live'
    g. Tiya-nku   live-3.PL   'They live'

(from facultad.pucp.edu.pe/ciencias-sociales/curso/quechua/gramatica.html#stop3)

(51) Japanese morphological paradigm

    a. Yom-ru   read-PRES   'read'
    b. Yom-ta   read-PAST   'read'
    c. Yom-anai   read-NEG   'not read'
    d. Yom-reba   read-COND   'not read'
    e. Yom-yoo   read-PROPOS   'let's read'
    f. Yom-(i)tai   read-DESID   'want to read'
    g. Yom-rare   read-PASS   'was read'
    h. Yom-sase   read-CAUS   'make read'

    (adapted from Jaeggli and Safir, 1989, 29)

(52) Chinese verbal paradigm

    Shi   'be (all persons)'

2.3.1 Consistent null subject languages

The Quechua/Italian/Spanish type of NSL shows a fairly systematic use of null subjects. In some sense, these null subjects are the default, whereas overt pronouns are typically used to indicate change of topic or contrast. For this

32 *The Null Subject Parameter: introduction*

reason, they have been called consistent NSLs. The traditional intuition has been that null subjects are possible due to rich agreement (see Taraldsen, 1980; Rizzi, 1986a and much subsequent work, as well as Section 4.2 below). This hypothesis works well for some rich-agreement languages, but formalizing the notion of rich agreement in a precise, predictive and accurate way has proven to be very challenging. For example, Jaeggli and Safir (1989) attempt to derive agreement richness by building on different properties of morphological paradigms. They define the notion of a **morphologically uniform** paradigm as in (53), establishing three general types of paradigms across languages: those whose forms are all morphologically derived, those that are fully underived, and those that are mixed. Derived forms have a root and one or more morphological affixes, as the Quechua form *tiya-ni* live-1.SG in (50). All of the forms in the Quechua paradigm and the Japanese paradigm in (51) are derived. Chinese forms, on the other hand, are fully underived (they consist of a root and no affixes), whereas English and French have some derived forms (*like-s* and some underived ones (*like*).

(53) **Morphological uniformity**
An inflectional paradigm P in a language L is morphologically uniform if P has either only underived inflectional forms or only derived inflectional forms. (from Jaeggli and Safir, 1989, 30)

Based on this division between derived and non-derived paradigms, they propose that only morphologically uniform languages can have null subjects (cf. (54)). This predicts that Quechua, Spanish, Italian, Chinese and Japanese will have null subjects, whereas English and French will not.[14]

(54) **The Null Subject Parameter**
Null subjects are permitted in all and only languages with morphologically uniform inflectional paradigms.

2.3.2   Discourse-related null subject languages
Since languages like Chinese or Japanese do not have verbal morphology that can identify a null subject, they must have a different mechanism. In this sense, Huang (1984) has proposed that null subjects are licensed through

---

[14] Jaeggli and Safir (1989) argue that the main difference between NSL Italian/Spanish and non-NSL German and Icelandic, which are also morphologically uniform (and arguably agreement-rich) stems from the fact that German/Icelandic, being V2 languages, have T and AGR in separate nodes, whereas Italian/Spanish do not. Jaeggli and Safir assume that AGR must case-govern the empty category to identify it. Since German/Icelandic have T and AGR split, and T is in C, AGR does not case-govern the null category, hence it is not identified.

2.3 Typology of Null Subject Languages 33

topics (hence their categorization as discourse-related null subject languages). In (55), the embedded null subject can be coreferential with the matrix subject *Zhangsan* or with "some other person whose reference is understood in discourse (i.e. the discourse topic)" (Huang, 1989, 187–188).

(55) Zhangsan shuo [*pro* hen xihuan Lisi]. (Chinese)
 Zhangsan say *pro* very like Lisi
 'Zhangsan said that he liked Lisi.' (from Huang, 1989, 187, ex. 4a)

More recently, Tomioka (2003) has proposed linking the availability of null subjects in discourse NSLs with independent properties of nouns in those languages. Tomioka notes that Japanese null pronouns have a wide range of semantic interpretations (referential uses, bound variable uses, E-type pronoun uses, indefinite uses, property anaphora, etc.) that can be correlated with the wide availability of bare NPs with many semantic interpretations in that language. Thus, for example, (56) shows a bare object NP that can be interpreted as an indefinite or definite singular or plural.

(56) Ken-wa ronbun-o yon-da (Japanese)
 Ken-TOP paper-ACC read-PAST
 'Ken read a paper/papers/the paper/the papers.'
 (from Tomioka, 2003, 328, ex. 19)

Tomioka proposes deriving the diverse meanings of *pro* through the same mechanisms proposed for the meanings of NPs. In particular, *pro* in languages like Japanese is the phonologically null version of a bare NP, suggesting the generalization in (57). This generalization applies to Japanese, Korean, Mandarin Chinese, Thai, Hindi, Turkish, and Brazilian Portuguese, among others.

(57) **Discourse pro-drop generalization**
 All languages which allow discourse pro-drop allow (robust) bare NP arguments. (from Tomioka, 2003, 336)

Although what constitutes a robust bare NP argument is not defined, the general idea is that bare NP arguments should be productively available in a variety of syntactic positions. Under this view, discourse NSs are the by-product of N' deletion/NP ellipsis, an operation that applies cross-linguistically, but whose results depend on the independent structure of nominals. Thus, in English, N' deletion/NP ellipsis leaves an overt D, as in (58a), whereas in Japanese it does not, as in (58b).

(58) (a) English-type (b) Japanese-type NP-ellipsis
      (DP-language)   (NP-language)

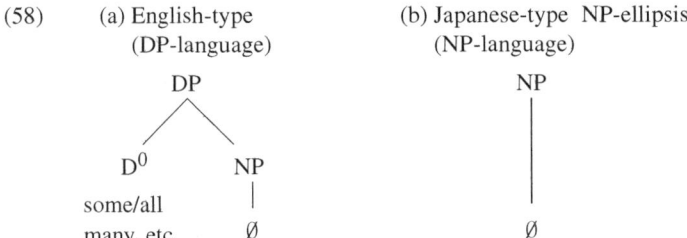

As Tomioka points out, this approach opens up several questions, among them, why languages with robust bare NPs (like English) do not allow NSs.

Another question raised by the analysis relates to partial NSLs like Shipibo (see immediately below), which have robust bare NPs in Tomioka's sense, but allow NSs only in 3rd person, not in 1st or 2nd.

2.3.3 Partial null subject languages

Certain languages fall in between the Italian/Quechua/Spanish type with generalized null subjects, and the English type with no null subjects. These intermediate languages, called partial null subject languages (see Borer, 1986, 1989; Vainikka and Levy, 1999; Elías-Ulloa, 2002; Holmberg, 2005; Holmberg et al., 2009; Shlonsky, 2009; Barbosa, 2010; Camacho and Elías-Ulloa, 2010, among others) are constrained along several dimensions, among them the expression of person, tense and referentiality and antecedent control. In Hebrew and Finnish, for example, referential null subjects are only productively possible with 1st and 2nd person. In (59a), a 3rd person verb cannot appear without an overt subject, whereas a 1st person instance can, as seen in (59b).

(59) a. *Nousi   junaan.   (Finnish)
          step-PAST.3.SG train-into
          '(He/she) boarded the train.'
      b. Nousin   junaan.
          step-PAST.1.SG train-into
          'I boarded the train.'   (from Vainikka and Levy, 1999, 614, ex. 1)

The same pattern exists in Hebrew past and future tense paradigms. In those cases, the verb is inflected for tense, number, gender and person, whereas in the present, person is not marked and overt referential subjects are obligatory in all persons (see Vainikka and Levy, 1999, 614–615). In (60a) we can see that a 1st person past verb can have a null subject, whereas a 3rd person past verb cannot (see (60b)). By contrast, (61) illustrates the present tense case, where the verb does not provide any morphological indication for person, hence overt pronouns are required for 1st, 2nd and 3rd.[15]

(60)   a. Aliti   al ha-rakevet.
        step-PAST.1.SG on the-train
        'I boarded the train.'   (from Vainikka and Levy, 1999, 615, ex. 2)

    b. *Ala   al ha-rakevet.   (Hebrew)
        stepped-PAST.3.SG.MAS on the-train
        '(He) boarded the train.'

(61)   *Lomed   Albanit.   (Hebrew)
    study.PRES.MAS.SG Albanian
    'I/you/he/she study Albanian.'   (from Shlonsky, 2009, 136, ex. 7)

In Shipibo, the partition is the opposite: 1st/2nd person subjects are obligatorily overt, as we see in (62a–b), whereas a 3rd person subject is optionally null, as seen in (62c) (see Camacho and Elías-Ulloa, 2010). Unlike Hebrew and Finnish, the verb in Shipibo does not have any overt person morphology in any tense (see *noko-ke* arrive-PERF for all persons).

(62)   a. Mia-ra Lima-n   noko-ke.   (Shipibo)
        2-EVID Lima-DIR arrive-PERF
        'You arrived in Lima.'

    b. Ea-ra Lima-n   noko-ke.
        1-EVID Lima-DIR arrive-PERF
        'I arrived in Lima.'

    c. Lima-n-ra   (ja) noko-ke.
        Lima-DIR-EVID he arrive-PERF
        'He/she went to Lima.'
        (from Camacho and Elías-Ulloa, 2010, 72, ex. 13)

---

[15] When the present tense appears with negation *eyn*, which can be inflected for person, the person asymmetry reappears (Shlonsky, 2009, 137), so that 1st/2nd persons can be null (cf. (i)) but 3rd persons cannot (cf. (ii)).

    (i)   Eyn-eni / eyn-xa   lomed   Albanit.   (Hebrew)
           NEG-1.SG / NEG-2.MAS.SG study.PRES.MAS.SG Albanian
           'I am/you are not studying Albanian.'

    (ii)   *Eyn-o   lomed   Albanit.
           NEG-3.MAS.SG study.PRES.MAS.SG Albanian
           'He is not studying Albanian.'

A third type of person restriction is illustrated by Marathi, which only allows NSs in 2nd person, according to Holmberg *et al.* (2009, 76). Interestingly, verbal morphology only unambiguously distinguishes the 2nd person singular.

Another source of variation relates to whether the null subject is in main or embedded clauses. In Shipibo, for example, 1st and 2nd subjects can be null so long as their antecedent is in the immediate clause (see Camacho and Elías-Ulloa, 2010). In Brazilian Portuguese, Finnish and Marathi, embedded subjects can be null if controlled (see Vainikka and Levy, 1999; Modesto, 2008; Holmberg *et al.*, 2009).

Finally, indefinite subjects can be null in Brazilian Portuguese, Finnish and Marathi (see Holmberg *et al.*, 2009). Both of these properties are illustrated in (63). In the first example, the null subject is interpreted as indefinite ('someone or other'), whereas in the second example, the embedded subject is interpreted as controlled by the main clause subject, so that *Ram* is the one buying the house.

(63) a. Unahlyat   lavkar utthavla jato.   (Marathi)
         summer-in early wake   go-PRES-3.SG.MAS
         'In summer one wakes up early.'
      b. Ram mhanala   ki ghar ghetla.
         Ram say-PAST.3.SG.MAS that house buy-PAST.3.SG.NEUT
         'Ram said that he bought a house.'
                                          (from Holmberg *et al.*, 2009, 60, ex. 1)

Barbosa (2010) extends Tomioka's (2003) proposal for discourse NLSs to partial *pro*-drop languages. In particular, she argues that partial and discourse NSLs have common properties that set them apart from consistent NSLs: In certain contexts, the null subject is optional in partial NSLs but obligatory in consistent NSLs. This is illustrated by the contrast between European and Brazilian Portuguese. In EP, a consistent NSL, the embedded pronoun *ele* 'he' in (64) cannot be interpreted as coreferential with the main clause subject *o João*, whereas in BP it can. By contrast, if the embedded subject is null, as in (64b), coreference is possible in both varieties. In other words, coreference obligatorily requires a null subject in EP but not in BP.

(64)   a. O João$_i$ disse que ele$_i$ comprou um computador.   (#EP, √BP)
          the Joao says that he   bought   a   computer
          'Joao says that he bought a computer.'
       b. O João$_i$ disse que *pro$_k$* comprou um computador.   (√EP, √BP)
          the Joao says that he   bought   a   computer
          'Joao says that he bought a computer.'   (from Barbosa, 2010, ex. 3)

Additionally, we see in (65a) that an intervening antecedent (*os moleques* 'the children') blocks the relationship between the main clause subject (*o João*) and the embedded null subject in BP but not in EP. As a result, the BP version of that sentence is ungrammatical because the NS requires an antecedent. The same pattern obtains in Hebrew, another partial NSL. In example (65b), *Itamar* is the intervening DP:

(65)   a. O João$_i$ disse   que os moleques   acaham   [que *pro*$_k$ é   esperto]
              the Joao   says   that the children   believe   that   is   smart.
                                                                                                      ($\sqrt{}$EP) (*BP)
              'Joao says that the children believe that he is smart.'
                                                                          (from Barbosa, 2010, ex. 8)
      b. * Talila$_i$ 'amra le-Itamar$_j$ še   *pro*$_k$ tavo.   (Hebrew)
          Talila said   to-Itamar that   will-come.FEM.SG
          'Talila said to Itamar that she will come.'
                                          (from Holmberg, 2005, 554, ex. 41b)

A third difference, already noted in Section 2.2.1, relates to the possibility of interpreting a 3rd person null subject as indefinite. Example (66a) illustrates that BP (a partial NSL) allows for this possibility, whereas consistent NSLs lack the option, as already mentioned. Instead, these languages resort to other strategies such as the clitic *se* in (66b).

(66)   a. É assim que faz   o   doce.   (BP)
            is so   that make.3.SG the sweet
            'That's how one makes the dessert.'
     b. É assim que <u>se</u> faz   o   doce.   (EP)
            is so   that CL make.3.SG the cake
            'That's how one makes the cake.'   (from Barbosa, 2010, exx. 18–19)

Based on these patterns, Barbosa (2010) argues that agreement is pronominal in consistent NSLs, and preverbal subjects are CLLD phrases (see Sections 4.2.1 and 8.1). In partial NSLs and discourse NSLs, null subjects are NP anaphoras.

2.3.4   Section summary

In this section, I have presented a typological distinction between consistent, agreement-based NSLs, discourse-based NSLs and partial NSLs. The latter type involves variation across several domains. NSs allowed depending on person and tense, or depending on whether they appear in main or embedded clauses. In this last respect, partial NSLs seem to have properties more consistent with discourse-based NSLs, where the NS is recovered through discourse. Finally, partial NSLs lack interpretive contrasts between overt and null pronouns.

2.4 Chapter summary

In this chapter, I have presented the cluster of properties proposed for the NSP, namely null subjects, null expletives, long wh-extraction, *that*-trace effect violations and alternative VS word order, as well as interpretive properties: OPC effects, absence of arbitrary readings with overt pronouns (in NSLs), the need to have additional strategies for generic readings with *pro* (in consistent NSLs), and the impossibility of referring back to CPs through *pro* in languages like Spanish/Greek.

Finally, I have presented two typologies of NSLs. First, the distinction between consistent NSLs (languages with rich agreement where NSs appear without systematic restrictions for person, number, etc.), discourse-related NSLs (those with no agreement and with NSs identified in discourse) and partial NSLs (those that have NSs in limited contexts, depending on person/tense, etc.). Among partial NSLs, we find those whose NSs correlate with explicit inflection (Hebrew, Finnish), and those that do not (Shipibo).

The second typology relates to whether the NSs are restricted to a main or embedded clause. Thus, Brazilian Portuguese, Finnish and Marathi restrict NSs to controlled instances in embedded clauses.

3 *The core content of the Null Subject Parameter*

3.1 Introduction

The notion of a macro-parameter suggests that several grammatical properties should cluster together around one core property, a conception that facilitates language acquisition (see Hyams, 1986, 1992; Liceras, 1989; Hyams and Wexler, 1993, among others) and makes fairly strict predictions about sequence of acquisition, possible and impossible grammars, etc.

In the case of the NSP, there have been several proposals regarding the core property (see Gilligan, 1987, 78–96 for a summary). Taraldsen (1980), for example, proposes that the subject position is potentially bound by AGR, which gives rise to the possibility of null non-thematic subjects. That availability of binding by AGR underlies *that*-trace filter violations: Since the subject position is bound in NSLs, extraction is licensed.

Rizzi (1982) modifies this notion, arguing that rich AGR binds the postverbal subject position, so the availability of *that*-trace effect violations in NSLs is related to the possibility of extracting from the postverbal position. Long wh-extraction and null resumptive pronouns also follow from this basic asymmetry: in languages like Italian, the postverbal subject position is licensed (technically, governed) in a way that the preverbal position is not in English. The availability of postverbal positions, in turn, is overtly manifested in free inversion (cf. Sections 2.1.3 and 2.1.5 above). Gilligan (1987) tests the typological predictions of Rizzi's early account, and reaches certain implicational correlations between having null subjects, free inversion and *that*-trace violations, which Roberts and Holmberg (2010) further refine.

In this section we review the implicational correlations proposed by Gilligan (1987) and Roberts and Holmberg (2010) and contrast them against empirical data from a number of languages, particularly Brazilian Portuguese, Dominican Spanish and Lubukusu and other Bantu languages.

Gilligan's (1987) study surveys the property cluster associated with the NSP in over 100 languages in order to establish whether the combinations predicted in (1) are the only attested ones.[1]

(1) Gilligan's (1987) typology of NSLs based on Taraldsen (1980), Rizzi (1982) and Safir (1985).

Null thematic subjects	Null non-thematic subjects	Subject inversion	*That*-trace filter violations
+	+	+	+
−	+	+	+
−	−	+	+
−	−	−	−

Although many of the studies he relies on are missing data on one or more of the properties, Gilligan (1987, 147) tentatively concludes that his survey supports the implications in (2).

(2) a. If a language has a thematic *pro*, it has expletive null subjects.
   b. If a language has free inversion, it has expletive null subjects (statistically significant correlation).
   c. If a language has free inversion, it has *that*-trace effect violations.
   d. If a language has *that*-trace effect violations, it has null expletive subjects.

These implicational statements predict certain possible and impossible combinations. Specifically, the combinations in (3a–d) should not be attested; however, in the previous chapter we have already seen examples of how some of these combinations may exist. Specifically, Finnish has obligatory overt expletives in some contexts, and restricted null thematic subjects in others.

(3) Combinations predicted not to exist by Gilligan's (1987) typology.

---

[1] (1) corresponds to Safir's analysis, which establishes less direct correlations between the different phenomena, in particularly taking into account languages where *that*-trace effect violations exist without null subjects, such as Dutch. Gilligan tests two additional patterns, both more restrictive, corresponding to Taraldsen (1980) and Rizzi (1982). For illustrative purposes, (1) should suffice. Gilligan's typology does not directly address the distinction between consistent, partial NSLs and discourse-oriented ones, in part because it tests hypotheses that preceded some of those distinctions. Whether some of the mismatches in Gilligan's typology could result from including disparate sets of NSLs remains a logical possibility that I will not explore here.

	Null thematic subjects	Null non-thematic subjects	Subject inversion	*That*-trace filter violations
(a)	Yes	No		
(b)		No	Yes	
(c)			Yes	No
(d)		No		Yes

Based on these results, Roberts and Holmberg (2010, 22) propose the implicational scale in (4), which defines the three types of languages represented in (5). Thus, a language may have expletive null subjects, but this does not imply *that*-trace violations or subject inversion based on the scale in (4). Haitian and basilectal Jamaican exemplify such a language.

However, if language has *that*-trace violations, it must also have expletive null subjects, but (4) does not imply subject inversion in that case. Examples of languages with this setting are Cape Verdean, Berbice Dutch, etc. Finally, a language could have all three properties, as Spanish, Italian and Greek do.

(4)   Subject inversion → (allow *that*-trace violations → expletive null subjects)

(5)   a. Has all three properties (Italian, Spanish, Greek, etc.)

b. Allows *that*-trace violations and has expletive null subjects (Cape Verdean, Berbice Dutch, Mauritian, Papiamentu, Saramaccan)

c. Only allows expletive null subjects (Haitian, basilectal Jamaican)

It is difficult to assess the empirical validity of both Gilligan's predicted impossible combinations and of Holmberg and Roberts's implicational scale (see Roberts and Holmberg (2010) on the limitations of typological predications like these), in part because in the absence of a specific analysis, in part because it is not clear what constitutes a *that*-trace filter violation or free inversion. Be that as it may, I will review some of the existing evidence in the following sections.

3.2   Null thematic subjects and no null expletives

The first correlation implies that one should not have languages like Spanish but with overt expletives. The issue that arises is whether languages or varieties that have partial thematic NSs and overt (but not obligatory) expletive subjects count as potential counter-examples, although Finnish is a potential candidate.

As already discussed in Section 2.1.1, this language has null subjects in 1st and 2nd person, as seen in (6), where the 1st person pronoun (*minä*) can be dropped.

(6)   (Minä) puhun englantia.   (Finnish)
    (I)   speak.PL English
    'I speak English.'

Finnish also has what seems to be optional expletives, as seen in the contrast between the obligatory presence of the expletive in (7a) and (7b). Note that the verb appears in 1st position in this last example, a position that is normally not tolerated in Finnish. The reason why this order is possible relates to the fact that *kiire* 'haste' cannot satisfy the EPP, so if one assumes that movement is costly, the adverb will not raise (and the EPP is suspended).

(7)   a. * (Sitä) Leikkii lapsia kadulla.
          EXP play children in-street
          'There are children playing in the street.'
    b. Tuli kiire.
       came haste
       'We/they are in a hurry.'

Like Finnish, certain varieties of Dominican Spanish have NSs and also an overt expletive, which is nevertheless optional, as we will see in the next section. By comparing this variety with other Romance and Spanish varieties, we will establish at least two types of expletives, one that competes with overt preverbal subjects, and one that is compatible with them. This distinction suggests that there are at least two positions for expletives, a CP-related one, and an IP-related one.

3.2.1   *Overt expletives in Dominican Spanish*

Dominican Spanish (henceforth DS) has a high proportion of overt subjects, particularly when compared with other varieties of Spanish. Thus, for example, in Otheguy *et al.*'s (2007) study of speakers of different Spanish varieties recently arrived in New York, Dominicans had 41% of overt pronouns vs. 27% for Ecuadorians, 24% for Colombians and 19% for Mexicans. In a separate study conducted in the Dominican Republic, Cabrera (2007) found a preference for overt subjects over null ones in 70% of sentences tested. In the following example, we find a sequence of several overt pronominals (*ellas* 'they.FEM') even though the topic does not change. Because topic continuation is usually related to null subjects and change of topic to overt pronouns in

NSLs, this example raises some questions about the status of null subjects in this Spanish variety.[2]

(8)   Hay unas muchachitas que están juntas conmigo, que **ellas** viven pa' fuera, entonces **ellas** vinieron a estudiar en la escuela del Pino, entonces **ellas** saben mucho inglés ... yo no me acuerdo en el país que **ellas** vivían.   (DSEC)
'There are some girls that are together with me, that they live outside, so they came to study in the Pino School, so they know a lot of English ... I don't remember the country in which they lived.'
(from Bullock and Toribio, 2009, 56, ex. 12b)

However, even in this Spanish variety, overt subjects are not obligatory, as the following example shows. In this sequence, all subjects that maintain the topic are null, even in the case of *hablaron* 'they spoke', which retrieves two separate topics (the referent of the first two subjects and his friend).

(9)   Se fue,   cogió un bastón, se encontró con   su compadre y   hablaron
      CL went, got   a   stick,   CL met   with his friend and talked
      tanto   que le salió   raíz al   ba'tón.   (DSEC)
      so much that CL came out root to-the stick
      'He left, got a (walking) stick, he ran into a friend, and they talked so much that the stick sprung roots.'   (from Bullock and Toribio, 2009, 63, ex. 26b)

As a conclusion, while DS has an increasing use of subjects, it still productively allows for null subjects.

The variety spoken in El Cibao (DSEC) also has an optional expletive *ello*, illustrated in (10) (see Henríquez Ureña, 1939, 1940/1975; Toribio, 1993; Silva-Villar, 1998; Hinzelin and Kaiser, 2006, 2007; Bullock and Toribio, 2009, among others). *Ello* covers at least the range of *there* and *it* in English, so it can appear with existential/presentational verbs (cf. (10a, b)), weather verbs (cf. (10c)), unaccusative verbs (cf. (10d, e)) and transitive verbs (cf. (10f)).[3]

(10)   a. Ello hay personas   que lo aprenden bien (el inglés)   (DSEC)
          EXP is   people.PL that CL learn.PL well (the English
          'There is people who learn it well (English).'

---

[2] The examples below are from the Dominican variety spoken in El Cibao, which will be relevant below. Whenever an example is explicitly from El Cibao, it will be marked as DSEC, otherwise, Dominican examples will appear as DS.

[3] DSEC presents a particular methodological challenge, because many of its features have a highly negative social connotation, and there is strong social pressure to eliminate them, particularly among educated, urban speakers. Since many studies rely on data from urban speakers, conclusions must be tentative. In this sense, Bullock and Toribio (2009) is especially valuable because it relies on data from rural and/or unschooled speakers from El Cibao.

b. Ello queda mucho tiempo todavía.
   EXP remains much time still
   'There still remains much time.'

c. Ello no está lloviendo aquí pero allá sí.
   EXP not is raining here but there yes
   'It's not raining here, but there, it is.'

d. Ello vienen haitianos aquí.
   EXP come.PL Haitians here
   'There come Haitians here.'

e. Porque si ello llega una gente de pa' fuera...
   because if EXP arrives some people.SG of outside
   'Because if there arrive people from the outside...'

f. Ello se hace bollos con coco.
   EXP CL make cakes with coconut
   'One makes cake with coconut.'

(from Bullock and Toribio, 2009, 57, ex. 14a–f)

However, expletives in DSEC are not obligatory, unlike in English or French. Thus, we also find examples like (11) with null expletives next to the ones with overt *ello* in (10).

(11) a. Había un viejo que tenía un gallo. (DSEC)
       was an old man that had a rooster
       'There was an old man that had a rooster.'
       (from Bullock and Toribio, 2009, 70, ex. 37)

     b. Como hubiera llovidos...
        since had rained
        'Since it had rained...' (from Bullock and Toribio, 2009, 64, ex. 30)

Furthermore, as Hinzelin and Kaiser's (2007) study shows, given the choice between an overt and a null expletive, urban speakers from the capital of El Cibao, as well as rural speakers from other regions in the Dominican Republic, chose the null expletive most of the time (between 67% and 93% of the time, depending on the construction).

Expletive optionality has led Bullock and Toribio (2009, 56, fn. 9) to propose that *ello* may be a left-peripheral discourse marker (see also Silva-Villar, 1998). Along these lines, the answer to a question like (12a) could be either (12b) with the expletive by itself, or (12c), with *sí/no* 'yes/no'. These examples suggest that *ello* may be connected to discourse functions in addition to (or maybe instead of) occupying the more traditional subject position.

(12) a. ¿Quiere bailar?   (DS)
         want   dance
         'Do you want to dance?'
      b. Ello.
         EXP
         'Yes.'
      c. Ello sí / no.   (DS)
         EXP yes / no
         'Yes/no.'   (from Hinzelin and Kaiser, 2006, 65)

Notice, however, that none of the examples of *ello* in the literature involve an overt preverbal subject (see in particular Hinzelin and Kaiser's (2006) extensive corpus of examples from different sources). Furthermore, (13) is ungrammatical, with a preverbal subject *unas personas* 'some people' preceding the verb. Since DS has an overwhelming SV word order tendency, the ungrammaticality of this example is surprising if *ello* is strictly a discourse-related expletive and not connected with the subject position.[4]

(13)   * Ello unas persona-s llegaron   ayer.   (DS)
           EXP some person-PL arrived.PL yesterday
           'Some people arrived yesterday.'   (from Jacqueline Toribio, p.c.)

Verbal agreement shows two patterns when *ello* appears. On the one hand, agreement can be 3rd person singular, particularly with existential *hay* '(there) is'. This pattern was illustrated in example (10a) above. A second pattern involves agreement with the postverbal subject as seen in (10d) above and in (14) below. In this example, the verb *llegan* 'arrive.3.PL.' agrees with *guaguas* 'buses'.[5]

---

[4] This makes these expletives crucially different from the ones described in for Northern Iberian varieties in section 3.2.2.
[5] There are examples with *ello*, a plural verb and a null subject, but as Hinzelin and Kaiser (2006, 69) point out, it is not possible to know whether *ello* is an expletive, or an instance of a referential pronoun *ellos* that has its final /s/ dropped. Elision of the final consonant in syllable codas is fairly well attested in Caribbean varieties.

(i)   Ello lo dijeron por radio.   (DS)
      EXP CL said   for radio
      'They said it on the radio.'   (from Toribio, 1993, 94, in Hinzelin and Kaiser, 2006, 69)

(14) Ello llega-n   guaguas hasta allá.   (DS)
      EXP arrive-3.PL buses   until there
      'Buses reach there.'

(from Toribio, 1993, 95, in Hinzelin and Kaiser, 2006, 69)

For examples with 3rd person singular agreement, is *ello* responsible for agreement, or is there an additional element that triggers agreement (cf. (15a) and (15b) respectively)? The second option would predict the existence of overt preverbal subjects, which, as we have suggested, are not attested in the literature. The first option, on the other hand, suggests that no overt preverbal pronouns should co-appear with *ello*, particulary if they occupy the same position.

(15)   a. [CP [IP *ello* hay]]
        b. [CP *ello* [IP *pro* hay]]

To summarize, the data from Finnish and DSEC suggest that the implicational (2a) 'thematic NS → expletive NS' does not hold.

3.2.2 *A CP-related expletive*

Certain Romance varieties show an overt expletive with a slightly different distribution from the one just presented.[6]

Like DS, these varieties are NSLs, and like DS, they have overt expletives of different types: weather-verb expletives like *it is raining*, expletives with extraposed clauses, as in *it is certain that* ... and expletives with existential verbs like *there is/there are* .... The first type is illustrated in (16), where a weather-verb (*orvalha* 'drizzle', *chove* 'rains', *moja* 'soaks', *lloverá* 'will rain' and *está lloviendo* 'is raining' respectively) appears with an overt expletive (*êle, el, ello, eso* respectively). Clausal extraposition cases are illustrated in (17), with a similar range of expletives as in the previous case, and (18) presents existential constructions.[7]

---

[6] These varieties include three distinct clusters: one, languages spoken in the Northwestern and Western Iberian Peninsula (Galician, spoken EP, Leonese), another, seventeenth- and nineteenth-century Spanish (see Silva-Villar, 1998 and references quoted there), and the third one, Central Colombian Spanish, henceforth CCS (as observed by myself). The precise geographical or social distribution of this expletive in these varieties remains unclear, although in CCS it seems to be an archaic but fully productive feature in the speech of older speakers. All examples from Northwestern and Western Iberian varieties come from Silva-Villar (1998), all CCS examples are my own.

[7] In the examples that follow, it is important to keep in mind that the expletive morpheme can have a separate referential interpretation, which should be discarded.

(16) a. Êle já   orvalha. (EP)
         EXP already drizzle
         'It is already drizzling.'
      b. El   chove. (Galician)
         EXP rains
         'It is raining.'
      c. Ello moja mucho. (Leonese)
         EXP soaks a lot
         'It is soaking wet.'
      d. Ello lloverá   sidra,   cigarrillos, corbatas, un   epatante
         EXP   rain-will cider,   cigarettes,   ties   a   dazzling
         solomillo. (19th-c. Spanish)
         sirloin
         'It will rain cider, cigarettes, ties, a dazzling sirloin.'
                              (from Silva-Villar, 1998, 252, ex. 8)
      e. Eso no está lloviendo tan duro. (CCS)
         EXP not is   raining   so hard.
         'It's not raining so hard.'

(17) a. Êle é certo que muitos se envergonhan de ... (EP)
         EXP is true that many CL shamed of
         'It is true that many people are ashamed of ...'
      b. E el   non em fermoso percorrer mundo? (Galician)
         Q EXP not was beautiful to-travel world
         'Wasn't it beautiful to wander the world?'
      c. Ello es necesario indagar que vida lleva. (18th-c. Spanish)
         EXP is necessary find-out what life leads
         'It is necessary to find out the type of life s/he is living.'
      d. Ellu foi que nun llegarun   a casa-si. (Leonese)
         EXP was that not ended-up-3.PL to marry-CL
         'It (just so) happened that they never ended up getting married.'
                              (from Silva-Villar, 1998, 252–253, ex. 9)
      e. ¿Eso no le parece que Gloria debe descansar? (CCS)
          EXP not CL seem   that Gloria should rest
         'Don't you think that Gloria should rest?'

(18) a. Pois ele havera castelhanos honrados? (EP)
         thus EXP will-be Castilians   honest
         'Are there honest Castilians?'
      b. Il   hai cecais outro   problema. (Galician)
         EXP is perhaps another problem
         'There is perhaps another problem.'

c. Ello hay por medio no sé qué papel de matrimonio.
EXP is involved not know.1.SG what document of marriage
(18th-c. Spanish)
'I don't know what kind of marriage document is involved therein.'
(from Silva-Villar, 1998, 253, ex. 10)

d. Eso allá hay mucha gente. (CCS)
EXP there is many people
'There is a lot of people there.'

These expletives appear productively in clause-initial position, but not in inversion contexts, for example in yes/no questions. We can see this property illustrated for EP and CCS respectively in (19)–(20): The order V-Expl is not possible in either case.

(19) * Chovera el hoije[sic]? (EP)
will-rain EXP today
'Will it rain today?' (from Silva-Villar, 1998, 254, ex. 12c)

(20) a. ¿Eso estará lloviendo? (CCS)
EXP will-be raining
'(I wonder:) is it raining?'

b. * ¿Estará eso lloviendo?
will-be EXP raining
'(I wonder:) is it raining?'

In CCS, the expletive *eso* cannot appear either immediately after the verb (see (21b)) or clause-finally, which is a possible position for subjects in yes/no questions.

(21) a. ¿Eso sabrá encontrar el restaurante? (CCS)
EXP will-know find the restaurant
'(I really wonder:) will s/he know how to find the restaurant?'

b. * ¿Sabrá encontrar eso el restaurante?
will-know find EXP the restaurant

c. * ¿Sabrá encontrar el restaurante eso?
will-know find the restaurant EXP

In embedded contexts, the varieties seem to split. Silva-Villar (1998, 255) reports that expletives are not possible in Galician and EP (see (22)), but in CCS they are under certain circumstances: whereas (23a) is not very good in this variety with an overt subject following the embedded expletive *eso*, (23b), with a null subject, is. Although the difference seems to be the presence of an overt subject in the first case vs. the second, it is not generally the case that overt subjects are not possible in embedded contetexts, as seen in (24).

(22) a. * Xa   sei   que el chove.
of-course know.1.SG that EXP rains
'Of course I know that it rains.'

b. * Foi   que ellu non legarun   a casa-si.   (Leonese)
happened that EXP not ended-up.3.PL to marry-REFLEX
'It so happened that they ended up not getting married.'
(from Silva-Villar, 1998, 255, ex. 13)

(23) a. * A mi me parece que eso Gloria no debe   salir.   (CCS)
to me CL seems that EXP Gloria not should go-out
'I think that Gloria should not go out.'

b. A mi me parece que eso no debe   salir.
to me CL seems that EXP not should go-out
'It seems to me that she/he should not go out.'

(24) Yo creo que eso la gente vive muy bien en esta ciudad.   (CCS)
I think that EXP the people live very well in this city
'I think that people live very well in this city.'

As the preceding two examples show, the expletive is compatible with an overt nominative preverbal subject. This is also the case for EP and seventeenth-century Spanish, as seen in (25) for other varieties. This has led Silva-Villar (1998, 267) to suggest that the expletive in these examples is discourse-related and appears in Spec, CP, as "the spellout of the deictically or contextually bound event argument referring to the given point in space and time."

(25) a. Ele os lobos anda-n com fame.   (EP)
EXP the wolves go-3.PL with hunger
'Wolves are hungry.'

b. Ello yo no se   porque mi padre no me   llamó   la torda
EXP I not know why   my father not CL.1.SG.ACC called.3.SG the thrush
o la papagaya.   (17th-c. Spanish)
or the parrot
'I don't know why I was not called either thrush or parrot by my father.'
(from Silva-Villar, 1998, 256–257 ex. 16)

To summarize the previous two sections, we have suggested that expletives can target at least two distinct positions: in DSEC, the expletive is incompatible with a preverbal subject, hence it must target a low position (IP or another subject-related position, cf. (15) above), whereas in CCS, Galician and other Northwestern Iberian languages, it targets a higher, CP-related topic position.

3.3 Subject inversion and no null expletives

According to Gilligan's implication in (2b), if a language has free inversion, then it should have null expletives. It follows that no language should be like Spanish or Italian (with SV/VS orders) and have overt expletives. In Rizzi's original analysis, if a language has free inversion, this implies that some other category satisfies its EPP requirement. Assuming some version of the Avoid Pronoun Constraint (one that states that overt pronouns should be avoided whenever possible), then such a language should not show overt expletives.

Overt expletives are a rarity among the world's languages. In Gilligan's (1987) survey of over 100 languages, he finds no case in which the expletive cannot be null.[8] Even in languages where overt expletives are present, we find a wide range of variation as to whether they are obligatory in all contexts. For example, expletives in Icelandic are only obligatory in clause-initial position (as are impersonal expletives in German and Yiddish), but must be null in non-clause-initial. This can be seen in (26a)–(28a), where það 'there' is not possible in three different types of expletive contexts in clause-internal position. By contrast, Norwegian det 'there', Danish der 'there', Swedish det 'there' and English it are obligatory in any clausal position in those contexts. Examples (26b)–(28b) illustrate the three contexts for Danish, (26c)–(28c) for Norwegian and (26d)–(28d) for Swedish.

(26) a. Þaðan   var (*það) skammt   til bæja.   (Icelandic)
        from-there was   there short-way to the-farms

    b. Derfra   var *(der) ikke langt til gårdene.   (Danish)
        from-there was   there not long to the-farms

    c. Derifra   var *(det) ikke langt til gårdene.   (Norwegian)
        from-there was   there not long to the-farms

    d. Därifrån var *(det) nära   till gårdarna.   (Swedish)
        from-there was   there short-way to the-farms
        'From there it was a short way to the farmsteads.'
                                        (from Platzack, 1987, 387, ex. 17)

(27) a. Nú er (*það) augljóst að Jón hefur barið Maríu.   (Icelandic)
        now is   it   obvious that John has   beaten Mary

    b. Nu er *(det) helt klart, at   John har slået   Maria.   (Danish)
        now is   it   very clear that John has beaten Mary

    c. Nå er *(det) åpenbart at   John har slått   Maria.   (Norwegian)
        now is   it   obvious that John has beaten Mary

---

[8] Although in his survey, several languages do not have data on this particular area.

        d. Nu är *(det) uppenbart att John har slagit Maria.   (Swedish)
           now is   it   obvious   that John has beaten Mary
           'It is obvious now that John has beaten Mary.'
                                            (from Platzack, 1987, 387, ex. 18)

(28)   a. Í   dag   hafa (*það) komið margir málvísindamenn hingað.
           in   today has   there   come   many   linguists   here
                                                                                      (Icelandic)
        b. I dag er *(der) kommet mange lingvister hertil.   (Danish)
           in today has   there come   many linguists here
        c. I dag har *(det) kommet mange lingvister hit.   (Norwegian)
           in today has   there come   many linguists here
        d. Idag har *(det) kommit många lingvister hit.   (Swedish)
           today has   there come   many linguists here
           'Today there have arrived many linguists.'
                                                      (from Platzack, 1987, 388, ex. 19)

It should be noted that none of these languages have null thematic subjects, although Icelandic has a fairly rich verbal paradigm (see Platzack, 2003, 331).

3.4   *That*-trace effects and overt expletives

The final implication from (2) predicts that languages should not have *that*-trace effect violations and overt expletives. Cabrera (2007) presented El Cibao speakers with a situation context and subsequently gave them a choice between an overt and a null complementizer in questions with a subject wh-word, as illustrated in (29a–b). Under those conditions, 80% of El Cibao speakers preferred the null complementizer version (29b) (see Cabrera, 2007, table 4.16). To the extent that this variety has overt expletives (see the discussion above), it seems to confirm the implicational.

(29)   a. ¿Quién dijiste que trabajó en el turno de noche?   (DS)
           who   said   that worked in the shift of night
           'Who did you say worked the night shift?'
        b. ¿Quién dijiste Ø trabajó en el turno de noche?
           who   said   Ø worked in the shift of night
           'Who did you say worked the night shift?'   (from Cabrera, 2007)

However, other native speakers of DS do allow for overt complementizers in those contexts, as seen in (30), suggesting that this implication does not hold universally. Although it is not clear why these conflicting results arise, I take them to mean that deletion is not obligatory in these contexts at least for some speakers (thanks to Jacqueline Toribio, p.c. for judgements).[9]

(30) ¿Quién tú dices que compró mangos?   (DS)
      who you say that bought mangoes
      'Who do you say bought mangoes?'   (from Jacqueline Toribio, p.c.)

Recall, however, that the original *that*-trace violation associated with the NSP should not be taken literally, but rather as the possibility of extracting from a postverbal position, an issue we will return to below.

3.5   Free subject inversion and *that*-trace effect violations

This implication follows in the traditional analysis, because *that*-trace effect violations (i.e. subject extraction in certain contexts) result from the availability of a postverbal subject position, also manifested in VS word orders (free inversion). The paradigmatic cases of this correlation come from Italian and Spanish. In these languages, it is possible to extract both subjects and objects without any changes in the complementizer system. In this sense, the subject wh-word *chi* in (31) does not induce deletion of the complementizer *che* 'that'.

(31) Chi credi che chiamarà questa sera?   (Italian)
      who think.2.SG that will call.3.SG this night
      'Who do you think will call tonight?'

Bavarian German, Övdalian, DS and Lubukusu also provide examples of this implication, but as I will argue below, both theoretical and empirical reasons question a direct connection between availability of a postverbal extraction site and *that*-trace effect violations. Additionally, Roberts and Holmberg (2010, 22, fn. 15) point out themselves that their proposed implicational seems to be counterintuitively backwards: free inversion is not a prerequisite for *that*-trace effect violations, but rather, *that*-trace effects imply free inversion. As we will see below, they suggest that this apparent puzzle can be resolved if Rizzi and Shlonsky's (2007) reformulation of what constrains subject extraction is correct.

3.5.1   Bavarian German and Övdalian

Bavarian illustrates a pattern where lack of inversion goes hand-in-hand with *that*-trace effects (see Bayer, 1984). Bavarian German, like general German,

---

[9] DS, like Puerto Rican Spanish, productively has the order SV in questions. See Ordóñez and Olarrea (2006), Comínguez (2012).

3.5 Free subject inversion and that-trace effect violations

has a fairly rigid V2 word order, so Italian-style free subject inversion is not possible, and the complementizer is dropped in subject extraction. In the example in (32a), when the wh-question *wer* 'who' is a subject, the complementizer *daβ* is absent, whereas when the question is about the object, the complementizer is present, as shown in (32b).

(32) a. Wer moanst du [mog d'Emma]? (Bavarian German)
    who think you loves Emma
    'Who do you think loves Emma?'

   b. Wer moanst du [daβ d'Emma mog]?
    who think you that Emma loves
    'Who do you think Emma loves?' (from Bayer, 1984, 210, ex. 2)

It should also be noted that Bavarian German is a partial NSL: only 2nd person subjects can be null (cf. (33a–b) vs. (c)).[10] However, violations of the *that*-trace filter do not correlate with the availability of NSs, suggesting that these two phenomena are not directly connected.[11]

(33) a. * Kumm-t *pro* noch Minga? (Bavarian German)
    come.3.SG *pro* to Munich
    'Will he/she/it come to Munich?'

   b. * Kumm *pro* noch Minga ...
    come.1.SG *pro* to Munich
    'If I come to Munich ...' (from Bayer, 1984, 239, ex. 68c–d)

   c. Kummst *pro* noch Minga, dann muaβt *pro* me b'suacha
    come.2.SG *pro* to Munich then must.2.SG *pro* me visit
    'If you come to Munich you must visit me.'
    (from Bayer, 1984, 211, ex. 7)

Övdalian, a variety of Mainland Scandinavian spoken in Sweden, shows a similar situation (see Rosenkvist, 2010b). In this language, 1st and 2nd person

---

[10] 2nd person morphemes are the only ones that uniquely encode person and number, as seen in the following table:

(i) Bavarian verbal suffixes (from Bayer, 1984, 239, ex. 69)

1SG, 2SG IMPER	2SG	1PL, 2SG/PL HON	3PL	2PL, 2IMPER	3SG
-∅	-st	-a		-ts	-t

[11] NSs are only possible in embedded clauses as seen in (33c) vs. (i) (Bayer, 1984).

(i) * In Bayern redt *pro* Bairisch
   in Bavaria speaks.3.SG *pro* Bavarian
   'In Bavaria, he speaks Bavarian.' (from Bayer, 1984, 211, ex. 6)

plural subjects can be null, as seen in (34), but the order SV is obligatory and the verb cannot precede the subject, as shown in (35).

(34)   a. Byddjum i Övdalim.   (Övdalian)
live.1.PL in Älvdalen
'We live in Älvdalen.'

b. Ulið fårå nų.
shall.2.PL leave now
'You ought to leave now.'   (from Rosenkvist, 2010b, 231, ex. 1)

(35)   a. * Ar kumið Lasse.   (Övdalian)
has arrived Lasse
'Lasse has arrived.'   (from Rosenkvist, 2010b, 239, ex. 10b)

b. Dier werd lie'ssner um Lasse int kumb.
they become sorry if Lasse not comes
'They'll be sorry if Lasse doesn't come (*sic*).'
(from Rosenkvist, 2010b, 242, ex. 16b)

Despite the partial availability of NSs, Övdalian has *that*-trace effects, as illustrated in (36). As the first example shows, the complementizer *at* 'that' must be dropped, or a resumptive pronoun must be inserted in the embedded clause (cf. (36b)). Alternatively, another complementizer *so* can be used, but this complementizer is also a conjunction.[12]

(36)   a. Ukin truo'dd du (*at) uld kumå?   (Övdalian)
who thought you would come
'Who did you think would come?'

b. Ukin truo'dd du at an uld kumå?
who thought you that he would come
'Who did you think would come?'

c. Ukin truo'dd du so uld kumå?
who thought you COMP would come
'Who did you think would come?'
(from Rosenkvist, 2010b, 240, ex. 12)

3.5.2 Levantine Arabic

Levantine Arabic shows *that*-trace effects like Bavarian and Övdalian, as Kenstowicz (1989, 264–265) points out. In this variety, the object wh-word can be extracted from the embedded clause, as seen in (37a), whereas the

---

[12] Övdalian verbs have identical forms for 1st, 2nd and 3rd person singular and 3rd person plural present tense and infinitive (*bait* 'bite'). In the plural, 1st and 2nd person are distinct (*baitum*, *baitið* respectively) (see Rosenkvist, 2010b, 237).

3.5 Free subject inversion and that-trace effect violations 55

subject wh-word cannot be extracted if the commplementizer *innu* 'that' is overt (cf. (37b)). If the complementizer is dropped, then subject extraction becomes grammatical, as (37c) shows.

(37) a. ʔayy fusṭaan Fariid kaal innu l-bint ištarat (Levantine Arabic)
 which dress Fariid said that the girl bought
 'Which dress did Fareed say that the girl bought?'

 b. * ʔayy bint$_i$ Fariid kaal innu e_i ištarat l-fusṭaan
 which girl Fariid said that bought the dress
 'Which girl did Fareed say that bought the dress?'

 c. ʔayy bint$_i$ Fariid kaal e_i ištarat l-fusṭaan
 which girl Fariid said bought the dress
 'Which girl did Fareed say that bought the dress?'
 (from Kenstowicz, 1989, 264, ex. 3a–c)

NSs are restricted to main clauses in Levantine Arabic (cf. (38a) vs. (b)). In embedded contexts, a pronominal subject is obligatorily cliticized on the complementizer (*-ha* in (38c)).

(38) a. (hiy) ištarat l-fusṭaan. (Levantine Arabic)
 (she) bought the dress
 'She bought the dress.'

 b. * Fariid kaal innu ištarat l-fusṭaan.
 Fariid said that bought the dress
 'Fareed said that s/he bought the dress.'

 c. Fariid kaal inn-ha ištarat l-fusṭaan.
 Fariid said that-she bought the dress
 "Fareed said that she bought the dress.'
 (from Kenstowicz, 1989, 264, ex. 4a–c)

While free inversion is possible in main clauses, the subject cannot be postverbal in embedded contexts with *innu*, as seen in (39a) vs. (39b). Since this is the environment crucial for licensing wh-extraction, then *that*-trace effects are expected.

(39) a. Fariid kaal innu l-bint ištarat l-fusṭaan. (Levantine Arabic)
 Fariid said that the girl bought the dress
 'Fareed said that girl bought the dress.'

 b. * Fariid kaal innu ištarat l-bint l-fusṭaan.
 Fariid said-she that bought the girl the dress
 'Fareed said that she bought the dress.'
 (from Kenstowicz, 1989, 264, ex. 5a-b)

3.5.3 Dominican Spanish

Dominican Spanish (DS) illustrates a similar pattern to Bavarian, Övdalian and Levantine Arabic: increasingly rigid word order (i.e. absence of free subject inversion) coexists with *that*-trace effect violations.

In his study of Caribbean Spanish, Ortiz López (2009, 88) finds that DS, Cuban and Puerto Rican speakers all overwhelmingly prefer the order SV (over 80% of the time) regardless of verb type or whether the subject is focused or not.[13] However, we do find evidence of alternative word orders in DS. In Bullock and Toribio's (2009) data, this order arises with presentational/existential sentences, such as (40). In (40a), the verb *haber* shows 1st person plural morphology, suggesting agreement with a null *pro*.[14] In (40b), we see plural agreement between the verb *hacer* and *tres meses* 'three months'. *Hacer* is typically used in two contexts: to denote a period of time in the past (as in the example), and to denote weather-related states (such as *hace frío* 'it is cold'). In other varieties, it does not agree with the DP: *Hace 25 grados* 'it is.3.SG 25 degrees'.

(40)   a. Habemos pocas familias en Los Compos.   (DSEC)
         be.1.PL few families in Los Compos
         'There are/we are a few families in Los Compos.'
         (from Bullock and Toribio, 2009, 54, ex. 5d)

       b. Hacían como tres meses que no llovía.
         be.3.PL approximately three months that not rain
         'It was was approximately three months since it hadn't rained.'
         (from Bullock and Toribio, 2009, 54, ex. 5a)

There are a few other instances of VS word order in non-presentational contexts, for example in (9) above, repeated below. In this example, the subject *raíz* is a bare noun in postverbal position.

---

[13] By contrast to Ortiz López (2009), Cabrera's (2007) study finds much lower frequencies of SV. In that study, speakers were presented with a contextually situated sentence with three possible variants, one option with a null subject, another one with a preverbal one, and a third option with a postverbal subject. Urban El Cibao speakers picked the null subject 33% of the time, the preverbal option 38% and the postverbal one 29%. It is not clear why Cabrera and Ortiz López's results vary so much. Part of it may be a test effect, but Ortiz López's results are more in line with general intuitions about Caribbean Spanish than Cabrera's. I take this to mean that DS is indeed losing free inversion.

[14] See the discussion of similar examples in other Spanish varieties the examples in (23)–(24) in Chapter 4.

(41)   Se fue, cogió un bastón, se encontró con su compadre y   hablaron
       CL went, got a   stick, CL met   with his friend   and talked
       tanto que le salió   raíz al   ba'tón.   (DSEC)
       so much that CL came out root to-the stick
       'He left, got a (walking) stick, he ran into a friend, and they talked so much
       that the stick sprung roots.'   (from Bullock and Toribio, 2009, 63, ex. 26b)

Given this increasingly fixed word order, one might expect DS to lose the ability to extract subjects over a filled complementizer and show canonical English *that*-trace effects, but this is not the case. Thus, subject extraction is acceptable in this variety without any changes in the complementizer system, as seen in (30).[15]

(42)   ¿Quién tú   dices que compró mangos?   (DS)
       who   you say that bought mangoes
       'Who do you say bought mangoes?'   (from Jacqueline Toribio, p.c.)

3.5.4   Brazilian Portuguese

Like DS, Brazilian Portuguese (BP) is an interesting variety to consider because it is increasingly losing many of the NS properties (see Duarte, 1993, 1995, 2000; Barbosa *et al.*, 2005). The European variety (EP) can have free inversion and null expletives, as shown in (43). Additionally, inversion is unrestricted, so for example, it is possible to have inverted definite subjects, as in (43a).

(43)   a. Telefonou o   João.   (EP)
             called   the Joao
             'Joao called.'
          b. Chove.
             rains
             'It is raining.'

By contrast, the VS word order in BP order is highly restricted, as Kato (2000, 250–251) points out: it is only productive with unaccusative verbs with indefinite subjects (cf. (44a)) and in existential constructions (cf. (44b)). As (45) shows, other types of verbs are ungrammatical in VS order. All of the ungrammatical examples in (44)–(45) are possible in EP (see also Figueiredo Silva, 1994).[16]

---

[15] Nevertheless, Cabrera's study found higher numbers of deleted complementizers, as already discussed in Section 3.4.

[16] Note, additionally, that the postverbal subject does not agree with the verb in the examples in (44a–b). The verb shows default 3.SG agreement.

(44) a. Tinha   chegado muitas cartas.   (BP)
         had.3.SG arrived   many   letters
         'There arrived many letters.'   (from Kato, 2000, 250, ex. 46a)
      b. Tem un gato embaixo da mesa
         has a cat under   of table
         'There is a cat under the table.'   (from Kato, 2000, 251, ex. 46b)

(45) a. * Cantam os pássaros / muitos pássaros.
            sing   the birds / many birds
            'The birds/many birds sing.'   (from Kato, 2000, 251, ex. 47c)
      b. * Respondeu a   pergunta a   Maria.   (BP)
            answered the question the Maria
            'Maria answered the question.'
      c. * Respondeu a   pergunta uma aluna.
            answered the question a   student
            'A student answered the question.' (from Kato, 2000, 251, ex. 47a–b)

Given this situation, does BP show *that*-trace effects? According to Menuzzi (2000), it does, but only when the NS is extracted from a preverbal position. In this sense, he is interpreting *that*-trace effects as the availability of long-distance subject extraction depending on the extraction site, regardless of the actual complementizer.

To show this, he uses a floated quantifier *todos* 'all' as a way of tracking extraction sites. With this in mind, consider (46). In this sentence, subject extraction is possible in the first example, and *todos* 'all' is located postverbally, suggesting that extraction has taken place from a postverbal position. When the floated quantifier is located preverbally, subject extraction is not possible, as shown in (46b). The corresponding structures appear in (47).[17]

(46) a. Que   rapazes, o Paulo desconfia [que gostem **todos** de Maria]? (BP)
         which boys   the Paulo suspects that like   all   of Maria
         'Which boys does Paulo suspect all like Maria?'
      b. * Que   rapazes, o   Paulo desconfia [que **todos** gostem de Maria]?
           which boys,   the Paulo suspects that (all)   like   of Maria?
           'Which children does Paulo suspect all like Maria?'
                                       (from Menuzzi, 2000, 29, ex. 33)

---

[17] Menuzzi (2000, 30) points out that (46a) has a "recherché feeling about it," but according to him, the contrasts are clear.

(47) a.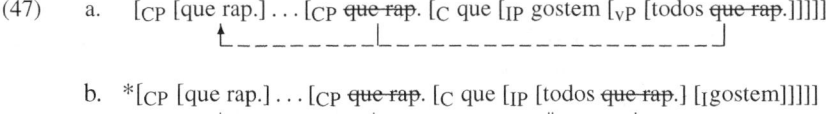

b. *[CP [que rap.] ... [CP que rap. [C que [IP [todos que rap.] [I gostem]]]]]

Menuzzi (2000) further asserts that extraction from a preverbal position becomes possible in contexts of inflected infinitives, as shown in (48). For these cases, he assumes that the verb has moved to C. He claims that *nada* in this example is dislocated to a position immediately dominating I′, because in finite clauses, the only possible order would be S–*nada*–V. Assuming that V is in I, and the subject is in Spec, IP, it follows that *nada* must be adjoined to I′. Transposing this idea to inflected infinitives, the result is the structure in (49), where the inflected infinitive is higher than the subject and the dislocated object.

(48) Que rapazes, o Manuel afirma terem todos nada oferecido de
 which boys the Manuel claims to-have.3.PL all nothing offered of
 presente pr'a Maria no aniversário dela?
 present to-the Maria in-the birthday of-her
 'Which boys does Manuel claim to all have offered nothing as a gift to Maria for her birthday?' (from Menuzzi, 2000, 35, ex. 40a)

(49)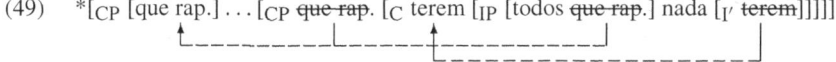

Below we will offer a slightly different account of these facts, but for now, note that if Menuzzi's analysis is correct, BP would be a case in which an increasingly fixed SV word order still allows for extraction from the postverbal subject position if the verb remains in I, or from either position if the verb moves to C.

3.5.5 Subject extraction in Lubukusu

Several Bantu languages show extraction asymmetries that bear a resemblance to *that*-trace effects. Among them, Lubukusu has NSs (Diercks, 2010, 172) and also alternative word orders (particularly with respect to locative inversion), but also has subject/object extraction asymmetries. This is unexpected under the implicational conditional being considered.

When a subject is extracted (both in wh-questions and relatives), it triggers obligatory agreement not only with the verb, but also with the complementizer (see (50)). In statements like (50a), the subject agrees with the verb (as signaled by verbal prefix *si-*), and this agreement is reproduced in the complementizer as well, as seen in (50b).[18] If the complementizer does not agree, as in (50c), the result is ungrammatical.

(50)   a. sii-tabu si-a-tib-a.   (Lubukusu)
            7-book 7-PAST-lose-FV
            'The book got lost.'

            b. siina si-sy-a-tib-a?
            what 7.WH-7.S-PAST-lose-FV
            'What got lost?'

            c. *siina sy-a-tib-a?
            what 7.S-PAST-lose-FV
            'What got lost?'   (from Wasike, 2007, 236)

By contrast, objects do not trigger complementizer agreement when they are extracted. Object questions can be formulated either in situ, or through movement. In situ wh-objects show the same pattern as regular SVO declaratives, as seen in (51a–b). Importantly, they do not trigger wh-agreement on the verb.

(51)   a. Nafula a-a-siim-a   Wafula.   (Lubukusu)
            1.Nafula 1.S-PRES-love-FV 1.Wafula
            'Nafula loves Wafula.'

            b. Nafula a-a-siim-a   naanu?
            1.Nafula 1.S-PRES-love-FV who
            'Who does Nafula love?'

By contrast, displaced object wh-words cannot follow this pattern, as seen in (52a), but must add an obligatory Comp-like element (glossed as PRED) as shown in (52b).

(52)   a. *naanu Nafula a-a-siim-a?
            who 1.Nafula 1.S-PRES-love-FV
            'Who does Nafula love?'

            b. naanu ni-ye Nafula a-a-sim-a?
            who PRED-1 1.Nafula 1.S-PRES-love-FV
            'Who is it that Nafula loves?'
                                    (from Wasike, 2007, 234, in Diercks, 2010, 85, ex. 5)

---

[18] Complementizer/wh-agreement is glossed as '7.WH' to distinguish it from subject agreement, glossed as '7.S'.

3.5 Free subject inversion and that-trace effect violations

While most of these facts are consistent with Gilligan's implicational universal that *that*-trace effect violations imply null expletives, and that free inversion implies *that*-trace effect violations (cf. (2) above), we find at least some languages that show free subject inversion and no *that*-trace violations. Additionally, as noted above, the implication seems to be backwards: if *that*-trace effect violations are possible because a language can have postverbal subjects, and postverbal subjects are possible whenever there is a null subject to license the EPP, then null subjects should be the condition for free inversion and for *that*-trace effects. As suggested, Roberts and Holmberg (2010) propose that Rizzi and Shlonsky's (2007) account provides a solution to these shortcomings, and this is also the solution proposed by Diercks (2010), as we will see in Section 4.4.2.

3.5.6 Summary

The data from the preceding sections suggest several conclusions:

1. Obligatorily overt expletives are typologically very rare.
2. Expletives may target an extended range of IP–CP positions.
3. Implications related to *that*-trace effects and free inversion are not directly connected with null subjects.
4. Implications related to *that*-trace effects and free inversion require a different formalization.

The first generalization leads to the conclusion that the requirement for obligatorily overt expletives is not directly connected to the NSP. Scarcity of expletives across languages also suggests that they may not be the product of a unique principle. This conclusion is supported by Sigurðsson's (2010) proposal that EPP effects fall under two distinct categories: NP-movement and a Filled Left Edge Effect (FLEE). Left edge refers to the highest clausal specifier, namely Spec, CP in full clauses, and Spec, TP in clauses without a CP layer, such as certain infinitival clauses. Recall that in Icelandic (and in German and Yiddish impersonal constructions), an overt expletive is only available in clause-initial position, but not otherwise. In the other Scandinavian languages (and in English), expletives are possible in other positions as well. For Sigurðsson (2010), this suggests that the syntax of certain expletives is driven by person agreement, which triggers their presence in several positions. Left-edge effects separate languages that have obligatory expletives only in root contexts from languages where expletives appear in non-root contexts.

I will return to *that*-trace violations in Section 4.4.2, although the proposal there will not be directly connected with the NSP.

3.6 Variation in logophoricity

Another important feature of the NSP that will have to be accounted for is variation in person. As I mentioned in the presentation of the typology of NSLs (see Section 2.3.3), several languages are sensitive to the 1st/2nd vs. 3rd person distinction. Specifically, we saw that Finnish and Hebrew allow for NSs under certain circumstances in 1st/2nd but not in 3rd person, and others like Shipibo allow the opposite pattern (overt in 1st/2nd and possibly null in 3rd). This has led several researchers to argue that 1st and 2nd person head a syntactic projection in the left periphery (Baker, 2008b; Shlonsky, 2009; Camacho and Elías-Ulloa, 2010; Sigurðsson, 2010, among others). In addition to those patterns, we also find evidence that subject extraction can be affected by person, and in this section we will consider three instances, inverted copular predicate in BP and in Spanish and locality of NSs in Shipibo.

3.6.1 Person effects in inverse copular clauses in Brazilian Portuguese and Spanish

Lima (2005) points out that subject–verb agreement, which is usually obligatory in BP, allows for two possibilities in inverted copular constructions, as illustrated in (53). If the predicate (*a causa da briga* 'the cause of the fight') appears in preverbal position, agreement can target either the postverbal subject (*as meninas* 'the girls') or it can be default, as in (53a), but if the predicate is postverbal, agreement with the subject is obligatory, as seen in (53b).

(53)   a. A causa da briga foi / foram as meninas.   (BP)
           the cause of-the fight was / were the girls
           'The cause of the fight was the girls.'

       b. As meninas foram / *foi a causa da briga.
           the girls were / *was the cause of-the fight
           'The girls were the cause of the fight.'   (from Lima, 2005, 1, exx. 1–2)

By contrast, Lima (2005) points out that 1st and 2nd persons trigger obligatory agreement with the subject, regardless of word order. In particular, (54a) does not allow for 3rd sg agreement (*e* 'is'), in contrast to (53a).

(54)   a. A causa da briga *e / sou eu.   (BP)
           the cause of-the fight *is / am I
           'The cause of the fight is me.'

       b. Eu sou / *e a causa da briga.
           I am / *is the cause of-the fight
           'I am the cause of the fight.'   (from Lima, 2005, 7, exx. 26–27)

The same patterns can be observed in Spanish, where the 3rd person verbal form *es* 'is' cannot appear with 1st person *yo* 'I' or 2nd person *tú* 'you', as seen in (55)–(56).[19]

(55)   a. Yo soy / *es la causa de la pelea.   (Spanish)
           I am / *is the cause of the fight
           'I am the cause of the fight.'

       b. La causa de la pelea soy / *es yo.
         the cause of the fight am / is I
         'The cause of the fight is me.'

(56)   a. Tú eres / *es la causa de la pelea.   (Spanish)
         you are / *is the cause of the fight
         'You are the cause of the fight.'

       b. La causa de la pelea eres / *es tú.
         the cause of the fight are / *is you
         'The cause of the fight is you.'

If one adopts Moro's (1993) proposal for copular sentences (as Lima (2005) does), they involve movement of either the subject or the predicate to preverbal position. Example (53a), the version where the verb agrees with the postverbal subject, can be analyzed as a case where inflection probes downwards and finds the subject. The default agreement case, in turn, can involve either a null expletive, or simply lack of agreement that is translated in to a default morpheme. In (53b), on the other hand, the closest agreeing category is the subject, so if one assumes that locality is relevant to determine agreement, then the proximity of the subject would make agreement obligatory. This, in turn would also require upwards probing.

In the case of 1st and 2nd person, we can follow a suggestion by Lima that "(first) person licensing may be obligatorily related to a position high in the clause," and adopt recent proposals (Baker, 2008b; Shlonsky, 2009; Sigurðsson, 2010) that a logophoric projection is located in the left periphery. As we will see later, if *pro* must be identified by an operator, and a 1st and 2nd person operator is situated in the left periphery, then the only option will be for *pro* to be interpreted as 1st and 2nd person, hence the agreement patterns in (54)–(56).

A similar pattern is seen in cleft-focus constructions in Spanish, as seen in (57) (see Camacho, 2001). The copular verb in these constructions must obligatorily agree with a 1st or 2nd person subject (*tú* 'you' in (57a–b)), but

---

[19] Spanish has distinctive 2nd person agreement, unlike BP.

when the focused predicate is not a subject, agreement is a default 3rd person, as seen in (57c).

(57)   a. Fuiste   tú   quien no vino.   (Spanish)
          were.2.SG you who not came
          'It was you who didn't come.'
       b. *Fue   tú   quien no vino.
          was.3.SG you   who   not came
          'It was you who didn't come.'
       c. Fue   a ti   a quien vimos.
          was.3.SG to you to whom saw
          'It was you who we saw.'

3.6.2 Person effects in Shipibo switch-reference clauses

A third case where extraction is sensitive to logophoricity is Shipibo NSs. Recall from Section 2.3.3 that Shipibo is a mixed NS language that only marks plural on the verb in the 3rd person, and that overt subjects are obligatory in 1st and 2nd person but optional in 3rd person. Thus, (58a) can be interpreted only as 3rd person because the subject is null, and all of the verb forms in (58) are identical regardless of the person of the subject.

(58)   a. Lima-n-ra   noko-ke.   (Shipibo)
          Lima-DIR-EVID arrive-PERF
          'He/she went to Lima.'
       b. Ea-ra Lima-n   noko-ke.
          1-EVID Lima-DIR arrive-PERF
          'I arrived in Lima.'
       c. Mia-ra Lima-n   noko-ke.
          2-EVID Lima-DIR arrive-PERF
          'You arrived in Lima.'
                                    (from Camacho and Elías-Ulloa, 2010, 72, ex. 13)

Embedded clauses in Shipibo are most frequently switch-reference clauses with a switch-reference morpheme, as illustrated in (59). As that example shows, 3rd person subjects can be null, whereas 1st/2nd person subjects must appear overtly at least in one of the clauses or in both, as seen with (en 'I' in (60a–c)). If no subject appears in those sentences (as in (60d)), the clause can only be interpreted as 3rd person.

(59)   Jawen atsabo oroṣon-ra   pei-bo   ate-ke.   (Shipibo)
          POSS yucca grow-PRIOR.SS.TR-EVID leave-PL cut-PERF
          'He grew yucca and cut the leaves.'

(60) a. En westiora ipo   chachi-şon   -ra en Quique kena-ke.
        IP a   carachama catch-PRIOR.SS.TR -EVID IP Quique call-PERF
                                                                (Shipibo)
        'I caught a carachama (type of fish) and called Quique.'
    b. En westiora ipo   chachi-şon   -ra Quique kena-ke.
        IP a   carachama catch-PRIOR.SS.TR -EVID Quique call-PERF
        'I caught a carachama (type of fish) and called Quique.'
    c. Westiora ipo   chachi-şon   -ra en Quique kena-ke.
        a   carachama catch-PRIOR.SS.TR -EVID IP Quique call-PERF
        'I caught a carachama (type of fish) and called Quique.'
    d. # Westiora ipo   chachi-şon   -ra Quique kena-ke.
         a   carachama catch-PRIOR.SS.TR -EVID Quique call-PERF
        'I caught a carachama (type of fish) and called Quique.'

In Camacho and Elías-Ulloa (2010), we analyze the 1st/2nd person paradigm in a similar way as we have proposed for BP and Spanish copular structures: they involve a logophoric head that must be overtly realized. In that analysis, the overt pronoun is the overt copy of a moved pronoun, which can surface in either position. Third persons, on the other hand, are recovered through the discourse, so they need not be overt.

3.7 Chapter summary

In this chapter, I have reviewed the empirical predictions of the different correlations of NSP properties, as proposed by Gilligan (1987). First, I have suggested that the correlation between null thematic and expletive subjects does not necessarily hold if one takes optionally overt expletives as counterevidence. Languages like Dominican Spanish from El Cibao have overt expletives despite having partial NSs. I have also argued that the DSEC expletive is best seen primarily as an IP-expletive, by comparison to other Romance varieties that have a CP-expletive. Regarding the correlation between subject inversion and null expletives, I have argued that the relative rarity of overt expletives in the world's languages suggests that these are independent properties. Furthermore, comparison within Scandinavian languages, some of which allow for expletive inversion and some of which do not, also suggests that the correlation between inversion and expletives is not tenable. Regarding *that*-trace effects, I have argued that DS shows a case of a language where *that*-trace effect violations do not hold and overt expletives still exist, regardless of whether *that*-trace effect violations are viewed as complementizer deletion or as subject extraction over a filled complementizer,

In the second part of the chapter, I have turned to the correlation between free subject inversion and *that*-trace effect violations, and I have suggested that it does not hold for at least some Bantu languages, and that *that*-trace effect violations may require an alternative explanation unconnected to the NSP. This alternative will be explored in Section 4.4.2.

Finally, I have argued that in addition to the EPP-related properties, the NSP must also account for the person effects that constrain the distribution of NSs in many languages, and in particular, the way they interact in cases of movement.

4 *The nature of the Extended Projection Principle and the Null Subject Parameter*

If one assumes the EPP, it follows that clauses without overt subjects must have a null one. One question this assumption raises is what category can satisfy the EPP in a NSL. Related to this question is the status of overt subjects: are they in an A or A′ position? Do they have properties similar to dislocated phrases?[1]

Several researchers have proposed a parametric version of the EPP. For example, Alexiadou and Anagnostopoulou (1998) argue that verb movement to I satisfies it in languages like Greek or Spanish that have rich agreeement. However, Holmberg and Nikkane (2002) point out that in Finnish, the verb also has rich inflection which licenses null subjects in many contexts and it moves to I, but overt expletives are still required in certain contexts. This leads them to propose two distinct requirements: one that can be satisfied by a verb moving to I, and another one that is active in some languages but not in others, that forces the Spec, IP to be filled.

Others like Manzini and Savoia (2002) propose that the EPP entails a D feature in IP. Languages like English lack a specialized element to realize D, hence a DP must surface. Consistent NSLs, on the other hand, have a weak D, so they need not realize it at PF. Finally, Northern Italian dialects, which have a subject clitic, have a strong D which surfaces as the clitic.

In the following sections, I will explore the three most prominent answers to the question of what fulfills the EPP in a NSL. After that, I will review the evidence for separate EPP requirements, and in Chapter 8, I will discuss the position of preverbal subjects in NSLs.

---

[1] The advent of bare phrase structure proposals casts some doubts on the theoretical viability of a unified EPP. Formulations of the EPP as a feature that attracts a category have the same problem: given the assumption that constituents that AGREE can do so at a distance, AGREE by itself cannot be the trigger for movement of the subject to a preverbal position, see Section 4.4. In Rizzi's (2005b) analysis (see also Rizzi and Shlonsky, 2007), the equivalent of the EPP, the Subject Criterion, assumes a Spec, head relationship, which is no longer considered a theoretically well-defined configuration (see below).

As Saab (2010) points out, the question of what satisfies the EPP in an NSL has been answered in three ways. The first and probably most prolific answer suggests that an empty category, *pro*, does (see Chomsky, 1981; Rizzi, 1982, 1986a; Rizzi and Shlonsky, 2007, and many others). The second one assumes that pronominal subjects are deleted versions of overt pronouns (see Perlmutter, 1971; Neeleman and Szendroi, 2007; Saab, 2009; Roberts, 2010a, among others). The third one assumes that the inflectional properties of the verb can be pronominal, hence they can satisfy the EPP (see Jelinek, 1984; Borer, 1986; Ordóñez, 1997; Alexiadou and Anagnostopoulou, 1998; Kato, 1999; Ordóñez and Treviño, 1999; Barbosa *et al.*, 2005; Barbosa, 2010; Sigurðsson, 2011, among others).

4.1   *Pro*

Assuming a formulation of the EPP in terms of a requirement to have a certain structural position filled, one is committed to the existence of a null pronominal (*pro*). For some researchers, *pro* is a syntactically distinct category, following Chomsky (1981). In this line, Rizzi (1986a) articulates a very influential theory of how *pro* fits into the general typology of referential elements. In his account, *pro* is subject to two independent conditions, presented in (1).

(1)   a. *Licensing of pro*: *pro* is governed by X^0.
   b. *Identification of pro*: let X be the licensing head of an occurrence of *pro*: then *pro* has the grammatical specification of the features on the X coindexed with it.   (from Rizzi, 1986a, 519–520)

In a NSL, a thematic subject *pro* is governed and identified by I^0. In English or French, on the other hand, I^0 is not rich enough to identify *pro*, so the identification condition fails and subjects must be overt. These same conditions could conceivably account for expletive *pro*, if one assumes that they must also be identified. However, given their non-thematic, non-referential status, one wonders why identification would be a requirement of expletives.

In some sense, the crucial debate with respect to *pro* has to do with whether there is a separate category that satisfies certain syntactic requirements, or whether these are satisfied by a feature on an inflectional or verbal category, as Holmberg (2005) points out.[2] In this section I will present several arguments

---

[2] The notion that inflection has argumental properties will be developed in detail in Section 4.2 below. Essentially, the idea is that inflection can receive a theta role and satisfy the EPP in certain contexts.

that are compatible with both proposals, although for the sake of presentation I will use the term *pro*. I will also point out where the two theories make distinct predictions, generally favoring an independent *pro* over pronominal agreement.

The two main theoretical arguments in favor of *pro* stem from Theta Theory and the EPP. If one assumes that theta roles must be discharged, it follows that there must be some syntactic category that receives the subject theta role, even when there is no overt subject, hence this category must be either *pro* or pronominal agreement. On the other hand, if all clauses must have a subject (regardless of their thematic structure), then even verbs that do not assign an external theta role must have an implicit expletive subject.

Other more empirically oriented reasons to propose *pro* are linked to the comparative distribution of overt and null subjects in a number of languages, a matter to which I turn below.

4.1.1 Presentational sentences

Burzio (1986, 129–130) notes that overt subjects must be postverbal in Italian presentational sentences (see also Cardinaletti, 1997, 36). For this reason, (2a), with the subject *io* 'I' in preverbal position is ungrammatical, whereas the counterpart with a postverbal subject presented in (2b) is fine. In that context, NS are not possible, as one can see in (cf. (3)).

(2)   a. * Io ci sono alla festa.   (Italian)
          I CL am at-the party   (from Cardinaletti, 1997, 37, ex. 8a)

    b. Ci sono io alla festa.
       CL am I at-the party
       'I am there at the party.'   (from Burzio, 1986, 130, ex. 106a)

(3)   * Ci sono alla festa.
      CL am at-the party   (from Burzio, 1986, 130, ex. 106b)

Spanish shows a similar situation. For example, if someone knocks at the door and I ask *¿quién es?* 'who is it?', the answer could be (4a), with a postverbal overt subject, but not (4b) with a preverbal one, or (4c), with a null subject.

(4)   a. Soy yo.   (Spanish)
       am I
       'It's me.'

    b. # Yo soy.
       I am
       'I am.'

c. # Soy.
   am
   'I am.'

In Spanish at least, this paradigm seems to follow from the assertion structure triggered by the question: *Who is it?* is only compatible with focus on the subject, which in that case must be clause-final (accounting for the contrast between (4a–b)). The ungrammaticality of (4c) can follow either because *pro* must be preverbal (as Burzio and Cardinaletti assume), or because it cannot bear the required nuclear stress to be focused.

Given that all of these forms have identical inflectional endings, these data present a challenge for the pronominal agreement analysis. One possibility more consistent with assuming pronominal inflection would explain the distributions just observed from nuclear stress placement, as suggested in the preceding paragraph. However, certain verb forms in Spanish are stress-final and stress falls on the vowel that indicates person/number. So if (4b–c) are ungrammatical in the context of (4a) because it is impossible to assign nuclear stress to the focused subject, a simple-minded extension of this analysis would predict that (5c) should be appropriate in the context of (5a), because the syllable that carries stress on the verb *fue* 'was' also conveys inflectional properties (3.SG.PAST), so the reference-bearing element would receive nuclear stress and therefore focus. However, only an overt subject is possible in that context (which triggers focus on the subject), as seen in (5b).

(5) a. ¿Quién fue el que rompió la puerta?   (Spanish)
        who was the that broke the door
        'Who was it that broke the door?'
     b. Fue   él.
        was.3.SG he
        'It was him.'
     c. # Fue.
        was.3.SG
        '(S/he) was.'

4.1.2 Copular sentences with nominal predicates

In Italian and Spanish, the order of the subject and the predicate can be reversed in copular sentences, as seen in (6). However, only the preverbal element can be null, whether it is the subject *io* 'I' in (7a) or the predicate *il presidente* 'the president' in (7b). Neither constituent can be null in postverbal position, as shown in (8), and this leads Cardinaletti (1997) to conclude that the null element (*pro*) is preverbal.

(6)   a. Io sono il presidente.   (Italian)
              I am   the president
              'I am the president.'
     b. Il   presidente sono io.
              the president am   I
              'I am the president.'   (from Cardinaletti, 1997, 40, ex. 27)

(7)   a. Sono il   presidente.
              am   the president
              'I am the president.'
     b. Sono io.
              am   I
              'It's me.'

(8)   a. * Io sono.
                I   am   (from Cardinaletti, 1997, 40, ex. 30)
     b. * Il   presidente sono.
                the president am   (from Cardinaletti, 1997, 40, ex. 29a)

Although these facts argue for the existence of *pro*, I can think of two objections to using them as evidence for the preverbal position of *pro*. First, by definition, the null category in (7b) is not the subject, since the verb agrees with *io* 'I'. It may be an expletive in Spec, IP required for independent reasons, but it doesn't agree with the subject. Second, Cardinaletti (1997, 40) acknowledges a potential alternative analysis to her own, quoting Solà (1992, 156), who points out that the copular construction "is precisely used to focalize the subject, hence it cannot be dropped." Cardinaletti counters that this explanation does not apply to (8a), because the postverbal predicate is not focalized, so whatever reason drives the ungrammaticality of (8), it cannot be that the constituent that should carry focus is null.

The Italian facts described until now are identical in Spanish, but in this language, the postverbal constituent would receive nuclear stress, if Zubizarreta (1998) is correct. This automatically discards *pro* from a postverbal position in the Spanish counterparts of (8). Consider the context introduced by (9a), which would be consistent with an answer that focuses the subject. In this context, the answer in (9b), the Spanish version of (8a), would be grammatical, as would be the alternative with emphatic stress on the subject pronoun *yo* 'I' in (9c). In both cases, the predicate (*el presidente* 'the president') is null and nuclear stress is no longer on the last constituent of the clause, hence the result becomes grammatical.

(9)   a. ¿Quién es el presidente?   (Spanish)
            who is the president
            'Who is the president?'
           b. Soy yo.
            am I
            'It's me.'
           c. Yo soy.
            I am
            'I am.'

The paradigm in (9) argues in favor of deriving the distribution of null predicates from focus and stress requirements, and not directly from the postverbal position of *pro*. However, one could claim that the pronoun in (9c), by virtue of being emphatic, is in a different position than in (8a) in Italian. However, this does not explain why the predicate can be null. Furthermore, if the predicate is overt, it must be postverbal, as shown by the ungrammaticality of (10a) shows. On the other hand, if the distributions in (6)–(9) follow from nuclear stress placement, then the grammaticality of (9c) also follows.

(10)   a. * Yo el presidente soy.   (Spanish)
             I the president am
           b. Yo soy el presidente
             I am the president
             'I am the president.'

These facts are not compatible with a pronominal agreement theory, since in all cases we have the same type of inflection and that theory cannot easily accommodate asymmetries based on word-order differences.

4.1.3   *Floated quantifiers*

Roberts (2010a, 72) quotes Rizzi (1987) as showing that only preverbal subjects license a floated quantifier in Italian. We can see this generalization in (11). In the first sentence, the preverbal subject can appear with a floated quantifier *tutti* 'all', but when the subject is postverbal, as in (11b), the floated quantifier cannot appear. In Sportiche's (1988) account, this contrast follows from a requirement that the element the floated quantifier associates with must c-command the quantifier, a configuration that happens in (11a) but not in (11b). Since a floated quantifier is grammatical with a null subject, as seen in (12), it follows that *pro* must c-command it, and must therefore be preverbal, assuming that the quantifier is located in the lower subject position. This contrast is not easy to explain if inflection is pronominal, since AGR/INFL c-commands the quantifier both in (11a) and (11b).

(11) a. I bambini sono andati tutti via. (Italian)
      the children are gone all away

   b. * Sono andati tutti via i bambini.
      are gone all away the children
      'All the children have gone away.'
      (from Roberts, 2010a, 72, exx. 20b–c)

(12) Sono andati tutti via. (Italian)
      are gone all away
      'They have all gone away.' (from Roberts, 2010a, 72, exx. 20b–c)

Cardinaletti (1997, 50–51) extends the floated quantifier test one step further to argue that *pro* occupies the specifier closest to I. She notes that in (13a), the preverbal quantifier is ungrammatical, even though the example has *pro* (*gli studenti* 'the students' is left-dislocated). This follows if *pro* does not c-command *tutti* 'all', suggesting a structure where *pro* is lower in the tree than the floated quantifier, as in (13b), and not one like (13c), where *pro* does c-command.³

(13) a. * Non so se gli studenti, questo libro, *tutti* l' hanno comprato.
         not know if the students, this book, all CL have bought
         (Italian)
         (from Cardinaletti 1997, 50, ex. 63)
   b. Non so se gli studenti, questo libro, [_Agrs1P_ *tutti* [_Agrs1P_ *pro* l' hanno comprato]]
   c. Non so se gli studenti, questo libro, [_Agrs1P_ *pro* [_Agrs1P_ *tutti* l' hanno comprato]]

However, the floated quantifier evidence for *pro* is not as compelling as it might seem at first sight, because if one extends the conclusions drawn from (13) to (11b), *pro* should also occupy Spec, IP, but in such case, it should be able to c-command the floated quantifier.

Alternatively, one could argue that *pro* does not occupy Spec, IP in general, and in (11b) in particular. If this is correct, something else must fulfill the EPP requirement, and the natural candidate would be for the overt subject *i bambini*

---

³ In Cardinaletti's proposal, Agrs1P and Agrs2P are different subject positions for strong pronouns, R-expressions and weak pronouns respectively.

'the children'. This assumption is consistent with Zubizarreta's (1998, 136) analysis of VOS word order in Italian, which she takes to be derived from the underlying SVO order, "where S is in the specifier of a Focus projection above TP" (p. 136) and TP is further adjoined to FP. If Zubizarreta is right, then the subject satisfies the EPP requirement, subsequently moving to FP. One immediate consequence of this line of analysis is that *pro* does not necessarily appear in (11b), hence this example is not evidence for its IP-position. The ungrammaticality of that example would then follow from the fact that the overt subject does not c-command the floated quantifier.

In Spanish, the floated quantifier evidence does not support the status of *pro* as adjacent to Spec, IP. In this language, the example corresponding to (11a) is also ungrammatical (cf. (14a)), however the one corresponding to (13) is not (cf. (14b)). One would expect the first example to be grammatical if *pro* occupies an IP position and can c-command the floated quantifier *todos/cada uno* 'all/each'. Conversely, if *pro* is lower than the preverbal floated quantifier in (14b), the sentence should be ungrammatical, as Cardinaletti proposes for Italian (cf. (13b) above).

(14) a. * Salieron todos/cada uno a la calle los niños. (Spanish)
went-out all/each one to the street the children

b. No sé si los estudiantes, este libro, todos / (cada uno) lo han
not know if the students, this book, all / (each one) CL have
comprado.
bought
'I don't know if the students have all/each bought this book.'

4.1.4 Agreement in the Ancona variety

Another argument for the preverbal position of *pro* stems from the Central Italian dialect spoken in Ancona (see Cardinaletti, 1997, 39–40). When the subject is postverbal, full agreement is optional, and the verb can show 3rd person singular morphology, as seen in (15a). Agreement between the verb and a preverbal subject, on the other hand, must fully match the features of the subject. As an illustration, the plural subject *i bambini* 'the children' triggers obligatory 3rd person plural agreement on the verb, as seen in (15b–c).

(15) a. Questo, lo fa sempre i bambini. (Ancona variety)
this.ACC CL do.3.SG always the.PL children.PL
'The children always do this.'

b. Questo, i bambini lo fanno sempre.
this.ACC the.PL children.PL CL do.3.PL always
'The children always do this.'

c. *Questo, i   bambini   lo fa   sempre.
   this.ACC the.PL children.PL CL do.3.SG always
                                     (from Cardinaletti, 1997, 39, ex. 21)

The agreement asymmetry related to the position of the verb provides a marker for the position of null subjects, which pattern like preverbal ones in requiring full plural agreement. As a result, (16a) cannot have a plural interpretation, and given the agreement asymmetry, the null subject must be preverbal. By contrast, (16b), with plural morphology on the verb must be interpreted as plural.

(16)   a. Questo, lo   fa   sempre.   (Ancona variety)
          this.ACC CL.ACC do.3.SG always
          'She/he always does this.' (not 'They always do this')
       b. Questo, lo   fanno   sempre.
          this.ACC CL.ACC do.3.PL always
          'They always do it.'   (from Cardinaletti, 1997, 39, ex. 22)

Notice that even when some element like a floated quantifier signals plurality of the null subject, the verb cannot show default 3rd person SG. This is exemplified with the floated quantifier *tutti* 'all' in (17): The verb can only be plural (*dimonstra* 'demonstrates' in (17a) vs. *dimonstrano* 'demonstrate' in (17b)).

If *pro* is always preverbal, agreement must be full as it is with overt subjects, hence both *pro* and the verb should be plural in (17a).

(17)   a. *Questo, lo   dimonstra   tutte.   (Ancona variety)
          this.ACC CL.ACC demonstrate.3.SG all.3.FEM.PL
       b. Questo, lo   dimonstrano   tutte.
          this.ACC CL.ACC demonstrate.3.PL all.3.FEM.PL
          'They always demonstrate it.'   (from Cardinaletti, 1997, 39, ex. 23)

Once again, this distribution poses a challenge to the pronominal agreement hypothesis. First of all, if agreement is always pronominal, one expects a referential clash between singular agreement and the plural DP in (15a). Second, the word-order asymmetries observed in (15a–c) are unexpected, if agreement is always argumental. As a consequence, the ungrammaticality of (17a) becomes surprising, given the grammaticality of (15a).

4.1.5   Section summary

This section has summarized arguments in favor of the existence of *pro* and the hypothesis that *pro* is preverbal. In particular, it has provided data from presentational sentences in Italian and Spanish, copular sentences with nominal predicates, floated quantifiers and agreement patterns in SV and VS orders in the Italian dialect spoken in Ancona. Although these arguments suggest the existence of *pro*, I noted that an alternative based on the idea that many of the ungrammatical cases follow because *pro* cannot be emphasized by stress challenge its obligatorily preverbal position. Data from copular and presentational sentences and word-order asymmetries in the Ancona variety raise additional challenges for the pronominal analysis. Finally, the agreement facts in the Ancona variety presents a solid argument in favor of the preverbal location of *pro*. However, the floated quantifier data do not immediately translate to languages like Spanish, and likewise can have an alternative analysis.

4.2 The pronominal agreement hypothesis

Holmberg (2005, 537–538), among others, has argued that the existence of *pro* as an independent category is undesirable, mostly for theoretical reasons. He points out that given certain minimalist assumptions about the way agreement works, *pro* can no longer be considered an independent category. In most versions of this framework, empty categories are assumed to be deleted copies of overt categories, so strictly speaking, there are no null categories specified in the lexicon. This means, according to him, that either AGR/INFL is interpretable (i.e. pronominal), or *pro* is the result of deleting an overt pronoun. In this section, we will consider the main proposals that have advanced the first alternative, namely that agreement has pronominal properties that satisfy both the Theta Criterion and the EPP.

The pronominal agreement hypothesis was initially rooted in Hale (1983), Jelinek (1984) and Borer (1986), although Rizzi (1982, 143) also proposes that INFL can be pronominal. The Hale–Jelinek version of this idea can be stated as in (18).

(18) Pronominal Agreement Hypothesis
    a. AGR/INFL verbal morphology may license the EPP.
    b. Morphological affixes can receive theta roles.

The specific instantiation of (18a) depends on the concrete formulation of the EPP, and on whether one assumes a checking theory of features or an AGREE version of syntactic concord, but for current purposes it does not matter. Example (18b) is explicitly proposed by Jelinek (1984, 44) and more recently by Holmberg (2005, 537). Thus, an example like (19a) would have the derivation in (19b–c). In (19b), the theta role is assigned by the verb to its pronominal person/number morpheme, and subsequent movement to I checks the EPP. Alternatively, I AGREES with the verb in an EPP feature, and movement is independently triggered.

(19) a. Despert-aron. (Spanish)
awake-3.PAST.PL
'They woke up.'

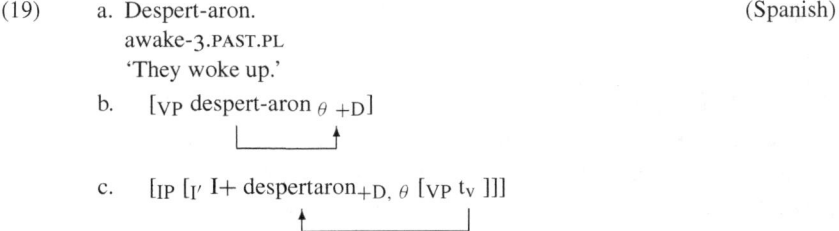

b. [VP despert-aron $_\theta$ +D]

c. [IP [I′ I+ despertaron+D, $_\theta$ [VP t$_V$]]]

An influential version of (18b) has been developed by Alexiadou and Anagnostopoulou (1998) (henceforth A and A).[4] Specifically, they make the claim that the EPP is parametric: it is satisfied by inserting an overt expletive in Spec, IP (cf. (20a–b)), or by merging a DP in that position (cf. (20c)) in languages with poor verbal morphology like English. In languages like Spanish or Greek, rich verbal morphology enables the verb to check the EPP by moving to I, as in (21a–b).

(20) a. There arrived a man.
b. [[IP there EPP [I [VP arrived a man]]]]
c. [IP A man EPP [I [VP arrived]]]

(21) a. Llegó una mujer. (Spanish)
arrived a woman
'A woman arrived.'
b. [IP [I′ I+ llegó+D [VP una mujer t$_V$]]]

Following Chomsky (1995), Alexiadou and Anagnostopoulou (1998) argue that the EPP should be formalized as a D(eterminer) feature present on the inflectional node that needs to be checked. Since the verb's inflectional endings are pronominal, then they can check the D feature on I. In English or French, on the other hand, the verb lacks this pronominal property, hence the D feature on I (the EPP feature) must be checked by a full XP raising to the Spec, IP. Alexiadou and Anagnostopoulou argue that the locus of EPP checking is AGRSP,

---

[4] Manzini and Savoia (2002) have a different version of how the EPP is satisfied. According to them, the EPP is a D feature in IP, which is realized or checked by a DP in English, not overtly realized in Italian/Spanish or instantiated as a clitic in Northern Italian dialects.

and that AGRSP only has a Specifier in non-NSLs, following Contreras (1991). Three consequences follow from these assumptions, as we will see below in detail: first, VS word orders in NSLs do not involve a null expletive, second, overt subjects do not occupy an A-position and third, arguably, only postverbal subjects should be considered in an A-position.

4.2.1 Pronominal agreement and reference

If agreement is pronominal, one expects to find cases in which it acts as the source of reference. Jelinek (1984, 43), following Ken Hale's insights, proposes that the node AUX (i.e. inflection, INFL in more current terminology) is "a constituent containing case-marked, fully referential clitic pronouns that serve as verbal arguments." As an example of how these clitics control reference and not the overt nominal, she points to example (22). The agreement clitic is *rlipa* '1.PL, inclusive, NOM', but the nominal *yapa* 'person' is 3rd person. The reflexive clitic *-nyanu* is also interpreted as a 1st person plural, suggesting that the agreement clitic and not the overt nominal controls co-reference.

(22) Puyukuyuku-puru, kula-lpa-rlipa-nyanu yapa-Ø nya
fog-WHILE NEG-IMPERF-1.PL(INCL)-NOM-REFL person-ABS see
-ngkarla. (Warlpiri)
-IRR

'We (plural inclusive) cannot see one another (as) person (s) (i.e., our shapes or figures) when it is foggy.'

(from Hale, 1983, 33, quoted in Jelinek, 1984, 46, ex. 17)

Jelinek (1984, 48) also quotes examples from Spanish that seem to pattern in a similar way as Warlpiri (see also Ordóñez and Treviño, 1999, 58). In an example like (23), a plural DP can appear as the subject of a 1st, 2nd or 3rd person verb and the subject's reference is interpreted depending on the values of inflection. Thus, in (23a), the subject includes the speaker among the set of students, whereas in (23b) it includes the addressees, but not the speaker. Example (23c) necessarily excludes the speaker, but it can be interpreted either as an equivalent of the 2nd person plural (in which case it includes the addressees), or as a true 3rd person, and in this interpretation it will also exclude the addressees. These facts apparently do not hold in Italian.

(23) a. Los estudiantes tene-mos mala memoria. (Spanish)
the students have-1.PL bad memory
'We students have bad memory.'

b. Los estudiantes ten-eis   mala memoria.   (Peninsular Spanish)
the students   have-2.PL bad memory
'The students have bad memory.'

c. Los estudiantes tien-en   mala memoria.
the students   have-3.PL bad memory
'The students have bad memory.'

This example, once again, suggests that the referential properties associated with the external theta role in (23) are determined by the verb's inflectional morphology and not by the overt DP. The examples in (24) lead to the same conclusion. In those cases, coreference between the main clause subject and the object in the adjunct clause depends on the main clause verb's inflection: If they match (as in (24a, c)), coreference is possible, if they don't (as in (24b)), coreference is not possible.

(24)   a. [Los estudiantes]$_i$ sali-mos de la reunión después de que nos$_i$
the students   left-1.PL of the meeting after   of that CL.3
acusara.   (Spanish)
accused.3.SG
'[The students]$_i$ left the meeting after s/he accused us$_{i/*j}$.'

b. *[Los estudiantes]$_i$ sali-mos de la reunión después de que los$_i$
the students   left-1.PL of the meeting after   of that CL.3
acusara.
accused.3.SG
'[The students]$_i$ left the meeting after s/he s/he accused them$_{*i/j}$.'

c. [Los estudiantes]$_i$ sali-eron de la reunión después de que los$_i$
the students   left-3.PL of the meeting after   of that CL.3
acusara.
accused.3.SG
'[The students]$_i$ left the meeting after s/he accused them$_{i/j}$.'

On the other hand, if the DP is not associated with an agreeing element, it recovers its ability to determine co-reference, as seen in (25). In this example, *los estudiantes* 'the students' is an object, and it is not associated with overt inflectional morphology, so it cannot be coreferential with *nosotros* 'us' because of the person mismatch.

(25)   Acusaron [a los estudiantes]$_i$, después de que él   se pelease   con
accused   to the students   after   of that CL.3 he fight.3.SG with
nosotros$_{*i/j}$.   (Spanish)
us
'They accused [the students]$_i$ after s/he fought with us$_{*i/j}$'.

These paradigms suggest that Spanish, like Warlpiri, fits best in the view that agreement is referential and therefore controls coreference. However, notice that this cannot be the whole picture. First, the patterns shown above are only possible with 3rd person, plural DPs, as seen in (26), where the 3rd person singular DP cannot be coreferential with a 1st person singular verb ending (contrasting with (23a)).

(26)   a. El estudiante tien-e   mala memoria.   (Spanish)
           the student   has-3.SG bad   memory
           'The student has bad memory.'
       b. *El estudiante teng-o   mala memoria.
           the students   have-1.SG bad   memory
           'The students have bad memory.'

Second, only DPs, not pronouns, or even a pronoun + DP combination show the pattern in (23). Thus, the overt pronoun *nosotros* 'we' in (27a) cannot appear with 3rd person verbal morphology, and requires obligatory 1st person inflection (*tenemos* 'have.1.PL'), as in (27b). Likewise, *ellos* 'they' in (28) is incompatible with 1st person morphology on the verb.

(27)   a. *Nosotros los estudiantes tien-en   mala memoria.   (Spanish)
           we   the students   have-3.PL bad   memory
           'We the students have bad memory.'
       b. Nosotros los estudiantes tene-mos mala memoria.
           we   the students   have-1.PL bad   memory
           'We the students have bad memory.'

(28)   a. *Ellos (los estudiantes) ten-emos mala memoria.   (Spanish)
           they (the students)   have-1.PL bad   memory
           'We the students have bad memory.'
       b. Ellos (los estudiantes) tien-en   mala memoria.
           they (the students)   have-3.PL bad   memory
           'We the students have bad memory.'

The mismatching possibilities observed in (23) reappear in infinitival contexts even with pronoun + DP combinations, as shown in (29), which is admittedly a marked construction.

(29)   Sugirieron   [hablar nosotros los estudiantes]   (Spanish)
       suggested.3.pl speak   us   the students
       'They suggested that we the students should speak.'

These additional facts in (26)–(28) suggest that aside from the role of inflection, one needs to take into account the ϕ-feature structure of DPs vs. pronouns, and perhaps the hierarchy of ϕ-features (see Shlonsky, 1997; Béjar, 2003; Harbour et al., 2008; Béjar and Rezac, 2009), to account for the number differences.

4.2.2   Pronominal agreement and ellipsis

One potential argument against the pronominal analysis of AGR/INFL comes from a generalization on ellipsis presented in Saab (2009, 2010, 2012). He points out that interpretable features never trigger partial identity effects under ellipsis. As background, he assumes the minimalist partition between interpretable and uninterpretable features, namely, between features with an import in the conceptual interface and those that are purely grammatical. He notes that when a verb is gapped, that verb's interpretable tense must be identical to its overt counterpart's. We can see an example of this in (30a), where the gapped verb is interpreted as having the same tense as the overt one (*aprendieron* 'learned'). In (30b), on the other hand, a mismatching tense interpretation renders the example ungrammatical.

(30)   a. Los estudiantes aprendieron mucho chino y   Antonio también
          the students   learned   much Chinese and Antonio also
          ~~aprendieron mucho chino~~   (Spanish)
          learned   much Chinese
          'The students have learned a lot of Chinese and Antonio too.'

   b. ?? Los estudiantes aprendieron mucho chino en el pasado y   Antonio
          the students   learned   much Chinese in the past   and Antonio
          en el futuro también ~~aprenderá mucho chino~~.
          in the future also   will learn much   Chinese

Gender does not require identity between the gapped item and the overt one, as seen in (31). In this example, the overt participle is masculine and the elided one is feminine.[5]

(31)   Juan fue localizad-o en el restaurante y   Marta también ~~fue~~
       Juan was located-MAS in the restaurant and Marta too   was
       ~~localizad-a en el restaurante~~.   (Spanish)
       located.FEM in the restaurant
       'Juan was located at the restaurant and Marta too.'

---

[5] Neil Smith (p.c.) notes that the corresponding example in English is subject to much variation, so that some speakers (including him) have the following pattern: *Bill lost his temper and so did John/*Mary*, whereas for others both options are possible. One possible explanation is that judgements may become more consistent if examples are presented with more context. The undesirable alternative is that gender is interpretable for some speakers but not for others.

If inflectional ϕ-features (person and number) are interpretable like Tense, then they should preserve strict identity under deletion, the way Tense was shown to do in (30). However, this is not the case, as seen in (32). In this example, the overt verb's person and number features are 3rd person singular, whereas the elided verb is interpreted as 1st person plural. To the extent that the generalization on identity of interpretable features holds, this is a strong argument against considering inflectional ϕ-features interpretable (i.e. pronominal).

(32) Juan fue al cine y nosotros también ~~fui-mos~~ ~~al~~ ~~cine~~.
Juan went.3.SG to-the movies and we too went-1.PL to-the movies
(Spanish)
'Juan went to the movies and we did too.'

Strict ϕ-feature identity is not required either in Jelinek's examples above, so (33a) can be interpreted either as (33b), with strict identity, or as (33c), with distinct person interpretation.

(33) a. Ayer, los estudiantes fuimos a la huelga, y hoy también los
yesterday the students went.1.PL to the strike and today also the
asistentes. (Spanish)
assistants.
'Yesterday students went on strike and today assistants did too.'

b. ... y hoy también los asistentes fuimos a la huelga.
'... and today (we) assistants also went on strike.'

c. ... y hoy también los asistentes fueron a la huelga.
'...and today assistants also went on strike.'

An interesting fact about Saab's generalization is that it doesn't immediately extend to *pro*. In the example above, both conjuncts have an overt subject (which is contrastive in the second conjunct). However, (34a), with a NS in both conjuncts, cannot be interpreted as (34b), with distinct persons on each verb. Intuitively, what prevents the non-identical feature interpretation in (34a) is that the second conjunct's person/number features are unrecoverable.

(34) a. #El sábado salimos al cine y el domingo, también
the Saturday went.1.PL out to-the movies and the Sunday too
~~salí~~. (Spanish)
went.1.SG out
'Saturday we went out to the movies and Sunday too (I went to the movie).'

b. El sábado salimos al cine y el domingo también
   the Saturday went.1.PL out to-the movies and the Sunday too
   salí al cine.
   went.1.SG out to-the movies
   'Saturday we went out to the movies and Sunday I went out to the movies also.'

But even in examples like (35a), where the anaphor should provide enough information to recover the content of the subject, the non-identical interpretation fails. The counterpart in which the subject is overt is marginal but clearly more acceptable than the one with *pro* (cf. (35b)).

(35) a. * El sábado, Andrés se molestó consigo mismo, y el domingo,
      the Saturday, Andres CL got upset with himself, and the Sunday,
      también me molesté conmigo mismo. (Spanish)
      too CL got upset with-me myself
   b. ? El sábado, Andrés se molestó consigo mismo, y el domingo,
      the Saturday, Andres CL got upset with himself, and the Sunday,
      yo también me molesté conmigo mismo.
      I too CL got upset with-me myself
      'Saturday, Andres got upset with himself and Sunday, I too, with myself.'

If we take the identity-of-interpretable-features-in-ellipsis hypothesis seriously, inflectional ϕ-features are interpretable only with a NS, but not with an overt one. Alternatively, inflectional features are never interpretable, and the subject (overt DP or *pro*) is interpretable.

Notice that these paradigms are very reminiscent of the Ancona facts presented in Section 4.1.4. In that case, a 3rd person singular verb could be compatible with a 3rd person plural overt DP, but not with a NS. Suppose that *pro* in (34a) must obligatorily gap with the verb because it is necessarily attached to it (in Cardinaletti's (1997) analysis, due to its weak pronoun nature). In that case, what makes that example ungrammatical is the fact that *pro*'s interpretable features are not identical with those of its antecedent.

4.2.3 Arguments from Irish against the pronominal agreement hypothesis
Irish has two distinct unaccusative constructions, which McCloskey (1997) calls salient and putative unaccusatives, illustrated in (36a–b) respectively. The most notable difference between them is that salient unaccusatives have a prepositional argument, which, according to McCloskey remains in a VP internal position. Putative unaccusatives, on the other hand, lack the preposition and the argument acts as an external argument.

(36) a. Neartaigh   ar a   ghlór.   (Irish)
       strengthened on his voice
       'His voice strengthened.'
    b. Neartaigh   a ghlór.
       strengthened his voice
       'His voice strengthened.'   (from McCloskey, 1996, 251, 23)

The account that rich inflection satisfies the EPP by verb-raising does not extend well to these cases. On the one hand, the fact that the internal argument remains in situ in (36a) suggests that it does not satisfy the EPP. On the other hand, since the verb is assumed to move to I, it could satisfy the EPP requirement. However, Irish has two types of verbal morphology, the so-called analytic forms and the synthetic forms (see McCloskey and Hale, 1984). Analytic forms lack ϕ-feature information, whereas synthetic forms have person and number content. NSs can only appear with synthetic forms, not with analytic ones. The fact that synthetic forms allow for NSs and analytic ones do not would classify the first type as rich and the second one as poor in Alexiadou and Anagnostopoulou's (1998) terms. In that context, one would expect that only synthetic forms would satisfy the EPP, however, all salient unaccusatives must appear in the analytic form (see McCloskey, 1996, 272).

4.2.4 Arguments from Finnish expletives against the pronominal agreement hypothesis

Holmberg (2005, 537) points out that if AGR receives the subject theta role, it is interpretable, hence referential. This means that it may also absorb nominative case. If *pro* exists as an independent entity, it would have to be expletive (because no theta role is available); however, in Finnish, overt expletives (like *sitä* in (37)) are barred from NS constructions.[6]

(37)   * Sitä puhun   englantia.   (Finnish)
        EXP speak.1.SG English
                                                    (from Holmberg, 2005, 543, ex. 21)

Holmberg (2005, 545) argues that the ungrammaticality of this example cannot be due to AGR checking the EPP and making the expletive redundant, since this would preclude sentences like (38a), where the expletive *sitä* is possible but AGR should also check the EPP. As seen in (38b), the expletive is not required.

---

[6] Finnish has productive NSs in 1st and 2nd person; see Vainikka and Levy (1999) and Section 2.3.3.

(38) a. Sitä olen   minäkin käynyt Pariisissa.   (Finnish)
       EXP be.1.SG I-too   visited Paris.INE
       'I have been to Paris, too (actually).'
                                            (from Holmberg, 2005, 543, ex. 19)
      b. Olen   minäkin käynyt Pariisissa.
         be.1.SG I-too   visited Paris.INE
         'I have been to Paris, too (actually).'
                                            (from Holmberg, 2005, 543, ex. 20)

He concludes that the contrast between (37) and (38) follows if AGR never checks the EPP. In (37), *pro* does, hence the expletive is redundant, and in (38a), the expletive checks it (because the pronoun *minäkin* 'I' is too low to do so). By contrast, the pronoun is in Spec, IP in (38b), so it checks the EPP and the auxiliary *olen* 'be' subsequently raises to C.

4.2.5   Word order asymmetries in agreement

All things being equal, the pronominal agreement hypothesis predicts that agreement asymmetries should not depend on word order, since agreement remains constant in the different word orders. Thus, a priori, Northern Italian dialects present a challenge in this particular domain (see Manzini and Savoia, 2002). Recall the data presented earlier from the Ancona variety (see (15)–(17)), which show that default singular agreement is possible in the order VS, but in SV order, full plural agreement is obligatory. Furthermore, the referential properties seem to be located on the overt DP, not on inflection. This conclusion is illustrated by (39a) and (39c), where subject reference is 3rd person plural, even though inflection is 3rd person singular in (39a). Note that these data are the mirror image of the Spanish examples in (23) above. Those data suggested that referential properties seem located on I.

(39)   a. Questo, lo fa   sempre i   bambini.   (Ancona variety)
          this.ACC CL do.3.SG always the.PL children.PL
          'The children always do this.'
       b. *Questo, i   bambini   lo fa   sempre.
           this.ACC the.PL children.PL CL do.3.SG always
       c. Questo, i   bambini   lo fanno sempre.
          this.ACC the.PL children.PL CL do.3.PL always
          'The children always do this.'   (from Cardinaletti, 1997, 39, ex. 21)

If referential properties are located on inflection, one would expect variation in reference between (39a)–(39c), given the difference in ϕ-features. However, reference remains constant in both examples.

To summarize this section, I have presented the pronominal agreement hypothesis through the implementation proposed by Alexiadou and Anagnostopoulou. This hypothesis assumes that the referential and/or thematic properties of an argument can be carried by the inflectional morphology of a verb, and certain distributional patterns of coreference taken from Warlpiri and Spanish fit well within this hypothesis. I have also presented several cases that seem to challenge this account, namely the generalization that only uninterpretable features can have different values in ellipsis (but inflection can). Additionally, the Irish analytic/synthetic distinction, in conjunction with the distribution of salient unaccusatives, argues against the notion that rich-agreement verbs can satisfy the EPP by raising to I. Finally, I have pointed out that the pronominal agreement hypothesis has difficulties explaining differences in verb agreement triggered by changing word orders (Ancona dialect), even though referential possibilities remain constant across examples.

4.3 Deletion

In this section, I turn to the third answer to the question of what satisfies the EPP. This answer assumes that *pro* is not an independent category, but a pronoun without overt phonological content. Within this general idea, we find at least two separate analyses. The first one is Holmberg's (2005) account of NSs in Finnish. The second one is Saab (2009, 2010, 2012), an account that extends otherwise well-attested mechanisms of ellipsis to the case of NSs. Finally, we will briefly recapitulate Tomioka's proposal regarding discourse NSLs, which also involves NP ellipsis.

4.3.1 Finnish expletives and NSs

Holmberg's analysis of the distribution of overt expletives in Finnish leads him to propose that NSs are the null counterparts of overt pronouns. Specifically, he advances a typology of null subjects with distinct levels of internal structure, as represented in (40). This typology corresponds roughly to Déchaine and Wiltschko's (2002) proposal for pronouns. If one assumes that the referentiality of a nominal expression is hosted in the determiner head (following Longobardi (1994), for example), then the only category that is fully referential in the pronominal typology in (40) is that of null DPs, not ϕPs or NPs.

(40)   a. D-less ϕPs (Null bound pronouns and generic pronouns in partial NSLs like Finnish and also Null subjects in Spanish, Greek or Italian)
   b. Null DPs (1st and 2nd person subjects in Finnish)
   c. Null NPs (NS in Chinese/Japanese)

Holmberg considers and rejects the pronominal agreement alternative, based on the following facts about Finnish. In this language, expletives have a limited distribution, for example, they can optionally appear in impersonal sentences like (41a), usually when nothing else can appear in first position.[7]

(41) a. Sitä meni hullusti. (Finnish)
 EXP went wrong
 'Things went wrong.' (from Holmberg, 2005, 543, ex. 20)
 b. Meni hullusti.
 went wrong
 'Things went wrong.' (from Holmberg, 2005, 542, ex. 17)

However, if any constituent in the clause can check the EPP, either that constituent moves to first position, as *nyt* 'now' does in (42a), or the expletive must appear, as seen in (42b), but the verb cannot be in initial position, as seen in (42c).

(42) a. Nyt meni hullusti. (Finnish)
 now went wrong
 'Now things went wrong.'
 b. Sitä meni nyt hullusti.
 EXP went now wrong
 'Now things went wrong.'
 c. *Meni nyt hullusti.
 went now wrong (from Holmberg, 2005, 541, ex. 13)

These examples show that Finnish has an overt expletive that surfaces in the expected position in order to satisfy the EPP, which is conceived as a requirement that the Spec of IP be filled. With this background in mind, suppose that we assume the pronominal agreement hypothesis for 1st and 2nd person, since Finnish only has productive NSs in these two persons. In that case, we predict that expletives should not be possible in those persons, a prediction

---

[7] In Finnish, arguments and certain adverbs (temporal, locative or instrumental) can check the EPP (i.e. move to preverbal position), whereas other adverbs (reason or manner) cannot do so. Holmberg (2005, 542) calls the second type "potential topics." Compare the grammaticality of (41b) with the ungrammaticality of (i), without adverbial movement and the grammaticality of (ii) with adverbial movement.

(i) *Leikkii lapsia kadulla. (Finnish)
 play children in-street
(ii) Kadulla leikkii lapsia.
 in-street play children
 'Children are playing in the street.' (from Holmberg and Nikkane, 2002, exx. 1c, 2b)

that isn't consistently borne out (cf. (43a) vs. (43b)). Given these contradictory results for expletives with 1st and 2nd person subjects, the pronominal agreement would be forced to claim either that inflection doesn't always satisfy the EPP, or that the EPP does not apply in all cases.

(43)   a. * Sitä puhun   englantia.   (Finnish)
             EXP speak-1.SG English

(from Holmberg, 2005, 543, ex. 21a)

        b. Sitä olen   minäkin käynyt Pariisissa.
           EXP be.1.SG I-too   visited Paris-INE
           'I have been to Paris, too (actually).'

(from Holmberg, 2005, 545, ex. 19b)

As an alternative, Holmberg (2005) proposes that Finnish has a null pronominal that checks the EPP, so the expletive is unnecessary in (43a), whereas in (43b), the expletive checks the EPP, because the overt pronoun is lower than Spec, IP. Note that the counterpart of (43b) without an expletive is also grammatical (cf. (44)), but in this case, the subject merges with IP, checks the EPP and the auxiliary incorporates to C. In other words, the difference between (43b) and (44) is structural: In the first example, the verb and the subject are lower than in the second one, as seen in (45).

(44)   Olen   minäkin käynyt Pariisissa.   (Finnish)
           be.1.SG I-too   visited Paris-INE
           'I have been to Paris, too.'   (from Holmberg, 2005, 545, ex. 24a)

(45)   a. [IP sitä [I [VP minäkin . . .]]]

        b. [CP olen [IP minäkin [I [. . .]]]]

As mentioned earlier, Holmberg assumes that finite 1st and 2nd person *pros* have the representation in (40b) above, that is, they are fully referential DPs. By contrast, generic NSs like (46) below, which cannot satisfy the EPP, have the representation in (40a).

(46)   Tässä istuu   mukavasti.   (Finnish)
        here sit.3.SG comfortably
        'One can sit comfortably here.'

Holmberg assumes that NSs in consistent NSLs have the same representation as generics in Finnish, but NSLs have a D feature in I, which is independent of AGR and Finnish does not. When I and a ϕP *pro* agree in a language like Greek or Spanish, the resulting category is [D ϕP], which makes it referential.

While Holmberg's account attempts to subsume *pro* into the class of overt pronouns assuming that they are the deleted counterpart of those pronouns, it is not clear to what extent this is explicitly done. On the one hand, the precise mechanisms for deletion of *pro*'s phonological content are not made clear, and on the other hand, one of the predictions this theory makes is that the types of *pro* we find should be at most the same as the types of overt pronouns, and at least a subset of those types. In practice, both Holmberg's and Saab's account (see below) restrict *pro* to the subset of weak pronouns, following Cardinaletti and Starke (1999). One lingering question is why this should be the case (i.e. why don't we have the null counterpart of overt, non-emphatic pronouns).

4.3.2   Pro *as ellipsis*

Saab (2009), Tomioka (2003) and Barbosa (2010) all develop different versions of the idea that NSs are elided instances of overt pronouns. Saab (2009, 2010, 2012) develops this idea within a much larger theory of ellipsis. Working in the framework of Distributed Morphology, he takes NSs to be deleted as a PF phenomenon only when they are adjacent to T. Formally, a (simplified) syntactic structure like (47a) is linearized as (47b), and D can be assigned a feature [+I]. This feature is added to elliptical heads under formal identity, and blocks lexical insertion rules, resulting in a null subject. Thus, the only difference between an overt pronoun and a null one is that the former lacks [+I] and gets content through lexical insertion rules, whereas the latter has [+I], which blocks the application of those rules.

(47)   a.   Syntax of *compramos* 'bought.1.PL'

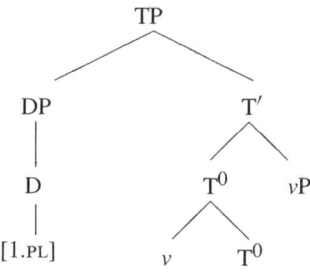

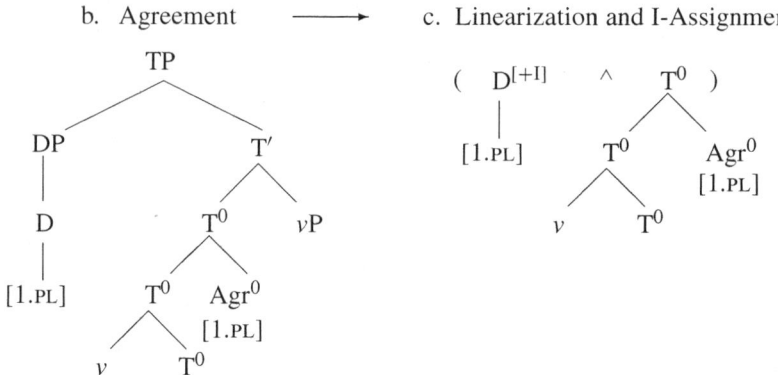

Since [+I] is assigned to subjects adjacent to T, for all intents and purposes, NSs are also the null equivalent of Cardinaletti and Starke's (1999) weak pronouns.[8]

4.3.3 Null/overt asymmetries

Both Holmberg's and Saab's deletion analysis of *pro* rely on Cardinaletti and Starke's (1999) assertion that *pro* is a weak pronoun. This raises the two following questions regarding the null/overt distinction. First, why is *pro* necessarily weak (at least in Spanish and Italian)? Second, why must it necessarily occupy a dedicated (Spec, IP) position?

To understand the relevance of the first question, consider that all languages that have *pro* also have overt pronouns, so it is puzzling that only weak pronouns can be null. There is a trivial answer to this question: phonological nullness is the weakest possible manifestation of a syntactic item, so in some sense, null pronouns simply deplete already deficient phonological content. However, the notion of weak pronoun also encodes semantic correlates, and in this sense, it is not clear why both things should go together. In Cardinaletti and Starke's analysis, pronominal deficiency stems from having fewer syntactic/functional projections, and this correlates with having less phonological content. As they put it: "[T]he more a pronoun is deficient, the less it has syntactic structure." (fn. 50). However, it should be clear that fewer syntactic/functional heads does not always mean less prosodic content, and

---

[8] Cardinaletti and Starke's distinction between weak and strong pronouns relies on a set of interpretive and prosodic properties. For example, weak pronouns cannot be modified by adverbs like *only*, or conjoined (see Section 7.1).

vice versa, less phonological content does not necessarily mean less syntactic complexity as Bayer (1999, 237) points out.

On the other hand, deletion is generally not concerned with the size of the deleted element, which can be as large and structurally complex as a whole IP in ellipsis contexts (see (48)), so the intuitive notion that NSs are null because they are syntactically simpler therefore phonologically smaller does not find a clear parallel in other areas where ellipsis is well defined.

(48) Doris compró una tartaleta de limón en la pastelería de San Antonio a
Doris bought a tart of lemon in the pastry-shop of San Antonio at
las 4 ayer y Samuel también ~~compró una tartaleta de limón en la~~
the 4 yesterday and Samuel also bought a tart of lemon in the
~~pastelería de San Antonio a las 4 ayer~~ (Spanish)
pastry-shop of San Antonio at the 4 yesterday
'Doris bought a lemon tart in the San Antonio pastry shop at 4 yesterday and Samuel too.'

A third point of contention is the following: if most of the semantic properties associated with strong pronouns have as a prerequisite some kind of prosodic prominence, then the reason why NSs do no have those properties is precisely because they cannot be prosodically prominent. In fact, Frascarelli (2007) explicitly argues for deriving the weak/strong distinction from the prosody of pronouns.

Cardinaletti and Starke (1999, 164) make a point of rejecting this alternative, noting that certain weak pronouns can bear stress (cf. for example clitics in Argentinean Spanish; see Huidobro, 2005), and that not all strong pronouns must be prosodically prominent (cf. French *Jean a vu seulement lui* 'Jean has seen only him', in which the pronoun is prosodically flat, according to Cardinaletti and Starke, 1999, 162). Additionally, they argue, if one were to derive prosodic weakness/strength separately from the semantic properties associated with those properties, one would miss the generalization that they tend to appear together. However, Cardinaletti and Starke (1999) themselves point to instances in which changes in semantic properties are not accompanied by changes in prosodic ones. For example, they suggest that weak pronouns usually cannot be used to point at something in the discourse, but if there is a salient antecedent in the discourse, then ostension becomes possible with weak pronouns. In other words, a weak pronoun can remain prosodically weak but show one of the properties of strong pronouns.

On the other hand, at least one of the properties they ascribe to strong pronouns (conjoinability) has no obvious correlate on the semantic side.

Furthermore, they explain the restriction on coordination by stating that it requires CP/DP and since weak pronouns do not project CP, they cannot be coordinated. By contrast, strong pronouns project a CP and can be conjoined. This leaves open the question of why overt verbal I'-levels can be coordinated in many languages. Additionally, in languages like Irish, *pro* can be conjoined (see (49)).[9]

(49)   da mbeinn   -se   agus tusa ann.   (Irish)
    if be.COND.1.SG -CONTR and you there
    'If you and I were there.'   (from McCloskey and Hale, 1984, 501, ex. 31a)

The data from Irish challenge the analysis of *pro* as a weak pronoun in general, because Irish *pro* lacks at least two of the properties of weak pronouns (it can be conjoined and it can appear with contrastive modifiers), but it is still null. To the extent that *pro* in Irish is necessarily linked to rich agreement (see McCloskey and Hale, 1984), one would assume that it occupies the same position as *pro* in other languages, but without the corresponding properties.

For languages like Spanish that disallow conjunction of *pro*, one can independently show that prosodic status determines coordination possibilities, as in the case of adverbs in *-mente* in Spanish (see (50)). In this example, two bound morphemes can be conjoined, and they happen to behave as two separate prosodic words (for example, they have independent stress; see Bosque (1987) and Camacho (2003, 67)). In other instances of bound morphemes, lack of conjoinability is associated with lack of prosodic independence. Extending the CP/IP analysis to these cases seems rather difficult.

(50)   a. La   boda   más   [ceremoniosa-   y   solemne]   -mente
    the   wedding   most   ceremonious-   and   solemn   -ly
    celebrada.   (Spanish)
    celebrated
    'The most ceremoniously and solemnly celebrated wedding.'

---

[9] In Irish, conjoined pronouns whether overt or null, have an added emphatic particle, as shown in (i)–(ii).

(i)   * mé agus tú   (Irish)
    I and you   (from McCloskey and Hale, 1984, 503, 35c)
(ii)   mise   agus tusa
    I.CONTR and   you.CONTR
    'You and I.'   (from McCloskey and Hale, 1984, 503, 36a)

b. La boda   más [ceremoniosamente y   solemnemente celebrada.
   the wedding most ceremoniously   and solemnly   celebrated
   'The most ceremoniously and solemnly celebrated wedding.'
                                                (from Camacho, 2003, 67)

To summarize, the deletion analysis faces the challenge of explaining why only weak pronouns can be deleted in NSLs. As an alternative account, it is possible that part of the distribution of *pro* comes from the fact that it is null, not from the contention that it is weak. I have also reviewed some evidence from Irish that not all instances of *pro* can be treated as weak.

4.4   Is the Extended Projection Principle universal?

In Section 4.4.2 and in previous sections of this chapter, I have assumed that the EPP is universal. The question we will address in this section is whether the EPP can be maintained as a unified requirement that some nominal category appear in Spec, IP. Part of the answer to this question crucially hinges on the status of null expletives. After all, if null thematic subjects are independently required by the θ-criterion, the sole remaining reason for postulating expletives would be that Spec, IP needs to be filled.[10] But if the EPP is not universal, then there is no need to postulate the existence of null expletives in NSLs. If that is correct, then the presence of overt expletives in languages that have them would have a different explanation not directly related to argument structure.

4.4.1   *Evidence for expletives in null subject languages*
For obvious reasons, empirical evidence for or against pure null expletives is very hard to find. Despite that difficulty, McCloskey (1996), has argued that Irish grammar shows no evidence of null expletives, and that the EPP does not hold in that language. First, Irish is consistently VSO in finite clauses, but McCloskey (1991, 1997) argues that the subject raises from its vP position to a position lower than IP. To reach this conclusion, he points out that subjects of finite clauses consistently place to the left of adverbs such as *go* 'often' in examples like (51). Assuming that the adverb signals the boundary for vP,

---

[10] Manzini and Savoia (2002, 162) point out that if one treats theta roles as independent features that can be merged with the corresponding argument, the need for thematic *pro* as bearer of a theta role disappears. However, proposing independent feature theta roles is not enough, one still needs to have something to associate that feature with, be it inflection or something else.

it follows that the subject must be higher than vP but lower than IP. At the same time, VP-ellipsis requires the subject to obligatorily elide, as seen in (52), where the second subject *muid* 'we' does not appear. This fact suggests that the subject and other VP-material form a constituent that excludes the verb, as shown in the structure in (53), where XP includes the subject and any other material to its right.

(51)   Chuala Róise go minic roimhe   an t-amhrán sin.   (Irish)
        heard   Róise often   before-it that-song
        'Róise had often heard that song before.'
                                            (from McCloskey, 1997, 219, ex. 50b)

(52)   Ní   tháinig muid 'na bhaile anuraidh ach tiocfaidh [muid 'na bhaile]
        NEG came   we   home   last-year but come.FUT   we   home
        i mbliana.   (Irish)
        this-year
        'We didn't come home last year but we will this year.'
                                            (from McCloskey, 1997, 211, ex. 23)

(53)   [$_{IP}$ V+I [$_{XP}$ Subj [$_{vP}$ Subj [$_{VP}$ V O ...]]]]

This suggests that subjects do not overtly occupy the cannonical Spec, IP subject position. Is this position occupied by an expletive? McCloskey believes that it is not. Recall from Section 4.2.3 that Irish distinguishes between salient unaccusatives, whose sole argument systematically remains inside VP, and putative unaccusatives, whose argument is external by all the relevant tests. The most notable difference between both classes is that the internal argument of salient unaccusatives has a preposition, as seen in (54a) vs. (54b).

(54)   a. Neartaigh   ar a   ghlór.   (Irish)
           strengthened on his voice
           'His voice strengthened.'
        b. Neartaigh   a   ghlór.
           strengthened his voice
           'His voice strengthened.'   (from McCloskey, 1996, 251, ex. 23)

If Irish has a null expletive to comply with the EPP, and expletive-associate chains must match in syntactic category, the existence of salient unaccusatives with a PP argument becomes problematic. As McCloskey (1997) points out, the same argument can be recreated for perfective passives. On the other hand, if Irish lacks expletives altogether, the existence of salient unaccusatives (and the perfective passive patterns) no longer becomes an issue.

4.4 Is the Extended Projection Principle universal? 95

For languages like Spanish or Italian, empirical evidence of null expletives is also very hard to come by. On the one hand, unlike thematic *pro*, expletives never alternate between overt and null forms, so it is hard to analyze the distribution of null expletives based on the distribution of overt ones. Even in varieties that seem to have overt expletives (cf. Sections 3.2.1 and 3.2.2), the evidence suggests that they are not uniquely related to the subject position, but potentially to a left-peripheral CP position.

Furthermore, I think one can find indirect evidence against null expletives. Consider, for example, extraposed clauses with verbs such as *resultar* 'turn out', shown in (55a). These clauses cannot be preposed, as seen in (55b), where *que Blanca va a venir* 'that Blanca is going to come' cannot appear before the verb. If the EPP holds in Spanish, one interpretation of this fact suggests that these clauses can never satisfy the EPP.

(55)   a. Resultó   [que Blanca va   a venir]   (Spanish)
               turned out that   Blanca is going to come
               'It turned out that Blanca is going to come.'
           b. ?* [Que Blanca va   a venir] resultó.
                that   Blanca is going to come turned out
                'That Blanca is going to come turned out.'

Other predicates that take extraposed clauses do allow for the clause to raise to a preverbal position, as seen in (56), where the clause *que Blanca va a venir* 'that Blanca is going to come' can appear pre or postverbally, although the preverbal position is not the preferred position, and tends to be interpreted as focused. The same pattern holds in English, but with the overt expletive *it*.

(56)   a. Es cierto [que Blanca va   a venir]   (Spanish)
               is true   that   Blanca is going to come
               'It is true that Blanca is going to come.'
           b. [Que Blanca va   a venir] es cierto.
                that   Blanca is going to come is true
                'That Blanca is going to come is true.'

As in the case of Irish unaccusative verbs, it is not clear why one type of predicate (*ser cierto* 'be true') allows for the extraposed clause to satisfy the EPP whereas another type (*resultar* 'result') does not.[11] Nevertheless, assume, for the sake of argument, that a null expletive appears obligatorily with *resultar*

---

[11] If one assumes that inflection can satisfy the EPP (see Section 4.2 below), then clausal raising must be unrelated to the EPP in (55)–(56), since in both cases inflection satisfies the EPP.

'turn out' (hence raising is impossible in (55b)), but optionally with *ser cierto* 'be true', hence the optional raising of the clause in (56). However, consider two more cases in the paradigm: when an adjective or adverb is added as a predicate of the main verb, then preposing the clause becomes possible with *resultar* 'result'. Thus, *resultó excelente* 'it turned out excellent' and *es bueno* 'it is good' both allow preposing of the clause, as seen in (57)–(58) respectively.[12]

(57)   a. Resultó excelente [que Luis viniera]   (Spanish)
        turned.out excellent that Luis come.SUBJ
        'It turned out great that Luis came.'

       b. [Que Luis viniera] resultó excelente.
        that Luis come.SUBJ turned.out excellent
        'That Luis came turned out (to be) great.'

(58)   a. Es bueno [que Luis venga]   (Spanish)
        is good that Luis come.SUBJ
        'It is good that Luis came.'

       b. [Que Luis venga] es bueno.
        that Luis come.SUBJ is good
        'That Luis comes is good.'

Given that the only difference between (55)–(56) and (57)–(58) is the presence of the adverb or adjective, it would seem that the possibility of preposing the extraposed clause is not related to the EPP. In fact, if anything, this contrast suggests a VP-internal EPP effect: if no adverb is present, the clause must remain in a VP-internal position, but if the adverb/adjective is present, the clause may move or remain in situ.

Existential constructions with *haber* 'be' also disallow an overt DP in preverbal position, both in Spanish and in English, as seen in (59)–(60). In (59), the existential verb *haber* 'be' must appear preverbally, just like *be* in (60). Even if an overt locative like *en la conferencia* 'at the conference' appears, the word order in (61a) is not possible (unless *tres personas* 'three people'

---

[12] Without a predicate, *ser* shows the same pattern as in (55). For example, if I ask ¿*por qué estás tan contento?* 'why are you so happy?' someone could reply (i) but not (ii).

   (i)   Es [que Blanca va a venir]
          is that Blanca is going to come
          'It's that Blanca is going to come.'

   (ii)   * [Que Blanca va a venir] es.
           that Blanca is going to come is

is focused), and the corresponding example in English lacks an existential, non-specific reading.[13]

(59) a. Habían   tres personas.   (Spanish)
        were.3.PL three people
        'There were three people.'
    b. * Tres personas habían.
         three people   were.3.PL

(60) a. There were three people.
    b. * Three people were.

(61) a. * Tres personas habían en la conferencia.   (Spanish)
         three people   were.3.PL in the conference
         'There were three people at the conference.'
    b. # Three people were at the conference.

Needless to say, there are multiple analyses of existential constructions. The main point here is that these contrasts raise issues about the universality of the EPP as a requirement to have a category in Spec, IP at least for languages like Spanish/Irish, where they do not interact with overt expletives and the syntactic distribution does not provide any independent evidence.

To summarize, the proposal that a null expletive fulfills the EPP requirement (as a requirement of Spec, IP) does not provide much explanation for the relative position of extraposed clauses, hence it questions whether the EPP is a universal requirement, in line with McCloskey (1997).[14] However, plenty of "EPP effects" have been described in the literature. In most cases, these remain a poorly understood cover term for situations in which some constituent must move to a clause-initial position, and perhaps these cases are best seen as the result of different PF constraints, in some instances, phonological alignment constraints; in other cases, they may be the result of interaction between assertion structure and prosody.

4.4.2   Positional freezing

In this section I present a slight detour that will take us to an alternative perspective for the correlation between VS word order and *that*-trace effects. This

---

[13] There are questions about whether the associate is an external argument. Rodríguez-Mondoñedo (2006) argues that it is an object, although it agrees with the verb.

[14] Since much of the distribution just discussed can be replicated in English, where an overt *it* does appear, the logical conclusion is that the EPP does not explain much of the English distribution either.

alternative is based on Rizzi (2005b) and particularly on Rizzi and Shlonsky (2007). Although this is not directly relevant to the NSP, since I have shown that NSs are not directly connected with *that*-trace violations, this detour allows me to explain some of the facts presented in Section 3.5.

Rizzi and Shlonsky present a different perspective on the EPP. Their proposal rests on the idea that the subject moves to a specialized position in the left periphery of the clause to signal to the interface systems that its specifier must receive a special interpretive property, in this particular case, [+aboutness] (Rizzi, 2005b). Thus, the requirement that a subject moves to the SubjP projection to receive an [+aboutness] interpretation is called the Subject Criterion. Because this movement is a last-resort movement, the category satisfies the criterion is frozen in that position, preventing it from further movement (so-called criterial freezing). The most important consequence of this freezing is that subjects cannot be extracted (if frozen in SubjP), giving rise to subject/object extraction asymmetries. In order to extract the subject, languages resort to alternative strategies, for example inflected complementizers. Another possibility is to satisfy the Subject Criterion with a category different than the subject, for example an expletive, among other possibilities, as we will see below. Expletives, however, are not what the sentence is about, but Rizzi (2005b, 213) suggests that they surface in order to satisfy a second requirement of the Subj dedicated position, namely the fact that it is part of the IP-layer, hence obligatory.

Returning to the freezing effect of the Subject Criterion, one possible by-passing strategy involves merging a nominal category with ϕ-features above the canonical IP subject position. The resulting configuration satisfies the Subject Criterion, according to RS. Two consequences follow: the complementizer shows some kind of agreement properties and subject extraction becomes possible.

For French, Rizzi and Shlonsky propose a representation as in (62). An agreement-bearing complementizer (*que*) merges with Subj′, producing a structure in which SubjP lacks an overt complementizer position, and where the Subject Criterion is satisfied by the agreeing complementizer (Fin + ϕ in (62)). This, in turn, allows for the subject to raise. Similar results obtain in English.[15]

(62) Subj extraction in French:

$[_{FocP}$ wh- [Foc $[_{FinP}$ wh- [Fin + ϕ [Subj ... $[_{vP}$ wh- ...]]]]]] Fin + ϕ = *qui*

---

[15] Both (62) and (63) below assume Rizzi's expanded structure for the left periphery, which includes, among others, a FocP, FinP (see Rizzi, 1997).

4.4 Is the Extended Projection Principle universal?

Following these ideas, Diercks (2009) proposes the following account for the Lubukusu paradigms presented in Section 3.5.5. Subject extraction in this language requires merging of an agreement morpheme above Subj to satisfy the Subject Criterion, as in French and English. As a result, complementizer agreement becomes obligatory whenever subject extraction takes place, as in (63).

(63)   Lubukusu subject extraction (after Diercks, 2010, 93, ex. 15)

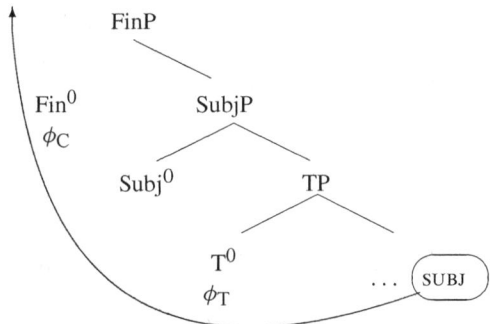

The extraction facts from BP in Section 3.5.4 pose a slightly more challenging problem for extending the freezing analysis. On the one hand, the data from inflected infinitives (see (48) from that section) seem to follow the Lubukusu pattern: whenever agreement is merged above Subj, extraction is licensed. On the other, if we adopt Menuzzi's (2000) proposal as is, extraction must take place from the preverbal subject position. Since this position would freeze the subject, according to Rizzi and Shlonsky's analysis, one would not expect extraction to be possible. However, I think there are reasons to argue for a slight reanalysis of the data. Menuzzi (2000) assumes that *nada* 'nothing' is adjoined to I′ because it precedes the inflected verb (as seen in (64a) vs. (64b)) but follows the subject. Since the subject is assumed to be in Spec, IP, it would follow that *nada* is adjoined to I′.

(64)   a. João nada   tinha feito ajudar Maria.   (BP)
            João nothing has   done help   Maria
            'João has done nothing to help Maria.'

        b. * João tinha nada   feito ajudar Maria.
            João has   nothing done help   Maria
            'João has done nothing to help Maria.'

                                                    (from Menuzzi, 2000, 34, ex. 37)

100 *The Extended Projection Principle and the Null Subject Parameter*

However, a different analysis is possible: if *nada* is dislocated, then arguably the subject is not in its SubjP position. In an articulated left periphery like the one in (65) (see Rizzi, 1997 and much subsequent work), *nada* would appear in TopP and the subject in a higher TopP. Alternatively, *nada* could be in Spec, SubjP.

(65) [$_{TopP}$ João [$_{TopP}$ nada [$_{SubjP}$ [$_{TP}$ tinha [feito ajudar Maria]]]]]

In the case of the inflected infinitive clauses, the verb must usually precede the subject (cf. (66a) vs. (66b)), a fact that Menuzzi (2000) takes to show V-to-C movement. However, whenever the object *nada* is dislocated, the verb can precede or follow the subject–object sequence (cf. (67a–b)), but it can not appear between the subject and the object, as seen in (67c).

(66) a. O Manuel recorda   [terem   os rapazes dado um presente pr'a
         the Manuel remembers to-have.3.PL the children given a   present to-the
         Maria].   (BP)
         Maria
         'Manuel remembers that the boys gave a present to Maria.'
      b. *O Manuel recorda   os rapazes terem   dado um presente
         the Manuel remembers the boys to-have.3.PL given a present
         pr'a Maria.
         to-the Maria
         'Manuel remembers that the boys gave a present to Maria.'
                                           (from Menuzzi, 2000, 32, ex. 34)

(67) a. João lamentou os rapazes nada   terem   feito para ajudar Maria.
         João regretted the boys nothing to-have.3.PL done to help   Maria
                                                                       (BP)
         'João regretted that the boys did nothing to help Maria.'
      b. ? João lamentou terem   os rapazes nada, feito para ajudar Maria.
           João regretted to-have.3.PL the boys nothing done to help Maria
           'João regretted that the boys did nothing to help Maria.'
      c. * João lamentou os rapazes terem   nada   feito, para ajudar Maria.
           João regretted the boys to-have.3.PL nothing done to help Maria
           'João regretted that the boys did nothing to help Maria.'
                                           (from Menuzzi, 2000, 34, ex. 38)

One possible account of these facts would have the verb in a constant position in all of these examples (for example, Rizzi's Fin^0 position), and the two arguments in different, dislocated positions above or below FinP, as in (68).[16]

---

[16] Merging Rizzi's (1997) left-periphery proposal with the Rizzi and Shlonsky SubjP proposal would result in the clausal template TopP > FocP > TopP > FinP > SubjP > TP.

4.4 Is the Extended Projection Principle universal?

(68) a. ... [FinP terem [TopP João [TopP nada [SubjP [TP feito ajudar Maria]]]]]
     b. ... [TopP João [TopP nada [FinP terem [SubjP [TP feito ajudar Maria]]]]]

Notice, though, that this means that the presence of the floated quantifier *tudo* 'all' in (48) in Section 3.5.4 above, repeated below as (69), no longer indicates that the extraction site is Spec, IP (or, in more precise terms, Spec, SubjP), but another topicalized position. The proposed structure for this example is presented in (70).

(69) Que   rapazes, o Manuel afirma terem   todos nada   oferecido de
     which   boys   the Manuel claims to-have.3.PL   all   nothing offered of
     presente pr'a   Maria no aniversário dela?   (BP)
     present to-the Maria in-the birthday of-her
     'Which boys does Manuel claim to all have offered nothing as a gift to Maria
     for her birthday?'   (from Menuzzi, 2000, 35, ex. 40a)

(70) BP inflected infinitive extraction

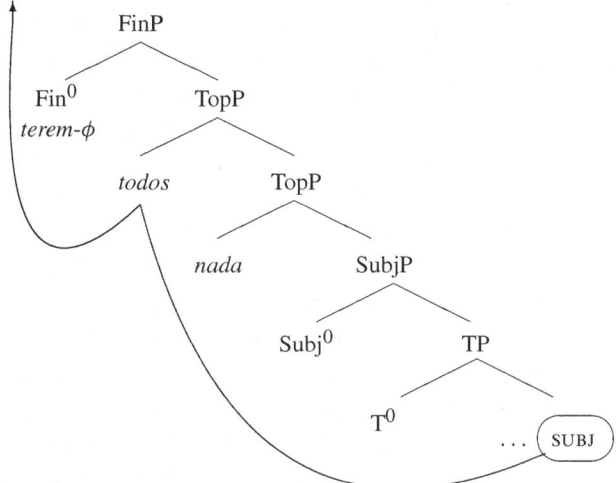

This analysis, in turn, raises the question of what satisfies the Subject Criterion in these examples, and two possible answers come to mind: one, it is still the verb + ϕ in Fin⁰, the other one, it is a null *pro*. In this sense consider the minimal pair in (71) given by Menuzzi. Subject extraction is possible if the floated quantifier *todos* appears postverbally (as in (71a)), but not if it appears preverbally, as in (71b). Following the logic developed so far, this must mean that *todo* 'all' in (71a) is in the canonical subject position, where it is frozen.

(71) a. Que   rapazes, o   Paulo   desconfia [que gostem **todos** de
         which boys   the Paulo   suspects   that like   all   of
         Maria]?   (BP)
         Maria
         'Which boys does Paulo suspect all like Maria?'
      b. *Que   rapazes, o Paulo desconfia que [**todos**] gostem de Maria?
         which boys   the Paulo suspects that all   like   of Maria
         'Which boys, does Paulo suspect that all like Maria?'
                                                (from Menuzzi, 2000, 29, ex. 30a)

4.4.3 The Subject Criterion revisited

In Rizzi and Shlonsky's proposal, merging of ϕ-features above SubjP satisfies the Subject Criterion, but why should this be?

The alternative I will propose is that the Subject Criterion may target a number of projections in the left periphery, which can vary depending on the language. Its default position will be SubjP, but it can also target positions higher in the structure. Thus, in Icelandic and in DSEC, expletives appear in Spec, TP (what corresponds to Rizzi and Shlonsky's SubjP), whereas in CCS and Northwestern Iberian languages, the expletive has the feature Top, merging directly in that position. In BP, English/French, Övdalian and Lubukusu, merging of an agreeing head over SubjP will satisfy the Subject Criterion and allow for subject movement.

Conceptually, formalizing the EPP as a requirement that targets a set of functional projections in the left periphery makes sense of the two independent properties associated with subjects. According to Rizzi and Shlonsky (p. 118), the DP in SubjP is interpreted as an aboutness topic ('about DP, I am reporting X') and also as the subject of a predication. But since these are independent properties, one expects them to be able to surface independently, and many researchers have argued that one of them has more prominence than the other depending on the language (see for example Li and Thompson, 1976). For this reason, separating each of them in different heads is conceptually attractive.

Specifically, I propose the constraints in (72)–(73). These requirements are alignment requirements and can be ranked with respect to each other.[17] Languages for which (72) is more prominent will typically yield

---

[17] Examples (72) and (73) differ from Rizzi and Shlonsky's proposal in two respects. First, they are seen as alignment constraints, not so much as constraints on matching content. This makes them more amenable to a theory that lacks Spec-head configurations. The alignment aspect of the proposal draws from Sigurðsson's (2010) Filled Left Edge Effect. Second, they interact in productive ways through constraint ranking, as suggested below.

4.4 Is the Extended Projection Principle universal?

non-topic-oriented languages like English, those for which (73) is will yield topic-prominent languages. If a language complies with both constraints, it will likely have expletives that are topic-oriented, as described above for Western Iberian languages.

(72)   Align DP with the edge of the Subj projection

(73)   Align XP with the edge of the Topic projection

The interaction between these two principles is best viewed in a ranking framework such as Optimality Theory. Thus, (72) will be ranked above (73) in some languages, and below in others. Other constraints may result in neither of these constraints affecting the output. This would be the case, for example, if faithfulness constraints are ranked higher, resulting in no movement. Presumably, this is the analysis for Irish and for extraposed clauses in Spanish, as well as for existential clauses.

Notice an important difference between the formulation of both constraints: whereas the first one requires a DP on the edge of the subject projection, the second only requires an XP. This difference captures a conceptual difference: subjects tend to be DP-like categories, but any category can be a topic (see Holmberg's 2005 analysis of Finnish).

4.4.4 Subject and topichood in Oromo

The proposed amendment to the Subject Criterion receives some support from the distribution of NSs and agreement in Oromo. In this language, the verb shows agreement with the subject in at least number and gender, as seen for feminine agreement in (74a) and number agreement in (74b) (see Clamons *et al.*, 1999, 60).

(74)   In response to *What did the girl and boy do?*
       a. Intal-t-ií-n   hoolaa bit-t-e.   (Oromo)
          girl-FEM-SUBJ-TOP sheep buy-FEM-PAST
          'The girl bought a sheep.'
       b. Intal-t-ií-n   -ifi gurbaá-n   wal   lol-an.
          girl-FEM-SUBJ-TOP- and boy-SUBJ-TOP each-other fight-3.PL.PAST
          'The girl and the boy were fighting.'
                                                 (from Clamons *et al.*, 1999, 60–1, ex. 1a–b)

This agreement, however, only exists when the subject is a topic. Thus, at the beginning of a story, where the subject is not the topic, we find examples like (75), which is a minimal pair with (74a) except for the agreement morphology on the DP (*intal-**t-ií-n*** 'girl-FEM-SUBJ-TOP' vs. *intala* 'girl') and the corresponding agreement on the verb (*bit-**t**-e* 'buy-FEM-PAST' vs. *bit-e* 'buy-PAST').

(75) Intala hoolaa bit-e. (Oromo)
      girl sheep buy-PAST
      'The girl bought a sheep.' (from Clamons *et al.*, 1999, 61, ex. 2a)

Objects are never marked for Case or topicality, as seen in (76). This sentence could appear immediately after the previous example, and given the discourse, the object is a perfect candidate for topic, but it is not overtly marked as such.

(76) [After *Intala takka-á magaalaa dhuf-e.* 'A girl came to the market']

(77) Nama tokko-ó   intala arke. (Oromo)
      person one.MAS-SUBJ girl   saw
      'A man saw the girl.' (from Clamons *et al.*, 1999, 62, ex. 3)

Clamons *et al.* (1999, 62) point out that topic marking in (74) is distinct from topicalization, a process that fronts any NP, and marks it with a different morphology than the one illustrated in (74). This is seen in (78a–b), where the fronted DP (*Salmaa*) is marked and interpreted as topicalized, regardless of whether it corresponds to the subject or the object of the clause.

(78) a. Yo Salmaa-ti, (isi-f-n)   dhuf-t-e. (Oromo)
         as for-Salma (she-SUBJ-TOP) come-FEM-PAST
         'As for Salma, she came.'
      b. Yo Salmaa-ti, gurbaa-n   isi ark-e.
         as for-Salma boy.SUBJ-TOP her see-PAST
         'As for Salma, the boy saw her.' (from Clamons *et al.*, 1999, 62, ex. 4)

These examples suggest that only subjects marked as topics agree with the verb. If we distribute the Subject Criterion requirement over several heads, we have a principled way of accounting for this pattern: only subjects that are marked as topics satisfy this requirement in Oromo, and hence trigger agreement. If topic and subjecthood are conflated as part of the Subject Criterion, then the facts from Oromo cannot be properly explained.

In sum, I propose that two interacting constraints underlie the Subject Criterion: subject alignment and topic alignment. In languages like English, the requirement applies to SubjP, and in languages like Chinese, plausibly to TopicP. In languages like Oromo, we see overt evidence of targeting TopicP in that only subjects marked as topics can agree with the verb.

This requirement is usually satisfied by the subject, and when it is, the subject is frozen in place. However, there are other ways to satisfy it, for example by merging an expletive with SubjP, which frees the subject for extraction. In other cases, a complementizer that has agreement properties appears in a left-peripheral position, also allowing movement of the subject.

As we will see in Chapter 5 (particularly in Section 5.5), the notion of the extended Subject Criterion will play an important role in accounting for why apparently very similar varieties have differential outcomes when licensing NSs.

4.5 The revised Null Subject Parameter

So, what is the NSP? Based on the evidence presented in previous sections, a successful analysis of NSLs and the NSP should at least take into account the following properties.

(79) a. **Typology of NSLs.** Certain languages have productive null subjects, others have restricted null subjects, others only have overt subjects.

  b. **NSs and agreement**

   i. The inflectional properties of a verb frequently correlates with the availability of null subjects, both language internally (i.e. Irish, Hebrew) and across languages (English vs. Spanish).

   ii. There is no universally valid notion of agreement-richness that serves as a sufficient condition for NS.

   iii. In some languages, NSs are identified in discourse.

  c. **Null expletives.** Null subjects do not imply obligatorily null expletives (cf. Finnish), and null expletives do not imply available null subjects (cf. German).

  d. *Pro* vs. **pronominal agreement.** Overall, the evidence argues in favor of *pro* as a separate syntactic category (Finnish expletives, agreement asymmetries in Northern Italian dialects).

  e. There is no convincing evidence for the universality of the EPP as a requirement to fill the Spec, IP position. Hence null expletives cannot be obligatory in NSLs.

Orthogonally to these properties, I have also assumed a revised version of subject extraction asymmetries based on Rizzi and Shlonsky, in which extraction asymmetries are the result of strategies for bypassing criterial freezing (induced by subject movement to SubjP).

We are now in a position to state the properties of the NSP as follows:

(80) a. *Pro* is a lexical entry available as part of Universal Grammar.
  b. *Pro* contains unvalued ϕ-features.
  c. The features of *pro* are filled in as part of AGREE.

The three properties in (80) are part of what Rizzi (1986a) termed identification, although, as we will see below, identification entails not only feature-valuation of *pro* but also discourse identification. What remains is to develop a specific theory of ϕ-feature valuation, and to see how this interacts with the discourse contexts.

4.6 Chapter summary

In this section, I have reviewed the three lines of analysis of NS that have been proposed in the literature: NSs as an independently defined category *pro*, NSs as deleted versions of overt pronouns, and NSs as pronominal affixes attached to the verb. I have argued that the evidence for *pro* is, overall, slightly more compelling than for the deletion analysis or the pronominal agreement proposal. As Roberts (2010a, 85) points out evidence for pronominal AGR/INFL comes mostly from interpretive facts (see more below), whereas the evidence for a separate null subject comes from syntactic paradigms. In order to distinguish the *pro* theory from the pronominal agreement theory, three general sets of facts appear particularly relevant. First, the distribution of overt expletives in Finnish. These expletives directly argue against the pronominal agreement hypothesis and in favor of an independent *pro*. Second, ellipsis seems to separate overt subjects (where person, number and gender appear not to be interpretable on INFL) from true NSs, where person, number and gender appear to behave like Tense, i.e. as an interpretable feature. Third, the facts from Italian dialects (represented by the Ancona dialect) suggest that in the general case reference does not track inflection but rather a separate category.

I have also argued that the EPP (or Subject Criterion) should be seen as two separate alignment constraints that interact through constraint ranking.

PART II
On identification

5 Identification and morphology

The intuition that NSs rely on the verb's morphology to recover the reference of the subject is very old. On the one hand, the verb in languages like Italian, Spanish or Swahili productively and distinctively encodes person and number, whereas in languages like French or English it does not. On the other hand, null subjects are possible in many languages only when they are recoverable from verbal information. As already mentioned, for example, NSs are possible in Irish in the synthetic form, which has person/number information (see McCloskey and Hale, 1984), but not in analytic form, with no person/number information.

Hebrew presents a different aspect of the same phenomenon. As I discussed in Section 2.3.3, this language only allows for NSs in contexts where person/number inflection is available (either on the verb or on some other functional category; see Shlonsky, 2009), which is typically in 1st/2nd person in the past and future tense, as well as with certain types of negation in the present.

A third type of example is illustrated by languages like Pashto (see Huang, 1984, 535). This is a split ergative language that follows a nominative–accusative pattern for present verbs. It has a rich agreement system, and the verb agrees with the subject in transitive and intransitive clauses, as illustrated in (1), where the verb *razi* 'comes' agrees with the person and number with the subject *Jān* and *zə* 'I' agrees with *xwr-əm* 'eat', respectively.

(1) a. Jān   ra-z-i.   (Pashto)
        John DIR-come-3.MAS.SG
        'John comes.'

     b. zə maṇa xwr-əm.
        I apple eat-1.MAS.SG
        'I eat the apple.'   (from Huang, 1984, 535, ex. 12)

For past events, the pattern is ergative, and the verb agrees with intransitive subjects (i.e. *Jān* and *ra-ğ-ay* 'came' in (2a)) and with transitive objects (i.e *maṇa* 'apple' and *wə-xwar-a* 'eat-3.FEM.SG' in (2b)).

(2)   a. Jān ra-ǧ-ay.   (Pashto)
          John ASP-come-3.MASC.SG
          'John came.'

       b. ma maṇa wə-xwar-a.
          I apple PERF-eat-3.FEM.SG
          'I ate the apple.'   (from Huang, 1984, 536, ex. 13)

When a null category appears, it tracks the verb's agreement morphology, thus the subject can be dropped in both (1a–b), as shown in (3), and in (2a) (cf. (4a)), but not in (2b), as seen in (4b).

(3)   a. *pro* ra-z-i.   (Pashto)
          DIR-come-3.MAS.SG
          'He comes.'

       b. *pro* maṇa xwr-əm.
          apple eat-1.MAS.SG
          'I eat the apple.'   (from Huang, 1984, 536, ex. 13)

(4)   a. *pro* ra-ǧ-ay.   (Pashto)
          ASP-come-3.MASC.SG
          'He came.'   (from Huang, 1984, 536, ex. 14a)

       b. * *pro* maṇa wə-xwar-a.
          apple PERF-eat-3.FEM.SG
          'Ate the apple.'   (from Huang, 1984, 536, ex. 16)

Conversely, the object can be dropped in (2b) but not in (1b), as seen in (5).

(5)   a. ma *pro* wə-xwar-a.   (Pashto)
          I   PERF-eat-3.FEM.SG
          'I ate it.'   (from Huang, 1984, 536, ex. 14b)

       b. * zə *pro* xwr-əm.
          I   eat-1.MAS.SG
          'I eat (it).'   (from Huang, 1984, 536, ex. 15)

Irish, Hebrew and Pashto illustrate that overt morphological agreement correlates fairly closely with the availability of NSs within single languages. Other languages where this correlation holds are Standard Arabic, Moroccan, Lebanese and Beni Hassan Arabic, Älvdalsmålet and Angami (see Cole, 2009, 574). Even in consistent NSLs like Spanish and Italian, NSs become impossible in tenses where the morphological paradigm is not distinct enough (see Lozano, 2002; Sheehan, 2007, and other references). As we can see in (6), the preterite and imperfect tenses differ with respect to the number of person distinctions. In the singular, 1st and 3rd person are identical in the imperfect, but distinct in the preterite.

(6)   Preterite and imperfect paradigm for Spanish *abrir* 'open'

	Preterite	Imperfect
1.SG	*abrí*	*abría*
2.SG	*abri-ste*	*abrías*
3.SG	*abri-ó*	*abría*
1.PL	*abri-mos*	*abríamos*
2/3.PL	*abri-eron*	*abrían*

In this context, when a subject is conjoined in one clause, as in (7), the subsequent clause can have a NS if the verb tense is preterite (cf. (7a)) but not if it is imperfect (cf. (7b)), and this takes place because the imperfect singular paradigm has homophonous endings for the 1st and 3rd persons.[1]

(7)   a. María y   yo llegamos a   casa. Yo / *pro* abrí   la   puerta.
           Maria and I   arrived   to home. I / *pro* opened.1.SG the door.
                                                                              (Spanish)
           'Maria and I arrived home. I opened the door.'
        b. María y   yo llegamos a   casa. Yo / ella / **pro* tenía   las llaves.
           Maria and I   arrived   to home. I / she / *pro* had.1/3.SG the keys
           'Maria and I arrived home. I found the keys.'
                                                          (from Sheehan, 2007, 84, ex. 158)

Although the correlation between NSs and agreement is clear, it is also well known that rich inflection is neither a necessary nor a sufficient condition for NSs, since many languages with rich agreement lack NSs (Icelandic is arguably one of them), and discourse-related NSLs with no agreement have productive NSs. Given this paradox, many have given up on the possibility of establishing a well-defined connection between overt morphological inflection and the availability of NSs (see for example Speas, 1995 and Alexiadou and Anagnostopoulou, 1998, 522–523, fn. 38). Rather, agreement richness is

---

[1] The unacceptability of (7b) with *pro* substantially improves if the second clause is negated, as in (i). I have no explanation for why this is.

(i)   María y   yo llegamos a   casa. *pro* no tenía   las llaves.   (Spanish)
        Maria and I   arrived   to home. *pro* not had.1/3.SG the keys
        'Maria and I arrived home. I/she didn't have the keys.'

stipulated as an abstract syntactic property of certain heads (see Speas, 1995) and the availability of NSs follows from that syntactic property. Cole (2009), on the other hand, proposes a theory that relativizes the notion of morphological richness to individual grammars, and this proposal allows him to capture general tendencies as well as cross and intra-linguistic variability in availability of NSs.

In the following sections, I will review and adopt Cole's (2009) proposal for morphological identification, which suggests that grammars set the minimal level of morphological specification at which a NS can be recovered, and this minimal level ranges from full ϕ-feature specification (person, number and gender) as in Tarifit, to no morphological specification whatsoever in Chinese. I will combine this proposal with a hierarchical approach to ϕ-features along the lines of Harley and Ritter (2002) and Béjar (2003), and a particular implementation of AGREE along the lines of Pesetsky and Torrego (2001, 2004, 2006, 2007) and Camacho (2011).

5.1 The minimal morphological threshold (MMT)

Cole's (2009, 569) point of departure is the following observation: in many languages, NSs are possible if uniquely identified by agreement morphology. If that fails, they are identified by reference to an antecedent in context, and if that is not possible, overt pronouns are used. This cascading strategy can be observed in the following Bengali examples. In this language, the subject and the verb agree for person and formality if they are nominative, but not for number; overt (redundant) pronouns are used for focus and to change topics. With this background, consider (8)–(10). Example (8a) introduces an overt subject *Iqbal*. The NS in (8b) is uniquely identified by verbal morphology (3.PAST) and naturally interpreted as coreferent with *Iqbal*, illustrating identification through verbal morphology.

(8) a. Iqbal Calcutta-e budhbar-e gœlo... (Bengali)
Iqbal to-Calcutta on-Wednesday go.3.PAST
'Iqbal went to Calcutta on Wednesday...'

b. Brihoshpothibar-e *pro* gari kinlo.
on-Thursday *pro* car buy.3.PAST
'On Thursday he bought a car.' (from Cole, 2009, 576, ex. 38)

By contrast, the same discourse structure is set up in (9), but the verbs in (9b) are both ambiguous between 2nd/3rd person, so morphology is not enough to identify the NS, which is retrieved from the discourse antecedent *Iqbal*. The

5.1 The minimal morphological threshold (MMT)   113

same situation arises with (10b), where the verb continues to be morphologically ambiguous between 2nd and 3rd person. Given the presence of an active discourse antecedent (*Iqbal*), if the intended interpretation of the third subject is 2nd person, there must be an overt pronoun (*tumi* 'you').

(9) a. Shonibar-e Iqbal Calcutta-e jabe... (Bengali)
     on-Saturday Iqbal to-Calcutta go-2/3.FUT
     'On Saturday, Iqbal will go to Calcutta.'

  b. *pro* gari kinbe.   *pro* Restaurant-e jabe.
     pro car buy-2/3.FUT *pro* to-restaurant go-2/3.FUT
     'He will buy a car. He will go to a restaurant.'
                                              (from Cole, 2009, 576, ex. 39)

(10) a. Shonibar-e Iqbal Calcutta-e jabe... (Bengali)
     on-Saturday Iqbal to-Calcutta go-2/3.FUT
     'On Saturday, Iqbal will go to Calcutta.'

  b. *pro* Gari kinbe.   Tumi restaurant-e jabe.
     car buy-2/3.FUT you-s to-restaurant go-2/3.FUT
     'He will buy a car. You will go to a restaurant...'
                                              (from Cole, 2009, 576, ex. 40)

This basic idea that recoverability first resorts to morphological identification, then to identification by antecedent and finally by inserting an overt pronoun, is combined with a variable scale of what constitutes successful morphological identification depending on the language. The general scale is presented in (11), and languages define at which point in the scale subjects can be recovered from the morphology (Cole's so-called "morphological maximality").

(11)   Recoverability scale

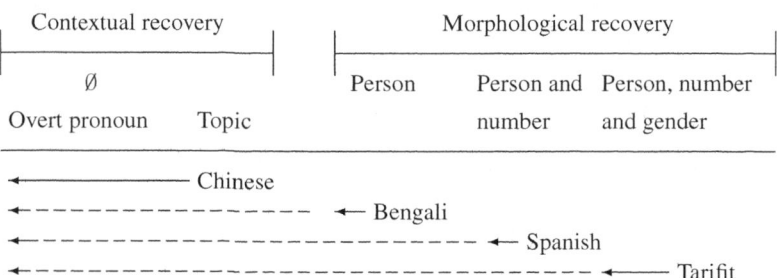

Thus, NSs are morphologically recoverable by a bundle of ϕ-features that include person, number and gender in Tarifit, otherwise by topic, otherwise an overt pronoun will be required. For Spanish, the morphological break-point is person and number, etc.

Under this perspective, what constitutes morphological richness to identify a NS is not uniformly defined for all languages, and a given language may define it as including person, while a paradigm that encodes the same distinctions in another language may not allow recoverability. I will call the point at which a language allows for morphological identification of a NS **minimal morphological threshold** (MMT) for NSs, as in (12). The MMT for Tarifit will be overt morphological encoding of person, number and gender, whereas for Bengali it will just be person.

(12)   The **minimal morphological threshold** (MMT) defines the minimal set of values overtly encoded in the morphology that a language requires to identify a null subject.

What happens to values to the right of the MMT setting? Consider the case of gender in Arabic. As Cole (2009, 579) points out, gender is restricted to a 2nd and 3rd person singular and plural in Arabic, but does not appear in 1st person, as illustrated by comparing (13a) with (13b–c). In the first case, the verb does not encode gender, whereas in the second examples it is marked for feminine or masculine. However, since NSs are possible in all persons, the MMT for Arabic cannot contain gender, otherwise NSs should not be possible in (13c).

(13)   a. (ʔanā)   raʔay-tu   zayd-an.   (Arabic)
          (I.NOM) see-PAST.1.SG.NOM Zayd-ACC
          'I saw Zayd.'

      b. (ʔanti)   takallam-ti
          (you.SG.FEM.NOM) speak-PAST.3.SG.FEM.NOM
          'You (fem.) spoke.'   (from Johns, 2007, 129, exx. 14, 15)

      c. (huwa)   ʤāʔ-a
          (he.NOM) came-3.SG.MAS.NOM
          'He came.'   (from Fassi Fehri, 1993, 115, ex. 48b)

Cole's solution involves assuming that "morphological maximality [in Arabic] is for person and number in the 1st person, but for person, number and gender in the 2nd and 3rd persons" (p. 579).

This issue raises the question of whether ϕ-features are simply listed, or whether they have internal structure that would derive which features are accessible to identify a NS in any given paradigm, an issue I will return to in Section 5.2.

Before doing so, it is worth discussing a consequence of this point of view: in languages with obligatorily overt subjects, identification by morphology fails, although it may do so in different ways. For example, in English, one might speculate that the MMT is set to have a person value of at least 1st or 2nd, so that even distinctive 3rd persons in the present do not identify a NS. In other languages, it may be specified as any person, so that even if the verb marks 1st, 2nd and 3rd persons distinctively, NSs will still not be identified.

However, if a NS is not morphologically identified in a language like English or German, why can't it be identified by a discourse antecedent, the way it is in Chinese? So why isn't (14b) possible as a continuation for (14a)?

(14)   a. Mary left last night and Bill left this morning.
        b. * As for John, is leaving tomorrow.

In Chapter 6, I will propose a solution to this question based on two ideas: the nature of NSs is different in Chinese-type and English-type languages and the locality requirements for identifying the antecedent are also different.

The proposed MMT also raises issues of learnibility: how does a child know which point of the scale the grammar falls into? I will return to this issue in Section 9.3.1.

5.2   The structure of ϕ-features

Cole's (2009) proposal does not specifically assume an internal hierarchy for ϕ-features, but as I pointed out in the preceding section, there may be reasons to think that ϕ-features are hierarchically organized. In addition to the issue of languages like Arabic, where gender is expressed in some persons but not in others, the scale in (13) seems to have an underlying structure: points of maximality display a certain implicational relation, such that number implies person and gender implies both person and number. It is thus worth considering whether research on the internal structure of ϕ-features can shed light on this issue.

5.2.1   *Φ-feature hierarchies*

Following Harley and Ritter (2002), Béjar (2003) proposes that ϕ-features are hierarchically organized as in the partial representation in (15).[2] One of the primary purposes of the hierarchy is to capture entailment relations among features. Thus, speaker entails participant, and inanimate entails class. Notice

---

[2] GROUP and MIN(IMAL) represent the different types of number systems.

that these representations are underspecified, and features are privative, i.e. they have or lack a given value (as opposed to having binary values).

(15)

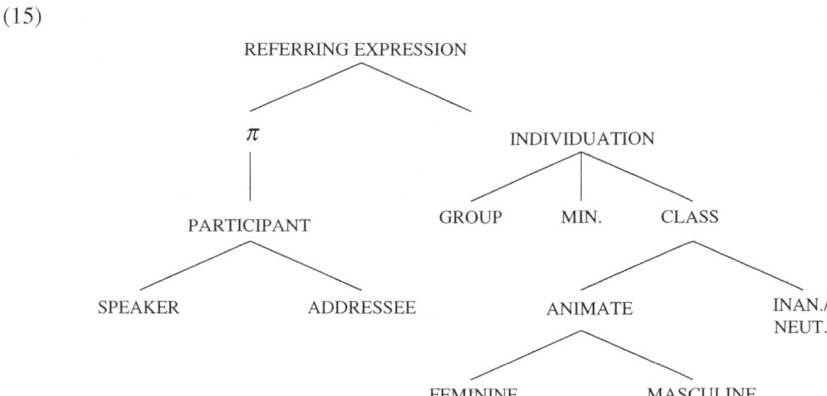

The hierarchy doesn't explicitly label any node as 1st or 2nd person, rather, those are represented as in (16). The tree is topped by a root node, which Béjar (2003, 45) takes to designate a REFERRING EXPRESSION. However, I will not assume referentiality to be encoded in R. These hierarchies apply both to nominals and ϕ-feature inflection, but there are non-referential nominal expressions (expletives, for example), and ϕ-feature inflection will be argued to also lack reference.

The feature π (person) is proposed on empirical grounds; if it did not exist, non-participants would be underspecified for everything but the root node (Béjar, 2003, 49).

(16) Person:

	3rd person	2nd person	1st person
	R	R	R
	π	π	π
	PART	PART	PART
		ADDR	SPKR

5.2 The structure of φ-features

This feature hierarchy is intended to be a general template that applies to elements bearing φ-features. However, verbal inflection and pronouns have two crucial differences: pronouns have potential referential capacity and categorial specification (as DPs, for example), whereas verbal inflection need not. In fact, if the arguments for *pro* given in Section 4.1 are correct, inflection does not have either property. This distinction is not reflected in (15) and (16) in any obvious way.

However, Béjar (2003, 49) suggests a way to capture reference by proposing the additional elements in the hierarchy (DEICTIC, DEFINITE, SPECIFIC and D), which have the entailments in (17) (see also Cowper and Hall, 2002).

(17) SPEAKER > PARTICIPANT > DEICTIC > DEFINITE > SPECIFIC > D > R(EFERENT)

Some of these features merit some additional comment. DEICTIC is introduced as a node separate from PARTICIPANT because deixis cuts across PARTICIPANT. On the one hand, the reference of participants depends on shifts in discourse, whereas that of non-participants does not. On the other hand, non-participants are inherently deictic but they do not shift. NPs, on the other hand, can be deictic but are not inherently so. DEFINITE is defined as referentially indexed in the discourse and SPECIFIC denotes a particular individual (see Cowper and Hall, 2002, 58). Finally, D provides the nominal with potential reference.

Béjar (2003, 49) takes the feature π to have a slightly different status, as a variable that ranges over the highest element in the hierarchy in (17). This means that in some languages, it can be all-inclusive (REFERENT), whereas in others, it could be DEFINITE.

The second problem, i.e. the categorial nature of pronouns, comes to light when considering languages like Chinese or Japanese, which seem to have argumental NPs (as opposed to DPs). This possibility clusters with four other characteristics in these languages, according to Chierchia (1998, 354, ex. 20): (a) generalized bare arguments (i.e. absence of determiners), (b) the extension of all nouns is mass, (c) absence of plural morphology and (d) generalized classifier system. Tomioka (2003), in turn, has argued that null pronouns are simply null counterparts of overt categories (cf. Hoji, 1998 and Tomioka, 1999).

One possible way to formalize the location of referentiality and the categorial nature of pronouns would be to assume that referentiality is not located in

118 *Identification and morphology*

REFERENT. One reason for this is that expletives can lack referential properties but have the same agreement properties as fully referential pronouns, as seen in (18).[3] There must be some way to signal that *it* lacks reference in the first case whereas it refers to *the tree branch* in the second case, and if this property is encoded in REFERENT, then we have no way of representing (18a). Based on this evidence, let us assume that R stands for ROOT, and that referentiality can be encoded in any of the features dominated by R up to DEICTIC.

(18)   a. It is snowing.
       b. I was walking under a tree branch when it fell and hit me.

Second, following ideas first suggested by Postal (1966) and Sommerstein (1972) and popularized by Abney (1987), we can assume that pronouns are Determiners, and that the feature geometry in (15) corresponds to D, with N/NP as a sister to D, as in (19). Note that following the comments above, π can range over any of the nodes from D to PARTICIPANT, which I indicate by putting it in parenthesis.

(19) ϕ-feature geometry for pronouns

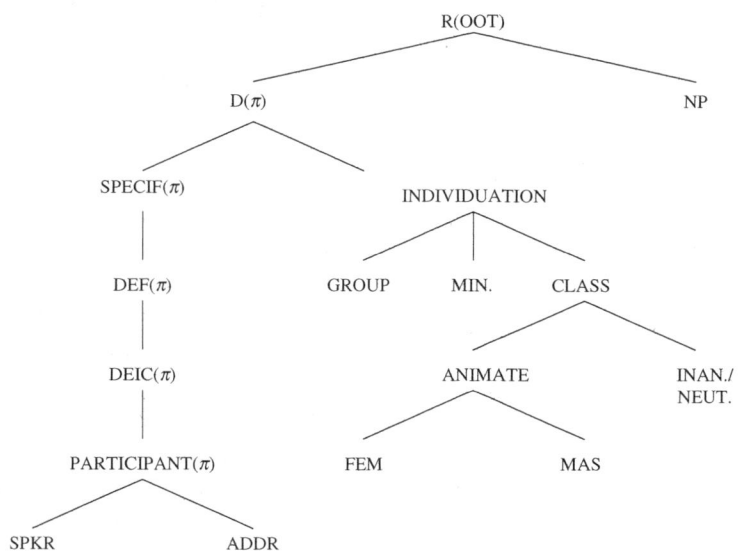

---

[3] As mentioned in Section 2.1.2, several authors have proposed that weather-verb expletives have referential properties, I will disregard that possibility.

5.2 The structure of φ-features 119

Inflectional φ-features, on the other hand, lack referential properties. This raises the question of whether nodes related to referential properties (D, SPECIFIC, DEFINITE and DEICTIC) should be present and represented, as in (19) or absent, as in (20).

(20) Impoverished φ-feature geometry for Infl

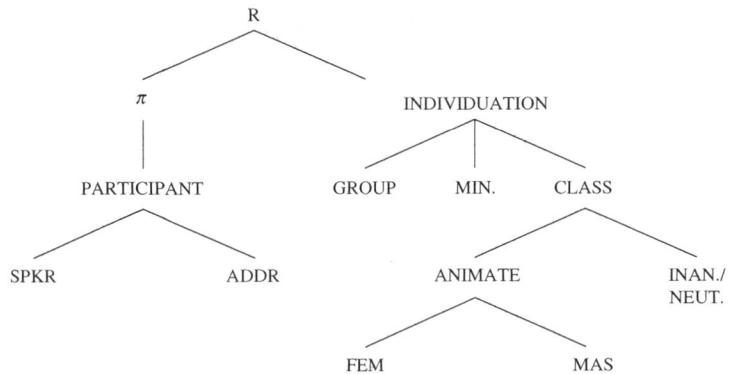

One argument in favor of including at least some of the nodes with referential properties in the representation for inflectional φ-features comes from the fact that several morphological systems are sensitive to definiteness, particularly with respect to objects. For example, Swahili definite objects trigger overt agreement but indefinites do not, as seen in (21) (see Linares, 2012 for other instances of definiteness agreement). In the first example, the verb lacks person agreement morphology and the object *kitabu* 'book' is interpreted as an indefinite, whereas in the second one, it is interpreted as definite, and the verb adds the prefix *ki-* '3.SG'. This would suggest that DEF should be present at least for the representation of object inflectional agreement in Swahili. Since we want the feature geometry to be as general as possible, I tentatively conclude that inflectional agreement should include the nodes in (19), although those nodes that have referential properties are uninterpretable.

(21)   a. U- me- leta kitabu? (Swahili)
        2.SG PERF bring book
        'Have you brought a book?'

    b. U- me- ki- leta kitabu?
       2.SG PERF 3.SG bring book
       'Have you brought the book?'
       (from Perrott, 1972, 38, quoted in Croft, 1988, 161)

120 *Identification and morphology*

One crucial difference between the pronominal φ-feature geometry and Infl's geometry is the absence of the NP branch in the representation for Infl. While it may make sense to match definiteness or deixis, I can't think of a reasonable counterpart of NP content in the realm of inflectional morphology. Rather, as we will see, I will propose that languages like Chinese or Japanese have pronouns that lack D but have NP, and in those languages we expect no agreement. Hence, the proposed geometry for Infl would be the one in (22).

(22)   φ-feature geometry for Infl

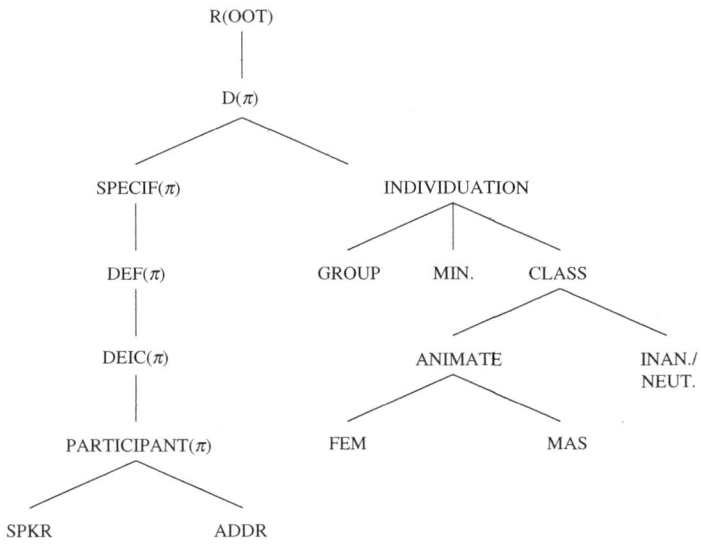

5.3   Agree

Béjar's (2003) analysis is built on the operation AGREE (see Chomsky, 2000, 2001), which involves at least two crucial steps: first, the probe and the goal must MATCH, then the goal VALUES the probe's features. The first operation is only possible if the features of the probe are a subset of the features of the goal as in (23) (see Béjar, 2003, 53).

(23)   a. MATCH is valued at the root (of the structure).

   b. Probe (F) and Goal (F') match if Goal (F') entails root Probe (F).

(from Béjar, 2003, 53, ex. 37)

5.3 Agree   121

Assuming the geometries in (19) and (22) for pronouns and inflection respectively, a variety of language-specific settings are possible, some of which are partially illustrated in (24). Thus, an Infl probe could be specified as SPECIF, and if the goal is specified as SPECIF, then the goal would entail the probe and they would MATCH. Likewise for the second row in the table. However, in the third row, because INDIV belongs to a separate branch than SPECIF in the feature geometry in (19), the goal would not entail the probe, hence there would be no MATCH.

(24)   Probe–goal match outcomes depending on feature specification
                                               (adapted from Béjar, 2003, 55, ex. 41)

[F] Probe	[F'] Goal	MATCH
[SPECIF]	[SPECIF]	Yes
[SPECIF]	[SPECIF[PART]]	Yes
[SPECIF]	[INDIV]	No

The second part of AGREE involves copying the features of a goal to a probe, and subsequently rendering the probe inert, as in (25).

(25)   AGREE: feature copying from goal to a probe   (after Béjar, 2003, 60, ex. 47)

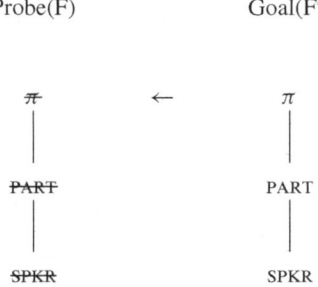

I adopt a the definition of AGREE presented in (26), which departs in important ways from the conception adopted in Chomsky (2000, 2001) and Béjar (2003) and builds on Pesetsky and Torrego (2001, 2004, 2006, 2007), Baker (2008b), Camacho (2010b, 2011) and Linares (2012). Specifically, the three most important differences with the Chomsky-based AGREE theory are the distinction between probes and goals, the distinction between interpretability and valuation and the elimination of c-command from the definition.

(26) A and B AGREE iff:
    a. At least one of the categories is functional and acts as a probe
    b. Both categories' ϕ-features MATCH
    c. A and B's ϕ-features are VALUED
    d. AGREE is locally constrained to the phrase that contains the matching categories

I assume, together with Béjar (2003), that the probe must be a subset of goal for MATCH, so that a probe specified as $[\pi]$ would match a goal specified as $[\pi[\text{PART}]]$, but not a goal specified as $[\text{INDIV}]$. VALUATION is defined as in (27).

(27)   a. VALUATION: when two categories have matching ϕ-features, the values of one can be copied onto the other.
    b. VALUATION can only specify the value of a node, not delete or change it.

In the conception of AGREE in (26), only the probe has to be functional, the goal can be functional or lexical. Thus, a Determiner (D) head probes a lexical Noun (N), but I (or v, depending on one's theory) probes a functional DP. Second, I assume that at the end of AGREE, both matching categories must have valued features, but the direction of copying can be from the probe to the goal or the goal to the probe. Which of the ϕ-feature structure is more specified determines directionality, so copying cannot delete or replace existing features, but it can append features to existing nodes. This is illustrated in (28).

(28)   Outcomes of VALUATION

Before Valuation		After Valuation		
A	B	A	B	Outcome
$[\pi]$	$[\pi[\text{PART}]]$	$[\pi[\text{PART}]]$	$[\pi[\text{PART}]]$	√
$[\pi[\text{PART}]]$	$[\pi]$	$[\pi[\text{PART}]]$	$[\pi[\text{PART}]]$	√
$[\pi]$	$[\pi[\text{PART}]]$	$[\pi]$	$[\pi]$	*
$[\pi[\text{PART}]]$	$[\pi]$	$[\pi]$	$[\pi]$	*

Finally, no c-command condition is built into the definitions. In Baker (2008b), the c-command condition is loosened to allow for cases in which either the Probe c-commands the Goal or the Goal c-commands the probe. Linares (2012) convincingly extends this conclusion, arguing that in general, agreement relationships are regulated by what he calls the Independence Principle, stated in (29). This principle generally leads goals to escape their base position in the tree and move to a position where they are not c-commanded by the probe.

(29)   *The Independence Principle:* A controller cannot be c-commanded by its target   (Linares, 2012, 80, ex. 27)

Linares notes that cyclicity independently constrains agreement patterns, ruling out many of the configurations where c-command has traditionally been invoked (see also Béjar, 2003). Consider, for example, cases in which an argument in base-position blocks agreement with a lower argument, but movement of the higher argument unblocks agreement, as schematically represented in (30). Cases like these are well documented in Icelandic (see Sigurðsson and Holmberg, 2008), and many other languages (see Béjar, 2003). These contexts are readily explained if one assumes that in (31), DP_{DAT} no longer intervenes because the probe (V) does not c-command it.

(30)   Exp V DP_{DAT} DP_{NOM}
                         *

(31) DP_{DAT} V   t DP_{NOM}
                          ✓

However, the contrast between (30) and (31) can also be explained if DP_{DAT} in (31) is outside of the agreement domain. To that effect, one of the dialects of Icelandic described by Sigurðsson and Holmberg shows the pattern in (32), where displacing the dative does not allow for full agreement with the nominative. If all that is at stake in (30) is the c-command configuration, then the available configuration in (32) comes as a surprise.

(32) DP_{DAT} V   t DP_{NOM}
                          *

124 *Identification and morphology*

On the other hand, Béjar (2003, §2.10–2.11) argues that a probe may extend its domain to the specifier position in some cases, and the specifier is not within the probe's c-command domain. Based on these types of evidence, I dispose of c-command as a requirement for AGREE in favor of cyclicity.

With these assumptions in mind, I propose that NS identification is a matter of valuing *pro*'s ϕ-features through AGREE. In this sense, the Null Subject Parameter is reduced to AGREE (in the spirit of Rizzi, 1986a). Whether AGREE is successful or not depends on the language-specific ϕ-feature geometry, a process that is consistent with the recoverability scale in (11). Let us see some concrete examples of how the system works.

5.4   Deriving null subjects in sample languages

In this section, I will show how the combination of the MMT, the proposed feature-geometries and AGREE account for distribution of NSs across several languages.

5.4.1   Minimal morphological threshold set to person, number and gender: Tarifit

As mentioned above, Tarifit requires person, number and gender to identify a NS. This means that the MMT is set to person, number and gender. As (33a) illustrates, the verb and the subject agree in these features, and as (33b) shows, subjects can be null, particularly when the topic is maintained (see McClelland, 1996, 37; Cole, 2009).

(33)   a. nəttæθ   t-   sən   a-   t-   snən
           3.SUBJ.SG.FEM   3.SUBJ.SG.FEM- know   IRR- 3.SUBJ.SG.FEM- cook
           səksu   (Tarifit)
           couscous
           'She knows [how to] make couscous.'
                                                        (from McClelland, 1996, 21, ex. 18)

       b. i-   ruh   ɣ-   rsuq
           3.SUBJ.SG.MAS- go   LOC- market
           'He went to the market.'   (from McClelland, 1996, 16, ex. 1)

The φ-feature geometry for the Infl probe in Tarifit is presented in (34). The feature GROUP appears in parenthesis to signal the singular (without GROUP) and plural contrast (with GROUP).[4]

(34) Finite φ-feature probes in Tarifit

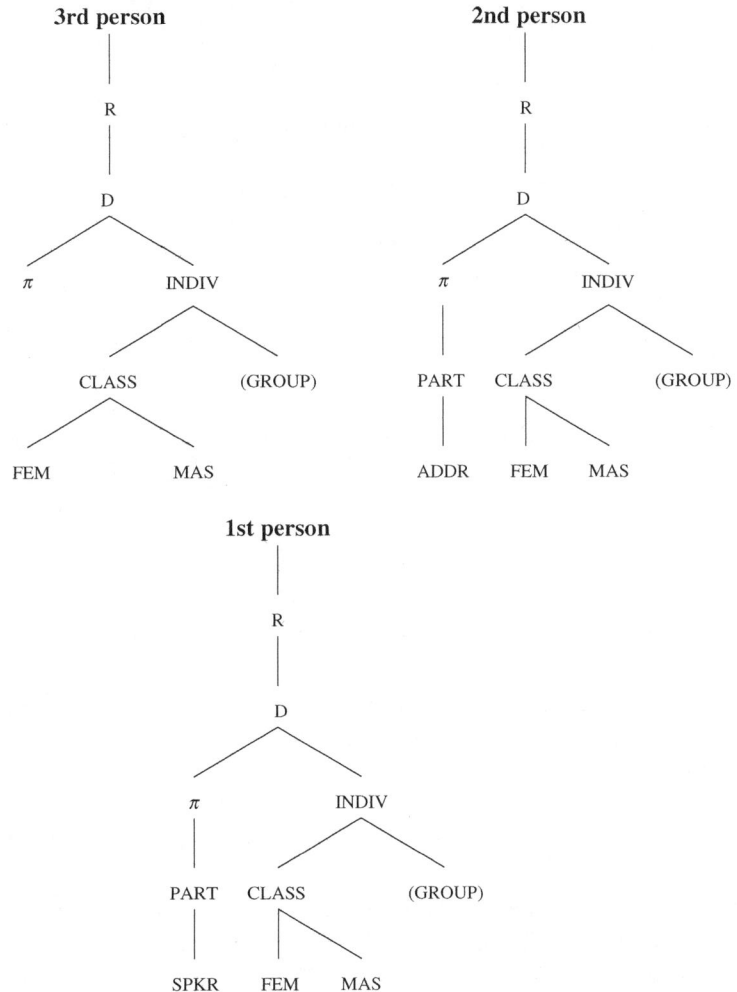

---
[4] Recall that π is variable that can range over SPECIF, DEF, DEIC and PARTICIPANT, in addition to D. In these representations, I have omitted one or more of those nodes because they are not relevant for establishing the MMT.

126 *Identification and morphology*

Assume that *pro* is generally specified as R, or perhaps R[D]. As a result, the AGREE operation would proceed as in (35) for 2nd person.

(35)   AGREE between 2nd person sg. Infl and *pro* in Tarifit

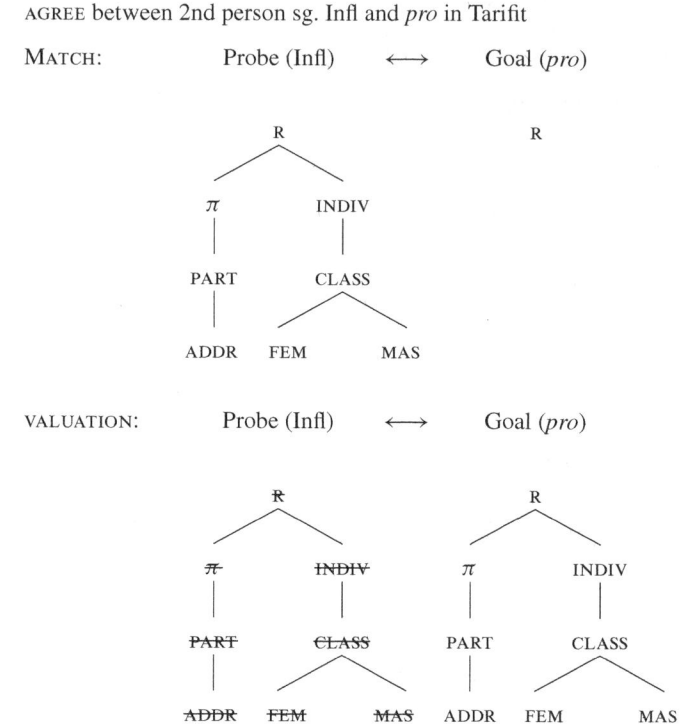

If the probe is underspecified, *pro* would be unvalued for some relevant node. As a result of how Tarifit defines the MMT, *pro* would not be sufficiently identified.

5.4.2   *Minimal morphological threshold set to person and number: Italian and Spanish*

In the case of Italian and Spanish, NS require at least person and number, as illustrated in (36). This means that MMT is set to person and number (i.e. D), for this reason, NSs are possible with inflected verbs (as in (36)) but not with absolute participles in out-of-the-blue contexts, as shown in (37). Arguably, participles have number but not person.

(36)   Comi-mos almendras.   (Spanish)
        eat-1.PL   almonds
        'We ate almonds.'

(37) *Construid-a-s,   el arquitecto se fue de vacaciones.   (Spanish)
       constructed-FEM-PL, the architect   CL went of vacation
       'Once constructed, the architect went on vacation.'

The φ-feature geometry for Spanish is the one proposed in (38) ignoring the intermediate nodes between R and π (recall that π ranges over several possible features).

(38)   Finite φ-feature probes in Spanish

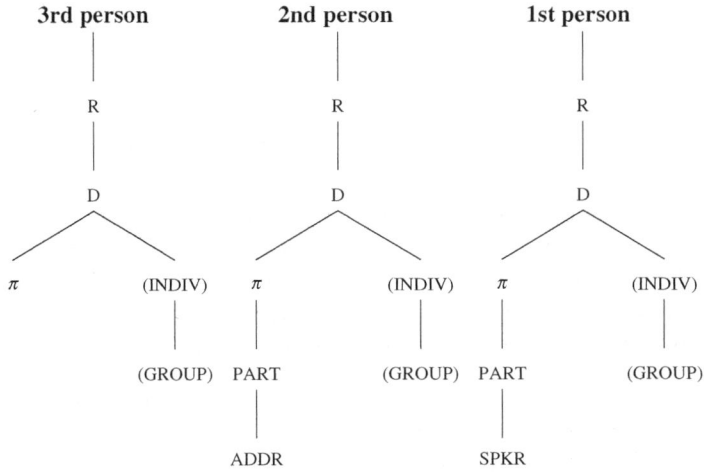

The *pro* identification process proceeds as in (39).

(39)   AGREE between 2nd person sg. Infl and *pro* in Spanish

           MATCH: Probe (Infl)   ⟷   Goal (*pro*)

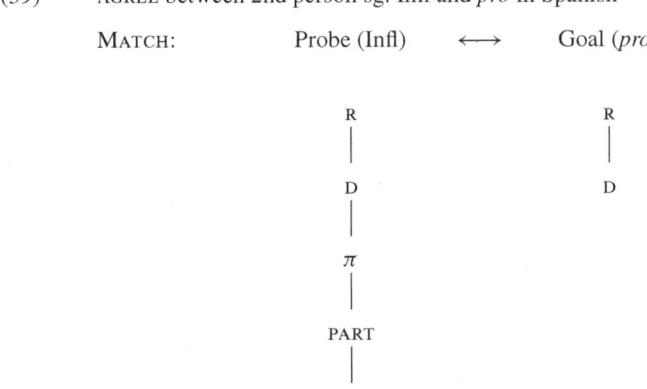

128 *Identification and morphology*

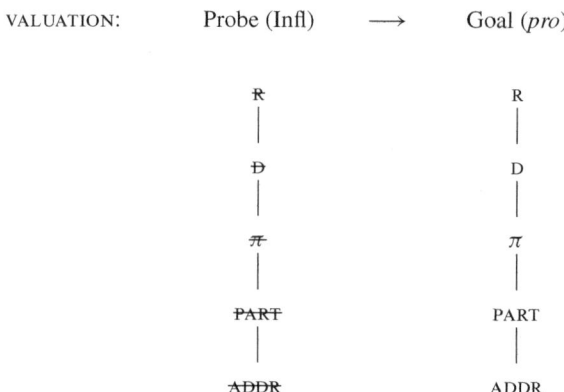

Notice that the resulting *pro* is not specified for CLASS, because the probe is unspecified for that feature. However, there is some reason to believe that *pro* can be potentially specified for gender, as in the case of secondary predicates or small clause subjects, illustrated in (40). In these examples, *pro* is necessarily identified as feminine because the secondary predicate is specified as feminine. For these cases, I take the feminine specification of *pro* to come from the overt morphology on the secondary predicate. However, as noted, gender is not enough to value/identify *pro*, as seen in (41).

(40) a. *pro$_i$* salió *pro$_i$* content-a.   (Spanish)
       pro   left   happy-FEM
       'She left happy.'

     b. La$_i$ consider-o   [*pro$_i$* atrevid-a]
        CL.FEM consider-1.SG   daring-FEM
        'I consider her daring.'

(41)   * Notamos [*pro* content-a]   (Spanish)
         saw   pro happy-FEM
         'We saw Ana happy.'

Assuming that the functional head associated with the adjective is specified as in (42), *pro*'s resulting specification will fail the MMT for Spanish.[5]

---

[5] Baker (2008b) argues that adjectival agreement fundamentally differs from verbal agreement in that the first type lacks 1st and 2nd person agreement. In his theory, this follows from two principles, first, structurally, verbs project a Specifier, whereas adjectives do not, and second, 1st and 2nd person agreement takes place in a specifier configuration (his SCOPA, p. 52). Both theories might converge in the following sense: some of the agreement mismatches Béjar (2003) analyzes are triggered when a target for agreement moves to the specifier of the probe, expanding the agreement search space. If adjectives lack a Specifier by design, these types of effects would be systematically absent with adjectives. I do not know if this prediction is correct.

(42) Representation for Adjectival φ-features in Spanish

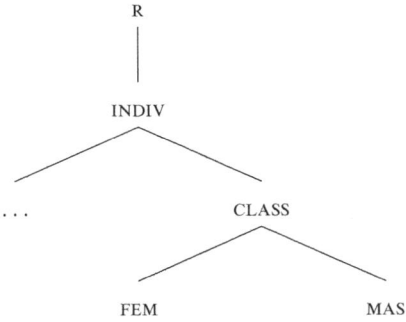

Hindi has a similar situation (thanks to Neil Smith for pointing this out). Overt pronouns do not encode gender features, but certain auxiliaries do, as illustrated in (43). The first example shows a present tense auxiliary *hai* 'is', unmarked for gender. In the past tense, the auxiliary shows a masculine/feminine distinction. In the current proposal, auxiliaries marked for gender would be specified for CLASS, although this would not affect the MMT, since NSs are possible with both types of auxiliaries.

(43) a. (vah) biimaar hai   (Hindi)
         he/she ill   AUX/COP
         'He/she is sick.'
      b. (vah) biimaar thaa
         he/she ill   AUX/COP.PAST.MAS
         'He was ill.'
      c. (vah) biimaar thii
         he/she ill   AUX/COP.PAST.FEM
         'She was ill.'   (from Neil Smith, p.c.)

5.4.3 *Minimal morphological threshold set to person: Bengali*

As pointed out in Section 5.1, Bengali verbs agree in person and formality with their subjects. This property is shown in (44), where the verb shows different morphological properties depending on whether the 2nd person is formal, neutral or intimate. However, formality does not seem to be necessary for identifying NSs, since the 1st person pronouns and verb forms do not encode differences in formality (cf. (45)), but NSs are still possible in that person.[6]

---

[6] I do not represent formality in the φ-feature hierarchy because it does not seem to participate in NS identification. I will not address, therefore, where it should appear in the φ-feature hierarchy. Three options come to mind: under person (given that it somehow classifies speech-participants in terms of social status, rather than discourse participation), under individuation (in the sense that it classifies, like genders and classifiers do), or under a separate branch.

(44) a. Apni   elen.   (Bengali)
        you.FORM came
        'You (formal) came.'
    b. Tumi   ele.
        you.NON-FORM came
        'You (neutral formality) came.'
    c. Tui   eli.
        you.INTIM came
        'You (intimate) came.'   (from Dasgupta, 2003, 404, my glosses)

(45) Verbal paradigm for Bengali *kenā* 'to buy' in the present (from Dasgupta, 2003, 404, 9.2)

	Not marked	Intimate	Neutral	Formal
1st	kini			
2nd		kiniš	keno	kenen
3rd		–	kene	kenen

Based on the paradigm in (45), I propose the following representations for Bengali inflectional probes. Once again, intermediate nodes between D and π have been omitted.

(46)   Finite ϕ-structure probes for Bengali

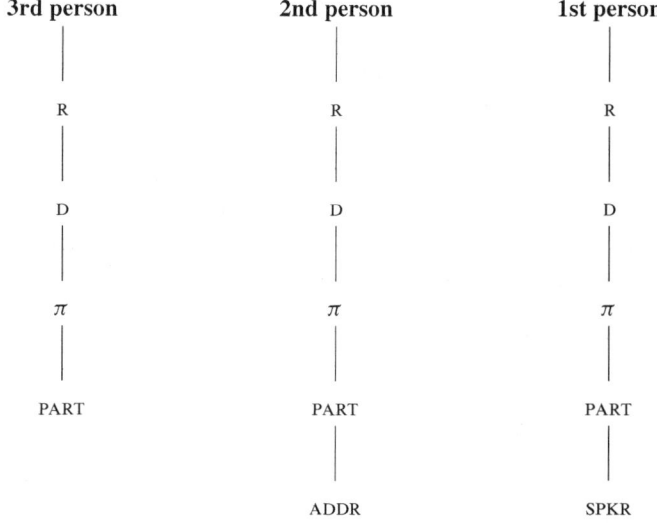

MATCHING and VALUATION in Bengali are represented in (47). As in the case of gender in Spanish, I do not assume that number is specified for *pro* in Bengali, although the corresponding overt pronouns do distinguish between singular and plural (see Sengupta, 1999, 278).

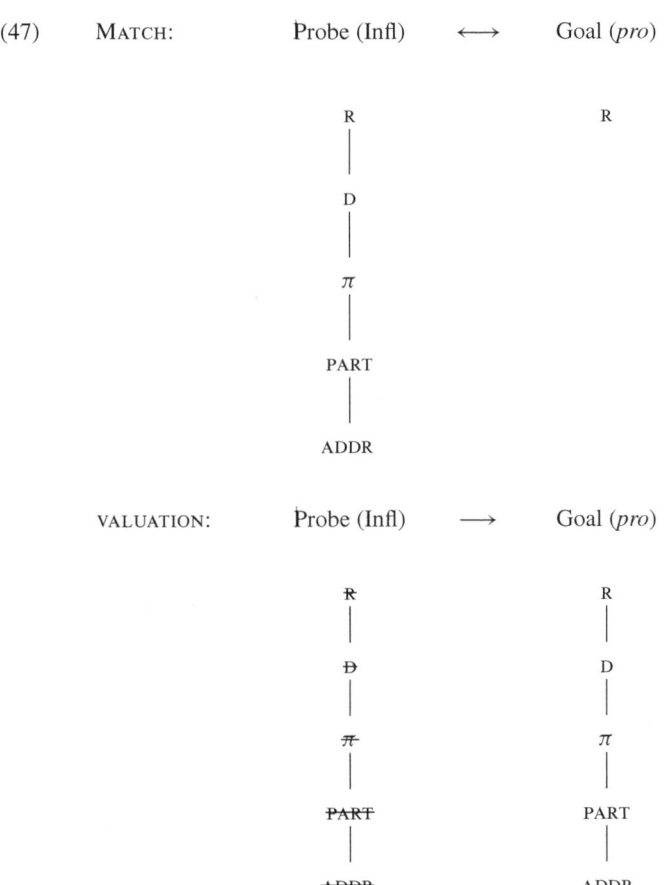

5.4.4 Gender in Arabic

Recall that Arabic 1st/2nd persons are specified for gender, whereas 3rd is not. In the current approach, this would be captured by distinct ϕ-feature hierarchies for each type of probe, as shown in (48) for the singular. Minimal morphological threshold in Arabic includes at least π, so all of those representations would value NSs that could be identified.

132 *Identification and morphology*

(48)   φ-structure for Arabic probes

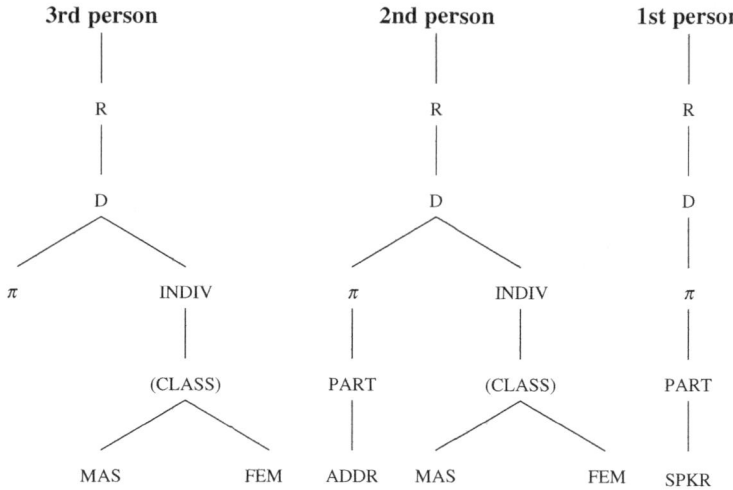

5.4.5 Mixed paradigm in Hebrew

In Section 2.3.3, we observed two types of partial NSLs, ones in which NSs are available depending on person and/or tense, and those in which NSs are restricted to main/embedded clauses. In this section, I consider the first type, in particular Hebrew, which shows three separate asymmetries that regulate the distribution of NSs (see Shlonsky, 2009, 133): the referentiality asymmetry, the person asymmetry and the tense asymmetry.

(49) a. The referentiality asymmetry: non-referential argumental NSs are possible in every tensed environment but one.

b. The person asymmetry: referential NSs are permitted with 1st and 2nd person inflection; 3rd person NSs are only possible in contexts of (non-standard) binding and/or Control.

c. The tense asymmetry: referential NSs are only possible in past and future tense clauses, not in present tense clauses (from Shlonsky, 2009, 133).

For present purposes, I will focus on the person and tense asymmetries, illustrated in (50)–(51) and (52) respectively. Example (50) illustrates that 3rd person pronouns cannot be null, regardless of the gender or number of the verb, whereas the examples in (51) show that verbs in 1st and 2nd person in the past allow for a null subject.

(50) a. * Lamad   albanit.   (Hebrew)
         study.PAST.3.MAS.SG Albanian
         'He studied Albanian.'
      b. * Lamd-da   albanit.
         study.PAST.3.FEM.SG Albanian
         'She studied Albanian.'
      c. * Lamd-du   albanit.
         study.PAST.3.PL Albanian
         'They studied Albanian.'

(51) a. Lamad-ti   albanit.   (Hebrew)
         study.PAST.1.SG Albanian
         'I studied Albanian.'
      b. Lamad-ta   albanit.
         study.PAST.2.MAS.SG Albanian
         'You (mas) studied Albanian.'
      c. Lamad-t   albanit.
         study.PAST.2.FEM.SG Albanian
         'You (fem) studied Albanian.'
      d. Lamad-nu   albanit.
         study.PAST.1.PL Albanian
         'We studied Albanian.'
      e. Lamad-tem   albanit.
         study.PAST.2.PL Albanian
         'You (pl) studied Albanian.'   (from Shlonsky, 2009, 135, ex. 5)

Finally, (52) illustrates the tense asymmetry: No person can be null in the present, regardless of gender and number.[7]

(52) a. * Lomed   albanit.   (Hebrew)
         study.PRES.MAS.SG Albanian
      b. * Lomed-et   albanit.
         study.PRES.FEM Albanian
      c. * Lomd-im   albanit.
         study.PRES.MAS.PL Albanian
      d. * Lomd-ot   albanit.
         study.PRES.FEM.PL Albanian   (from Shlonsky, 2009, 136, ex. 7)

Shlonsky (2009) analyzes these two asymmetries in the following way: the ϕ-feature matrix of the present and future Tense lacks the slot for [person].

---

[7] The person asymmetry reappears in the present with negative *eyn*, which carries inflection. In these contexts, only 1st/2nd are possible (see Shlonsky, 2009, 137).

134 *Identification and morphology*

First and 2nd persons, on the other hand, are taken to head a separate syntactic projection, a Speech Act Participant Phrase located above TP, in the left periphery (see Sigurðsson, 2010 for a similar proposal for Finnish). "Sap^0 is filled by a pronominal clitic, moved from the position of the thematic subject" (Shlonsky, 2009, 142). The clitic is moved to Sap^0, and the verbal complex in T adjoins to that head. In essence, Shlonsky suggests that Hebrew lacks covert 1st and 2nd pronouns, but it has 1st and 2nd clitics. In the approach I have proposed here, Hebrew would set the MMT to [PART].

Regarding the tense asymmetry, Shlonksy's suggestion that ϕ-features lack [person] means that it lacks the relevant [PART] node, as illustrated in (53). In this representation, *pro* does not have a value that satisfies Hebrew's MMT, and additionally, D is not deleted on Infl.

(53) AGREE between 2nd person sg. present Infl and *pro* in Hebrew

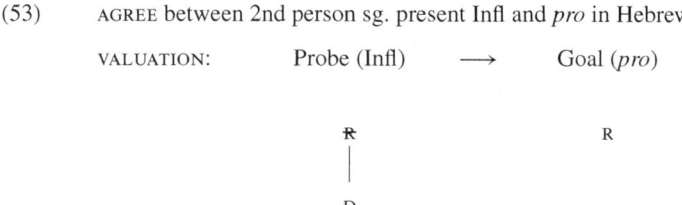

The account correctly predicts that *pro* should not be possible in the present. In the past and future, Infl values *pro* so that it satisfies the MMT only in 1st and 2nd person, because only those persons are specified for [PART], whereas 3rd person lacks the relevant feature, as seen in (54)–(55).

(54) Hebrew 2nd person sg. past Infl

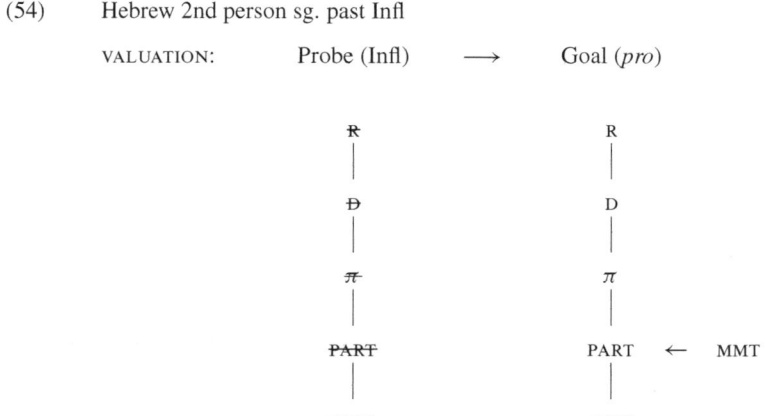

5.4 Deriving null subjects in sample languages 135

(55)   Hebrew 3rd person sg. past Infl

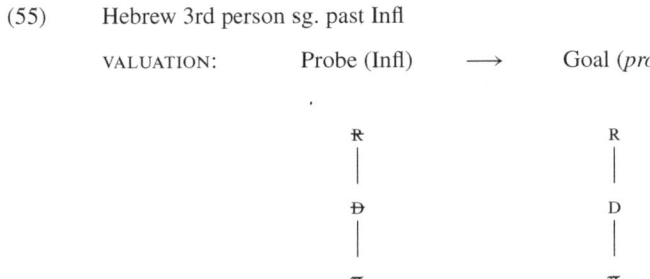

Shlonsky (2009) argues that 3rd person NSs are possible when controlled by another argument, an issue we will return to below. For now, these cases illustrate that in the relevant agreement domain, 3rd *pro* cannot be identified, as predicted by the theory.

The Hebrew paradigm presents an interesting case study to test how learnable the theory is (cf. also Chapter 9). Suppose that a child starts with a minimal grammar compatible with the data, namely, that Hebrew is not a NSL. Null Subjects in the input will be associated with morphological forms that comply with the person and tense asymmetries, and those forms will provide positive evidence to set the MMT to PART. Any other form that does not have such overt morphology will not appear with NSs, hence nothing will trigger resetting of the parameter.

5.4.6 Mixed paradigms in German vernaculars

A similar account applies to Schwabian, Zurich German (ZG) and Övdalian (see Fuß (2005) and Rosenkvist (2009, 2010a, 2010b) for general details and references). In Schwabian and Zurich German, null subjects are only possible in 1st and 2nd person singular, as illustrated in (56)–(57). In Övdalian, on the other hand, only 1st and 2nd person plural subjects are possible, as seen in (58).

(56)   a. ... daß scho   des Buch kauft   hasch.   (Schwabian 1st/2nd sg.)
           that already the book bought have.2.SG
           '... that you already have bought the book.'

        b. Geschtern han-mr   en Bobbel Eis   kauft.
           yesterday have-1.SG.me.CL a ball ice cream bought
           'Yesterday I bought myself a ball of ice cream.'
                                                    (from Rosenkvist, 2009, 164, ex. 13)

        c. * Kommt   net.   (from Trutkowski, 2011, 213, ex. 26c)
             comes.3.SG not

(57) a. Ha der das nöd scho verzellt? (ZG, 1st/2nd sg.)
have.1.SG to-you it not already told
'Haven't I told you that already?'

b. Wänn nach Züri chunnsch, muesch mi bsueche.
when to Zurich come.2.SG must.2.SG me visit
'When you come to Zurich, you must visit me.'
(from Rosenkvist, 2009, 164, ex. 15)

(58) a. ... dar wilum glåmå min wennanan. (Övdalian)
when want-to.1.PL chat with each-other
'... when we want to chat with each other.'

b. Nų irið iema.
now are-2.PL. home
'Now you are home.' (from Rosenkvist, 2009, 169, ex. 22)

c. * ir unggrun nų, kanenda!
is hungry now indeed
'He/one is indeed hungry now!' (after Rosenkvist, 2010b, 236, ex. 2)

As the inflectional paradigms of these varieties show (cf. (59)), the person and number forms that allow for null subjects (shown in bold) show distinctive morphology: *chume, chunnsch* 'to come.1.SG/2.SG' respectively in Zurich German, *komm, kommsch* 'to come.1.SG/2.SG' in Schwabian, and *kumum, kumið* 'to come.1.PL/2.PL' in Övdalian. However, some 3rd person forms also show distinctive inflection (*-t* for ZG and Schwabian and *kumå* in Övdalian) but do not allow for NSs. Rosenkvist (2009, 171) argues that one additional factor to take into account is that 3rd person sg. subjects "in general are not fully identified solely by person and number features on an agreeing element; it is common that 3p singular pronouns also have gender features."

(59) Verbal inflection paradigm for *to come* in Schwabian, Zurich German and Övdalian (adapted from Rosenkvist, 2009, 171, table 3)

	Singular			Plural		
	1	2	3	1	2	3
Zurich German	**chume**	**chunnsch**	chunnt	chömed	chömed	chömed
Schwabian	**komm**	**kommsch**	kommt	kommet	kommet	kommet
Övdalian	kumb	kumb	kumb	**kumum**	**kumið**	kumå

5.4 Deriving null subjects in sample languages   137

The distribution of NSs in Zurich German, Schwabian and Övdalian fits well in the proposed analysis, according to which all three varieties set the MMT to [PART]. This predicts that none of them will allow for NSs with 3rd person probes. All persons in the plural lack a [PART] node in Zurich German and Schwabian, given that they are identical (cf. (60)). In Övdalian, on the other hand, the reverse situation holds: all persons in the singular are identical, so they are underspecified for [PART]. Finally, Zurich German and Schwabian 1st and 2nd person singular geometries specify [PART], as does Övdalian 1st and 2nd person plural.

(60)   φ-structure for Zurich German, Schwabian and Övdalian:

Singular: **ZG and Schwab 1st/2nd person**   **Övd 1st/2nd/3rd person**

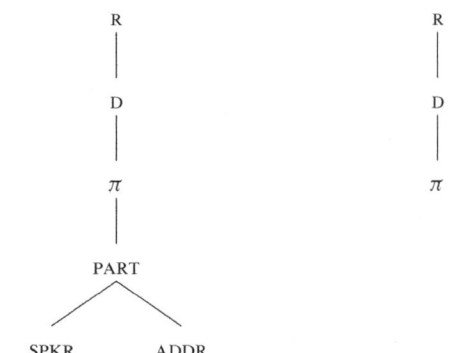

Plural: **ZG and Schwab 1st/2nd/3rd person**   **Övd 1st/2nd person**

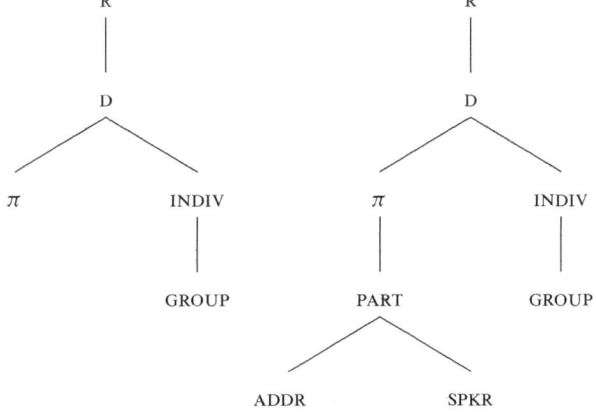

138   *Identification and morphology*

Regarding the fact that 3rd persons show distinctive morphology but do not license NSs, the current approach does not present a problem, since the MMT is set to PART, but those forms are not specified for that setting.

5.4.7   Summary

In the preceding sections, I have adopted the idea that NS identification is constrained by Cole's recoverability scale in (11), a scale that ranges from morphological recovery to contextual recovery. Each language sets a minimal morphological threshold (MMT) to recover a NS. I have applied the notion of MMT, combined with the feature geometry to Tarifit (MMT set to person, number and gender), Italian/Spanish (MMT set to person, number), Bengali (MMT set to person) and to mixed paradigms such as Hebrew and German Vernaculars (MMT set to participant).

I have also argued that ϕ-feature bundles are best viewed as structured hierarchies, rather than lists. Additionally, I have adopted the idea that agreement between two categories involves copying of the probe's feature root node to the the goal's root node. These assumptions have as a consequence that agreement will not target intermediate nodes in the hierarchy.

5.5   Identification and locality

All of the instances of identification by morphology presented in the preceding section involve AGREE between a probe and a goal within the same clause. In other words, subjects agree with the verb in their own clause, not with another verb. So, for example, (61) cannot mean 'I think that I left', with a structure in which the embedded *pro* is identified by the matrix probe.

(61)   *pro* cre-o   que *pro* sali-ó.   (Spanish)
        pro think-1.SG that *pro* left-3.SG
        'I think that s/he left' not 'I think that I left.'

In general, then, AGREE is locally constrained to IP/CP. In this section, I analyze the contrast between Standard German and Germanic vernaculars as a difference in the location of the agreeing probe. This distinction derives from the fact that German does not license NSs despite having strong agreement, whereas vernaculars do.

5.5.1   On the locality of head-agreement: Standard Germanic vs.
          C-agreeing German Vernaculars

Standard German is frequently quoted as a problem for accounts that link agreement richness with the ability to have a NS. Specifically, despite the distinctive endings for all persons in the German inflectional paradigm (shown in (62)), this variety lacks NSs, as shown in (63), which requires an overt *ich* 'I' pronoun.

(62)   Verbal inflection in Standard German for *arbeiten* 'to work' (from Jaeggli and Safir, 1989, 28, ex. 38)

Singular			Plural		
1	2	3	1	2	3
arbeit-e	arbeit-est	arbeit-et	arbeit-en	arbeit-t	arbeit-en

(63)   Sie kenne *(ich) nicht.   (Standard German)
        her know   I   not
        'Her I do not know.'   (from Rosenkvist, 2009, 151, ex. 3)

At the same time, several regional varieties of Germanic do have NSs, as already shown in (56)–(58) above. Another set of German varieties, including Bavarian, Lower Bavarian and Frisian, also have restricted NSs depending on person and number (see Bayer, 1984; Fuß, 2005). Thus, Bavarian only allows for 2nd person SG/PL NSs (see (64)–(65)), whereas Lower Bavarian, also allows for 1st person PL NSs in addition to 2nd person, as seen in (66). Finally, (67) illustrates 2nd person SG NSs in Frisian.

(64)   a. w... obst   noch Minga   kummst.   (Bavarian 2nd sg. and pl.)
           if.2.SG to   Munich come.2.SG
           'Whether you come to Munich.'

        b. * ... ob noch Minga   kummst.
              if   to   Munich come.2.SG

(65)   a. Hobbds   khoa geld   nimma.
           have-2.PL no   money not-anymore
           'You have no money any more.'   (from Rosenkvist, 2010a, ex. 9)

        b. * Hobb   khoa geld   nimma.
             have-1.PL no   money not-anymore
             'We have no money any more.'   (from Ursula Atkinson, p.c.)

(66)   Fahr-ma   noch Minga?   (Lower Bavarian 2nd sg./pl. and 1st pl.)
        travel-1.PL to   Munich
        'Are we going to Munich?'

(67) a. Miskien moatst   my helpe.   (Frisian 2nd sg.)
       perhaps must.2.SG me help
       'Perhaps you must help me.'
    b. Ik tink   datst   my helpe moatst.
       I think that.2.SG me help must.2.SG
       'I think that you must help me.'   (from Rosenkvist, 2009, 167, ex. 19)

Null Subjects in Bavarian, Lower Bavarian and Frisian are only possible if C is inflected (by contrast to Zurich German, Schwabian and Övdalian). Thus, we saw in (64) that the complementizer *obst* 'if.2.SG' is inflected for person and number, whereas in (68), the complementizer *ob* 'if' lacks inflection, although the verb still has it.

(68) a. * Ob *pro* noch Minga kumm-st.   (Bavarian)
         if   to   Munich come.2.SG
     b. * Ob *pro* noch Minga kumm-ts.
         if   to   Munich come.2.PL   (from Bayer, 1984, 240)

Bayer (1984) and Fuß (2005) give convincing evidence that the C-related morphemes of Bavarian and Lower Bavarian are inflectional morphemes, not independent clitics. For example, whereas 2nd person morphology on C is compatible with an overt pronoun in Bavarian, it is not in other varieties, as seen in (69)–(70). Furthermore, other subject clitics in Bavarian cannot be doubled by a full pronoun, as seen in (71) (see Fuß, 2005, 159).

(69) a. kumm-st?   (Bavarian)
        come-2.SG
        'Are you coming?'
     b. kumm-st du?
        come-2.SG you
        'Are you coming?'   (from Bayer, 1984, 249, ex. 100c–d)

(70) a. kumm-st-de?   (Non-Standard German)
        come-2.SG
        'Are you coming?'
     b. * kumm-st-de du?
          come-2.SG you   (from Bayer, 1984, 250, ex. 101c–d)

(71) a. ob-e   (*i) noch Minga   kumm   (Bavarian)
        whether-CL.1.SG I   to   Munich come-1.SG
     b. ob   i noch Minga kumm
        whether I to Munich come-1.SG
        'Whether I come to Munich.'   (from Fuß, 2005, 159, ex. 2)

Second, 2nd person forms are obligatory in all contexts, so they cannot be replaced by the relevant full forms (see Fuß, 2005, 158). Other subject clitics are not obligatory.

(72) a. ob-st noch Minga kumm-st (Bavarian)
whether-2.SG to Munich come-2.SG
'Whether you come to Munich.'
b. *ob du noch Minga kumm-st
whether you.SG to Munich come-2.SG (from Fuß, 2005, 158)

Finally, Fuß (2005, 159) quotes Altmann's (1984, 207) observation that 2nd person forms are transparent when it comes to determining whether a clause-initial verb is interpreted as V1 or V2, whereas 1st and 3rd person forms unambiguously force a V1 interpretation.

In sum, abstracting away for the moment from the person restrictions, we seem to have three patterns: those that have NSs in the I-field (Zurich German, Schwabian and Övdalian), those that have NSs in the C-field (Lower Bavarian, Bavarian and Frisian) and those that lack NSs (Standard German). One possible way to account for these differences would be to relativize licensing of *pro* to the two distinct areas, IP and CP. Suppose, then, that the I-field languages identify *pro* in IP, hence MMT is defined with respect to probes in Infl. Following this idea, since Zurich German, Schwabian and Övdalian have probes specified for [PART] in Infl, 1st/2nd person subjects can be null.

In Bavarian and Lower Bavarian, on the other hand, the probe is located in C, so only 2nd person SG/PL, 2nd person SG/PL and 1st person PL NSs will be possible because these are the only combinations specified at the C-level, as seen in (73).

(73) C-related inflectional paradigm in Bavarian and Lower Bavarian

	Singular			Plural		
	1	2	3	1	2	3
Bavarian		-st			-ts	
Lower Bavarian		-st		-ma	-ts	

This means that recoverabilty in these two dialects is set as in (74), whereas π-feature geometries for probes are the ones in (75). Consequently, only 2nd person SG/PL in both varieties and 1st person PL in Lower Bavarian will satisfy morphological maximality.

142 *Identification and morphology*

(74) MMT in Bavarian and Lower Bavarian: [R [D [π [PART]]]]

(75) Probe φ-structure for Bavarian and Lower Bavarian

Singular: **2nd person 1st/3rd person**

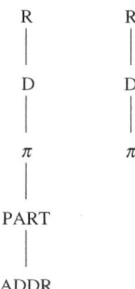

Plural: **Bavarian/Lower Bavarian   Bavarian   Lower Bavarian**

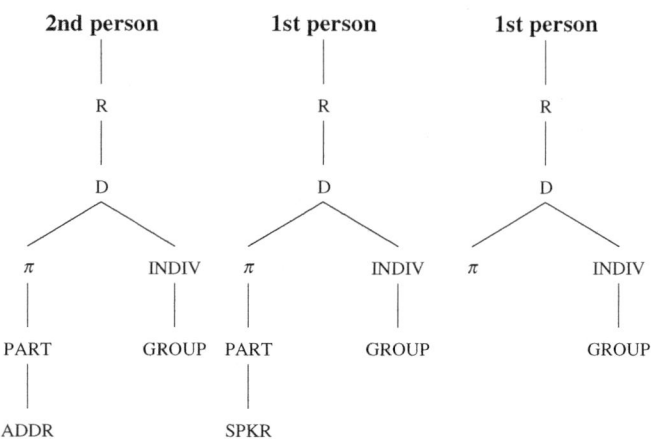

Consistent with this account, Bavarian displays *that*-trace effect violations, as illustrated in (76). Under the Rizzi–Shlonsky freezing approach, this is expected, since one of the ways to bypass *that*-trace effect violations is to have an agreeing complementizer.

(76) a. Wer moanst   du [*t* mog d'Emma]?   (Bavarian)
         who think.2.SG you   loves Emma
         'Who do you think that loves Emma?'

b. Wer moanst du [daß *t* d'Emma mog]?
   who think.2.SG you that Emma loves
   'Who do you think that loves Emma?'

c. Weam moanst du [daß d'Emma *t* mog]?
   who.ACC think.2.SG you that Emma loves
   'Who do you think that Emma loves?'   (from Bayer, 1984, 210, ex. 2)

Turning now to Standard German, we can assume that like Bavarian and Lower Bavarian, the probe that agrees with the subject *pro* is in C, but in Standard German, C-agreement does not have inflection, hence the probes are unspecified for [PART]. If the MMT is the same for all three varieties, it follows that referential NSs are not identified in Standard German.

To summarize, the proposed analysis locates the crucial difference between German/Bavarian and ZG/Schwabian in where the probe for subject agreement is located: in German/Bavarian, in C, in ZG/Schwabian (or Italian/Spanish) in I/T. German and Bavarian, in turn, vary because of how specified the probe is in each language. It follows, then, that while German shows a rich inflectional paradigm on the verb, it does not have referential NSs, whereas another one with an essentially identical inflectional paradigm to Standard German does.[8]

5.5.2 Local agreement vs. distant reference: 1st and 2nd person shifted readings

The so-called shifted readings of Slave and Amharic show instances in which an embedded 1st/2nd person is fully valued within its clause, but it is interpreted as if it had the features of a matrix antecedent (see Rice, 1989; Schlenker, 2003; Baker, 2008b). This suggests that in addition to valuation, there is an independent mechanism that determines actual discourse anchoring.

Person shift is illustrated in (77). As Baker (2008b, 124–150) points out, the embedded 1st or 2nd person subject is interpreted as if coreferential with a 3rd person antecedent in these examples. In addition to that reading, there is a non-shifted one, where the 1st person refers to the speaker and not to the matrix subject.[9]

---

[8] I must assume that V-to-C movement of the verb in German is not enough to identify a NS in that variety, although the equivalent configuration still does in Bavarian.

[9] Although the shifted reading has a similar interpretation to that of a direct quote in English (*Tony said 'I eat fish'*), its syntactic properties distinguish direct quotes from shifted readings in Slave and in Amharic (see Schlenker, 2003; Baker, 2008b).

(77) Tony łue ghǫshéohtį́   enį́dhę̀.   (Slave)
      Tony fish 1.SG.SUBJ.OPT.eat 3.SG.SUBJ.wants
      'Tony wants to eat fish.' (Lit. 'Tony wants I eat fish')
                                (from Rice, 1989, 1273, quoted in Baker, 2008b, 129)

In Slave, we find three types of main verbs with respect to shifted readings: those that allow for shifting of 1st persons (as in (77)), those that also allow for shifting of 2nd persons, and those that do not allow for shifting at all. Whether a given verb is of one type or another is a lexical property. For example, the equivalent of 'know' does not induce shifting, whereas the equivalent of 'think' does. One important syntactic property that distinguishes shift-inducing verbs from those that do not allow person shifting is that the first type lacks a complementizer, whereas the second type must have one.

At first sight, it might look like shifted readings involve two instances of AGREE, one local (between *pro* and the embedded verb/probe) and one non-local (between the antecedent in the main clause and *pro*). As a consequence of these two instances, the ϕ-feature values of the second iteration of AGREE are superimposed on the first iteration. However, I don't think this is the right way to view these cases. From the point of view of the theory I have proposed, such an analysis would involve erasing an already specified ϕ-feature node, something that would predict overgeneration in other cases. Empirically, this solution would not explain why the morphology is the way it is: the embedded verb and subject (if overt) show 1st person morphology, not 3rd marking. Finally, if erasure of ϕ-features is involved, it is not immediately obvious why it is restricted to 1st/2nd persons, so on this view, we would expect that an embedded 3rd person could be interpreted as coreferential with a matrix 1st, but this does not seem to happen.[10]

For these reasons, I will suggest that the mechanisms underlying person shift in Slave are fundamentally distinct from AGREE. Baker's (2008b) analysis is consistent with this conclusion (although his overall proposal is different in other respects). In his account, shifted readings arise indirectly through control.

---

[10] Note that while all the research on person shift readings goes to great lengths to point out that they are not cases of direct quotation, the interpretive patterns are very similar to direct quotation cases; thus a 1st person inside a quotation can be interpreted as referring to a 3rd person matrix subject, as in (i), but a 3rd person inside a quotation cannot be interpreted as referring to a 1st/2nd person matrix subject (cf. (ii)). These common patterns remain unexplained if person shifting is completely independent from quotations.

(i) Peter said 'I am going away' (where I = Peter).
(ii) #I said 'He is going away' (where he = I).

The embedded clause has a speech-act participant operator S (for speaker) or A (for addressee) that binds the embedded subject, yielding a 1st and 2nd person interpretation respectively.[11] In shifted readings, the embedded S also binds the embedded subject, yielding a 1st person, but S is controlled by the subject of matrix clause, resulting in coreference, as shown in (78).

(78)   [CP1 [Tony [CP2 S2 [TP *pro*   T[1.SG]...]   want]]]

Thus, shifted readings are a consequence of control across clausal boundaries, whereas as agreement is a locally bound type of AGREE.

5.5.3 Chapter summary

In this chapter, I have advanced a proposal about the relationship between morphological richness and null subject identification. I have argued that ϕ-features are organized in hierarchies, and that the grammar of a language will determine what is the minimal morphological threshold (MMT) in the ϕ-feature hierarchy for a null subject to be recovered. This threshold may change from grammar to grammar, so that Tarifit requires person, number and gender, whereas Spanish and Italian only require person and number and Bengali requires person. Additionally, the MMT may also be checked at different levels (IP vs. CP), giving rise to minimal distinctions between very close varieties like Bavarian, Lower Bavarian and Frisian on the one hand, and Zurich German, Schwabian and Övdalian on the other.

---

[11] In Baker's analysis, absence of binding by S or A results in 3rd person interpretation.

6 *Discourse identification*

In this chapter, we turn to discourse identification of *pro*, which is well-known to be topic-oriented (see Givón, 1983; Huang, 1984; Samek-Lodovici, 1996; Grimshaw and Samek-Lodovici, 1998; Frascarelli, 2007; Camacho, 2011; Sigurðsson, 2011). We will study two separate cases: instances in which *pro* is identified by inflection and also by a topic, and cases in which *pro* is identified only by a topic. In order to understand the discourse conditions of *pro*, we will review Frascarelli's (2007) proposal for Italian. This will lead me to reassert Rizzi's double requirement of licensing and identification, recast in terms of valuation and discourse linking. I will then present cases within NSLs where morphological valuation fails, and only topic linking applies. Then I will turn to obligatorily overt subject languages with limited cases of NSs (topic drop), and after that I will review Chinese-type discourse NSLs. Finally, I will develop the analysis that one of the relevant differences between agreement-based and discourse-based NSLs relates to *pro*'s specification.

6.1   Topics and *pro*

A number of researchers have noted that *pro* is topic-oriented. Samek-Lodovici (1996, 29) explicitly states that NSs must be licensed by topic antecedents, noting that a complement of a *by*-phrase cannot be an antecedent to an NS in Italian, Chinese, Hebrew or Greek. Example (1) shows that in Italian, a *by*-phrase (*da Gianni* 'by John') in the first clause cannot serve as the antecedent for the NS in the second clause. Example (2) shows the same point for Chinese. Because *by*-phrase adjuncts are independently known not to be topics, one natural explanation of this observation would be that only topics can be antecedents of NSs.

(1) a. Questa   mattina,   la   mostra   è   stata   visitata da
        this   morning   the   exhibition has been   visited   by
        Gianni$_i$.   (Italian)
        John
        'This morning, the exhibition was visited by John.'
     b. Piú   tardi, pro$_{*i}$ / egli$_i$ / lui$_i$ ha visitato l' università.
        more late   pro   / he   / he   has visited the university
        'Later on, he visited the university.'
                                        (from Samek-Lodovici, 1996, 31, ex. 3)

(2) a. Zuotian   na yizhi beizi bei Lisi$_i$ dapo le.   (Chinese)
        yesterday that one cup   by Lisi   break ASP
        'Yesterday, that cup was broken by Lisi.'
     b. Jintan pro$_{*i}$ / ta$_i$ dapo le   linwai yizhi.
        today pro   / he   break ASP another one.
        'Today he broke another one.'   (from Samek-Lodovici, 1996, 31, ex. 6)

Conversely, an overt preverbal subject in a declarative sentence can serve as antecedent to a subsequent NS in all four languages, as shown for Italian in (3), where *Gianni* can be the antecedent of the subject of *ha visitato l'università* 'has visited the university'. In Italian, the most natural configuration for co-reference in this context would be to have an NS, whereas in Hebrew and Chinese, an overt pronoun can also appear (cf. *hu* 'he' in Hebrew in (4b) and *ta* in Chinese in (5b)).

(3) a. Questa mattina, Gianni$_i$ ha visitato la mostra.   (Italian)
        this   morning, John   has visited the exhibition
        'This morning, John visited the exhibition.'
     b. Piú   tardi, pro$_i$ / ?egli$_i$ / ??lui$_i$ ha visitato l'università.'
        More late, pro   / he   / he   has visited the university
        'Later, he visited the university.'

(4) a. Ba-slos   a be Juli   ha-nasi$_i$ xatam al ha-xoze
        in-three   in   July   the-president   signed on the-contract
        ha-ze.   (Hebrew)
        the-this.
        'The third of July, the president's brother signed this contract.'
     b. Lemoxorat pro$_i$ / hu$_i$ xatam al xoze   xadas.
        the next day pro   / he   signed on contract new
        'The next day he signed a new contract.'
                                        (from Samek-Lodovici, 1996, 33, ex. 9)

(5) a. Zuotian, Lisi$_i$ dapo le yizhi beizi. (Chinese)
yesterday, Lisi break ASP one cup
'Yesterday, Lisi broke a cup.'

b. Jintian pro$_i$ / ta$_i$ dapo le linwai yizhi.
today pro / he break ASP another one
'Today he broke another one.' (from Samek-Lodovici, 1996, 33, ex. 10)

We can reach the same conclusion from another angle by looking at cases where *pro* cannot be uniquely identified by morphology in agreement-rich languages. In such cases, the topic becomes essential for determining *pro*'s reference. As we mentioned earlier, Cole (2000) (quoted in Sheehan, 2007, 158) notes that the subject of the second clause in (6a) can be null, because *abrí* 'opened.1.SG' uniquely identifies it as a 1st person. However, in the imperfect shown in (6b), *tenía* 'had.1/3.SG' is ambiguous between 1st and 3rd person morphology. In that context, the antecedent becomes crucial for identifying the NS, but that particular example does not have an unambiguous antecedent because the preceding subject has two conjoined DPs, so the NS cannot be identified, and it is not possible.

(6) a. María y yo llegamos a casa. Yo / *pro* abrí la puerta.
Maria and I arrived to home. I / *pro* opened1.SG the door
(Spanish)
'Maria and I arrived home. I opened the door.'

b. María y yo llegamos a casa. Yo / ella / *pro* tenía las llaves.
Maria and I arrived to home. I / she / *pro* had.1/3.SG the keys
'Maria and I arrived home. I/she found the keys.'
(from Sheehan, 2007, 84, ex. 158)

The same kind of situation is pervasive in the subjunctive in several languages, since agreement paradigms are impoverished in that mood. For example, Cardinaletti (1997) notes that the present subjunctive verb form in Italian does not distinguish between 1st/2nd/3rd person. In that context, 2nd persons cannot be null, as seen in (7). We will return to these cases below.

(7) a. Che possa riuscir-ci non è chiaro. (Italian)
that can.SUBJ.SG manage-CL not is clear
'It isn't clear that I/*you/he can manage it.'

b. Che tu possa riuscir-ci non è chiaro.
that you can.SUBJ manage-CL not is clear
'It isn't clear that you can manage it.'
(from Sheehan, 2007, 83, exx. 154–155)

These examples suggest that *pro* is crucially identified by a topic. Is topic identification a sufficient condition for NSs in all languages? Frascarelli (2007) argues that it is, but this is too radical a conclusion, since reducing NS identification to the availability of a topic cannot account for the contrast between (6a) and (6b), where the only relevant difference is the inflectional paradigm of the imperfect vs. the preterit. Thus, I suggest two conditions on NSs, as in (8).

(8) Conditions on referential categories
   a. Referential categories must be contentful.
   b. Referential categories must be discourse-linked.

Overt nominal categories comply with (8a) automatically, whereas their corresponding null counterparts do so through valuation as described in the previous chapters. We can think of this condition as a prerequisite for a referential category to be discourse-linked. The second condition is intrinsically connected to topic linking, as suggested earlier. We will now turn to the specific details of topic linking in Frascarelli's proposal.

6.2   Typology of topics

Frascarelli (2007) builds on the observation that NSs are usually topic-oriented, and proposes that *pro* is always bound by a topic. Although her proposal is very specific to Italian, it constitutes a clear and detailed account of the prosodic properties of NS antecedents in actual discourse. Her analysis is partly based on the discourse distribution of NSs and partly on the prosodic properties associated with them. Based on these, she proposes that NSs are bound by an Aboutness Shift Topic, which has an intonational contour L*+H. These elements introduce a new topic or shift from a previous one. For example, in (9), the phrase *l'ultima unità* 'the last unit' is a new topic introduced after a general description of the materials of a self-learning course, and it is a CLLD.

(9)   Il materiale era tantissimo quindi all' inizio l' ho fatto tutto di corsa cercando di impiegarci il tempo che dicevate voi magari facendolo un po' superficialmente pur di prendere tutto – **l'ultima unità** la sto facendo l'avevo lasciata un po' da parte ...   (Italian)
   'The material was quite a lot, so at the beginning I did it all in a rush, trying to do it in the time that you had fixed, perhaps a little superficially, so as to do everything – I'm doing the last unit now, I had put it aside before ...'
                                                               (from Frascarelli, 2007, 698, ex. 8)

In addition to Aboutness Shift Topics, Frascarelli (2007) distinguishes two other kinds: Contrastive topics and Familiar topics. The first type has an H pitch, and provides an alternative to an existing topic, as seen in (10), where *a lei* 'to her' presupposes that alternative possibilities for the speaker position were available in discourse.

(10) Invece **a lei** non l'   ha   presa   come speaker.   (Italian)
      instead to her not CL.3.SG have.3.SG taken.FEM as   speaker
      'On the contrary he didn't choose her to be the speaker.'
                              (from Frascarelli and Hinterhölzl, 2007, 96, ex. ix)

Finally, a Familiar topic "refer[s] to given information in the discourse" (Frascarelli, 2007, 699), it is D-linked (i.e. it relates to referential sets pre-established in discourse), and it is "used to refer to background information, for topic continuity (cf. Givón, 1983) or in the right periphery, as an 'afterthought' (p. 699)". Thus, in (11), *la conferma* 'the check' is first introduced by speaker A, then resumed by speaker B and repeated as a right-hand topic by student A.

(11) A: Io dovevo studiare le regole qui e lì fare solo esercizio, invece mi aspettavo di trovare dei punti a cui far riferimento ogni volta per vedere la regola, questo mi è mancato praticamente: **la conferma** di ricordare tutto insomma.   (Italian)
      'I was supposed to study the rules here and do the exercises at home, while I expected to find some outlines I could refer to, at any point, to check the relevant rule, this is what I missed: the check that I could remember everything.'
      B: Comunque quelle domande ti davano **la conferma** che avevi capito.
      'However those questions gave you **a check** for your understanding.'
      A: Ma ... magari non me la-non riesco a darmela da sola **la conferma**.
      'Ah well, maybe I cannot do **this check** on my own.'
                                                    (from Frascarelli, 2007, 699, ex. 9)

Frascarelli (2007) proposes that these three topics are projected in an expanded C-domain, as seen in (12), following Rizzi (1997) and subsequent work. Each of these topics is a based-generated CLLD phrase, associated with a clitic (see Cinque, 1990).

(12) [ForceP [**ShiftTopP** [GroundP [**ContrastTopP** [FocP [**FamTopP** [FinP ...]]]]]]]

As mentioned, *pro* is assumed to be bound by a local Aboutness Shift Topic or a silent local copy of it. As an example, the antecedent of the first *pro$_i$* in (13) is *il mio capo* 'my boss', the Aboutness Shift Topic. If this topic is maintained

6.3 Topic identification in an inflection-rich null subject language

from clause to clause, a silent copy of it appears in FamP and locally binds *pro*, as in (14) (see Frascarelli, 2007, 709).

(13)   [il mio capo]$_i$ come diceva Carlo ... *pro*$_i$ è un exreporter ... *pro*$_i$ è stato in giro per il mondo ... (Italian)
'My boss as Carlo used to say ... *pro*$_i$ is a former reporter ... *pro*$_i$ has been all over the world.'

(14)   [$_{AboutShiftTopP}$ [il mio capo]$_i$ ... [$_{AgrSP}$ [$_{vP}$ *pro*$_i$ è un exreporter]] [$_{FamP}$ Top$_i$ [$_{AgrSP}$ [$_{vP}$ *pro*$_i$]]]

Frascarelli's topic typology has very clearly defined phonological properties that allow us to identify them in Italian. Clearly, extending this typology (and the accompanying stress contour markers) to other languages requires more evidence than is currently available.

Let us now turn to instances in which morphological valuation fails in an otherwise consistent NS language. In such cases, as predicted, discourse identification is the only available option.

6.3   Topic identification in an inflection-rich null subject language

Although Spanish and Hebrew typically have NSs valued by inflection, in both languages certain adjunct clauses have NSs not valued by inflection.

6.3.1 *Absolute clauses in Spanish*

Absolute clauses in Spanish (see Pérez Jiménez, 2007; Camacho, 2011, among others) illustrate a case where NSs are not valued by verbal inflection. In the current framework, the probe lacks the minimal ϕ-feature specification (D).

Absolute clauses are adjunct clauses that consist of a predicate of any type (a participial, a PP, an AdvP or a DP) and a subject, and they obligatorily appear in the order Pred-S. As pointed out in Camacho (2011), since the subject can be null (see (15)), the question arises as to how it can be identified, since the predicate lacks person and potentially number values, as in the case of (15b), where the adverb *lejos* lacks person, number and gender features.

(15)   a. Incómodo   por el incidente, Jaime evitó   encontrarse con su jefe.
uncomfortable by the incident, Jaime avoided run into   with his boss
(Spanish)
'Uncomfortable about the incident, Jaime avoided running into his boss.'
(from Camacho, 2011, 990, ex. 3c)

b. Lejos ya   en el tiempo, la guerra perdió importancia en la vida
   far already in the time, the war   lost   importance in the life
   diaria.
   daily
   'Once distant in time, the war lost relevance in day-to-day life.'

As Camacho (2011) points out, absolute-clause NSs show common properties with *pro* and *PRO*. Specifically, like *pro*, they alternate with overt subjects, they are case-marked in the way overt subjects are and they allow for split antecedents. Like obligatorily controlled *PRO*, they must have an antecedent, and it must be local, as seen in (16): in (16a), the feminine gender of the adjunct-clause predicate renders the main-clause subject unavailable as an antecedent, so the NS is not recoverable. The fact that the clitic is also unavailable as an antecedent illustrates another property: the antecedent must be a topic, and the clitic cannot serve as one. This contrasts with cases where a doubled dative DP appears, in these cases, illustrated in (16b), the doubled dative DP (*a Ana* 'to Ana') can serve as an antecedent to the NS of the absolute clause. Finally, like controlled *PRO*, absolute-clause NSs have obligatory *de se* readings.

(16) a. *Cansada por el paseo, Miguel le sirvió un café.   (Spanish)
        tired.FEM by the walk, Miguel CL served a   coffee
        'Tired by the walk, Miguel served her coffee.'
     b. Cansada por el paseo, Miguel le sirvió a Ana un café.
        tired.FEM by the walk, Miguel CL served to Ana a   coffee
        'Tired by the walk, Miguel served Ana coffee.'

Since the MMT for NSs in Spanish is set to [D] and probes for absolute-clause predicates lack that specification, this means that *pro* will not be valued by the probe. However, if *pro* is linked to the topic antecedent, then that process establishes a chain between the topic, *pro* and the probe, yielding agreement. The topic can, in turn, be null, but since the topic is located at the edge of the CP-phase, it can be discourse-linked to an antecedent, as in (17).

(17)   [CPmain ... φ ... [CPabs   [TopP Top$_i$ [TP T$_i$ pro$_i$ ...]]]]

If Camacho's (2010) analysis of absolute-clause NSs is correct, it yields three interesting conclusions. First, even in an agreement-rich language like Spanish,

NSs are not always identified by rich agreement, but by a topic antecedent. Second, this NS–antecedent relationship, which seems to be long-distance, can be reduced to shorter, phase-bound links, all subsumed under the valuation version of AGREE. Third, it confirms Cole's (2009) intuition that agreement recoverability and topic recoverability are parts of a continuum.

6.3.2 Adjunct clauses in Hebrew

Shlonsky (2009, 146–151) discusses a fairly similar situation in Hebrew (see also Borer, 1989; Gutman, 2004). In (18), the embedded NS "is obligatorily dependent on a nominal in the matrix clause" (p. 146).

(18)   Dani$_1$ kibel   mi-Dafna ve-Rina matana yafa   axarei
       Dani received-3.MAS.SG from-Dafna and-Rina present pretty-FEM.SG after
       še   pro$_{1/*2}$ siyem   et ha doktorat   (Hebrew)
       that   finished.3.MAS.SG ACC the doctorate
       'Dani received a fine present from Dafna and Rina after he had finished his doctorate.'   (from Shlonsky, 2009, 146, ex. 18)

Like in Spanish, the embedded NS in these clauses can have several possible constituents as antecedents, and according to Shlonsky (2009, 148) "Gutman [Gutman, 2004, J.C.] views the accessibility of the antecedent as a necessary condition for the grammaticality of sentences with covert subjects. One of the factors that determine accessibility is the discourse salience of the antecedent." Thus, like in Spanish absolute clauses, a main-clause passive agent is not a good antecedent for the embedded NS. Shlonsky (2009, 149), following Borer (1989), assumes that these cases of non-standard binding/control entail assigning a [person] feature to the NS. This feature, which makes the NS referential, is copied to T's ϕ matrix through a mechanism he calls feature synchronization. Synchronization is possible because matrix T and the embedded NS are in a probe–goal relation.

Regardless of the specific mechanics of each proposal, the configurations of Spanish absolute clauses and Hebrew non-standard binding/control are very similar. In both languages, control by a discourse-salient antecedent is obligatory and in both cases valuation in the embedded domain is not possible because inflection lacks the relevant specification (in Hebrew, 3rd persons do not license NSs in general).

6.3.3 Subjunctive clause null subjects

As we saw earlier, several tenses across the Spanish or Italian conjugation do not distinguish between two or more persons. Consider, for example, the present subjunctive or the imperfect indicative in Spanish, where 1st and 3rd person verb endings are identical, and 2nd person is distinct in the singular, as seen in (19).

(19)   Spanish present subjunctive and imperfect indicative sg. paradigms

	Present subjunctive	Imperfect subjunctive
1/3.SG.	*consiga*	*conseguía*
2.SG.	*consigas*	*conseguías*

Assuming that 1st/3rd persons are identically represented, they should lack [PART], as in (20). If so, *pro* will remain unvalued for [PART] in its clause. Nevertheless, 1st/3rd NSs are possible in out-of-the-blue contexts with subjunctive mood (cf. (21a)) and with imperfective tense (cf. (22)).

(20)   Spanish singular present subjunctive ϕ-feature geometry

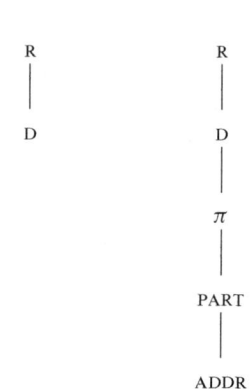

(21)   a. Que lo consiga   no es claro.   (Spanish)
          that CL manage.1/3.SG.SUBJ not is clear
          'It is not clear that I/he/she will manage it.'

       b. Que lo consigas   no es claro.
          that CL manage.2.SG.SUBJ not is clear
          'It is not clear that you will manage it.'

(22)   Durante   ese   verano,   cada   día   salía   a   buscar   el
       during   that   summer,   each   day   went.out.IMP to   look.for the
       periódico.   (Spanish)
       newspaper
       'During that summer, I/he/she went out to look for the newspaper every day.'

How is *pro* discourse-linked in (21a) and (22)? The proposal is that both 1st and 3rd persons are derived by default. In the case of 3rd person, it is frequently the default morphological setting, as we showed for the case of Ancona Italian and other Italian dialects in Section 4.1.4.

Regarding the 1st person, I also assume that it has a special status. While a number of researchers have argued that both 1st and 2nd persons are represented as syntactic heads in the left periphery (see Poletto, 2000; Speas, 2004; Sigurðsson, 2004, 2010, 2011; Baker, 2008b; Sigurðsson and Holmberg, 2008), which bind the corresponding pronouns, Safir (2004) argues against this view, and suggests that 1st and 2nd persons pick out an individual in the context through a constant function, rather than through binding. I will assume that 1st persons are subject to a constant function, that is, a function that gives the same extension in a given context, but, contrary to Safir (2004, 138), I do not extend this proposal to 2nd persons. Whereas the 1st person can always be contextually recovered (i.e. the speaker), the 2nd person cannot always be recovered, because the reference of the 2nd person addressee requires some pointing gesture. Consider, for example, the situation described by Safir (2004, 138) in which "a squad leader is assigning tasks to his or her assembled group, s/he might point to each member saying *you do this, you do that*." In that context, if the squad leader walks into the room looking at the ceiling and says, without any gesture, *you do that*, the addressee is not uniquely fixed, but if s/he says *I'll do that*, there is no question as to who the speaker is. This suggests an asymmetry between the way in which reference to 1st person is assigned (through a constant function) vs. how reference to 2nd person is derived.

Consequently, in the examples above, the 1st person interpretation comes from the constant function, which can be seen as a last-resort operation that allows the underspecified [D] output of (20) to be interpreted as a 1st person.[1]

Extending this analysis to cases where underspecification affects all three persons reveals some interesting properties. Recall that the Italian present subjunctive is one of those cases, but Cardinaletti (1997, 51) notes that in out-of-the-blue contexts, an NS can be interpreted either as 1st or 3rd person, but

---

[1] As we will see below, topic drop in Swedish (cf. (i)) tends to be identified as 1st person by default, see Sigurðsson (2011, 279).

(i) Kommer strax. (Swedish)
     come   right.away
     '(I'll) be there in a minute.' (from Sigurðsson, 2011, 279, ex. 23b)

not as 2nd person, as already mentioned in (7), repeated as (23): without an overt subject, (23a) can be 'I' or 'he/she', but not 'you'. For the 2nd person interpretation, an overt pronoun is required, as in (23b).

(23)   a. Che possa   riuscir-ci   non è chiaro.   (Italian)
             that can.SUBJ.SG manage-CL not is clear
             'It isn't clear that I/*you/he can manage it.'
       b. Che tu   possa   riuscir-ci   non è chiaro.
             that you can.SUBJ manage-CL not is clear
             'It isn't clear that you can manage it.'
                        (Cardinaletti, 1997, 51, ex. 66, quoted in Sheehan, 2007, 83)

The proposed analysis for the Spanish cases above carries over fairly well to these cases: inflection does not value *pro*, hence either the constant function adopted from Safir (2004) assigns a 1st person interpretation, or the default 3rd person interpretation comes into play, but nothing yields the 2nd person interpretation.

In this context, it is worth pointing out that even contextual saliency does not allow for 2nd person interpretation in Italian present subjunctive examples, as noted by Rizzi (p.c. to Sheehan, 2007, fn. 40). Thus, in (24), the second clause introduces an NS that is clearly identified by the verb *hai* 'have.2.SG.' as 2nd person. However, this is not enough to interpret the subjunctive clause's subject as referring to a 2nd person as well.

(24)   # So   [che   hai   provato] ma non   è   facile [che possa
           know   that   have.2.SG   tried   but not   is easy   that can.SUBJ
           riuscir-ci]   (Italian)
           succeed-CL
           'I know that you've tried but it's not going to be easy for you to succeed.'
                        (from Rizzi, p.c., quoted in Sheehan, 2007, 83, fn. 40)

This is a fairly robust effect, as the following examples show (thanks to Vieri Samek-Lodovici for judgements; glosses and translations are my own). Thus, regardless of whether the potential antecedent is an overt or null subject pronoun (cf. (25)–(26)), preverbal or postverbal (cf. (25a) vs. (b)) or a CLLD object or a topic (cf. (27)), a 2nd person interpretation is not possible.

(25)   a. * So   che   tu   hai   provato ma non è facile che possa
              know that you have2.SG tried   but not is easy   that can.SUBJ.SG
              riuscir-ci.   (Italian)
              succeed-CL
              'I know that you have tried but it's not going to be easy for you to succeed.'

6.3 Topic identification in an inflection-rich null subject language

    b. * So che (ci) hai provato tu, ma non è facile che possa
        know that CL have2.SG tried you but not is easy that can.SUBJ
        riuscir-ci.
        succeed-CL
        'I know that you have tried but it's not going to be easy for you to succeed.'

(26) a. * So che (tu) vuoi andare ma non credo che possa far-lo.
        know that you want go but not think.1.SG that can.SUBJ.SG do-CL
                                                                                                  (Italian)
        'I know that you want to go but I don't think that you will be able to.'

    b. * So che (tu) provi spesso a chiamar-mi, ma non sembra che
        know that you try frequently to call-CL but not seems that
        riesca a trovar-mi.
        succeed.SUBJ to find-CL
        'I know that you frequently try to call me but it doesn't seem that you succeed to find me.'

(27) a. * A te, non te l' ho mai detto, ma non è facile che possa
        to you, not CL.2 CL.3 have ever told, but not is easy that can.SUBJ
        riuscir-ci.   (Italian)
        succeed-CL
        'You, I have never told you this, but it's not easy for you to succeed.'

    b. * Tu, fra tutti noi, so che avresti desiderato molto
        you, among all us, know.1.SG that would-have wanted much
        aiutar-lo, ma non credo che possa riuscir-ci.
        help-CL, but not believe that can.SUBJ succeed-CL
        'You, among all of us, I know that you would have very much wished to help him, but I don't think that you can succeed.'

Spanish is partially similar, in the sense that (21a) above (with a morphologically ambiguous 1st/3rd verb ending) cannot be interpreted as if it were the polite form of talking to an addressee (corresponding to the pronoun *usted* 'you-formal'). Thus, (21a) cannot mean the same as (28).[2]

(28)   Que usted lo consiga no es claro.   (Spanish)
        that you-FORM CL manage.1/3.SG not is clear
        'It is not clear that you will manage it.'

This confirms that there may be something special about the way an addressee is picked in discourse, whether it is morphologically 2nd or 3rd person. However, Spanish and Italian differ because Spanish is much more liberal when

---

[2] Thanks to Liliana Sánchez (p.c.) for pointing this out.

158   *Discourse identification*

it comes to identifying an addressee by a salient antecedent, so that (29) is acceptable, by contrast to the Italian examples in (25)–(27) above.

(29)   Se   que usted   lo ha   intentado, pero no creo que lo
         know.1.SG that you-FORM CL have.3.SG tried   but not think that CL
         consiga.   (Spanish)
         manage.1/3.SG
         'I know that you've tried it, but I don't think that you will manage it.'

6.3.4 Topic drop

Topic drop is a phenomenon in which a subject or an object can be dropped provided that the Spec, CP is null (see Sigurðsson, 2011). For example, in German, it is possible to drop the subject in (30a), which would be interpreted as 1st person, but only if nothing precedes the verb. If something does, like *jetzt* 'now' in (30b), then topic drop is no longer possible.

(30)   a. (Ich) kenne   das nicht.   (German)
           (I) recognize that not
           '(I) do not recognize that.'
        b. * Jetzt kenne   das nicht.
             now recognize that not
             'Now (I) do not recognize that.'
                                        (from Sigurðsson, 2011, 271, exx. 8a, 9a)

The phenomenon, which occurs in a range of Germanic languages, does not generally depend on verb agreement, although agreement may constrain identification (see Sigurðsson, 2011, 279). Thus, although both Swedish and Icelandic have topic drop with similar properties, in Swedish (without agreement), null topics can be construed as different persons depending on the context, whereas in Icelandic (with agreement), they are constrained by agreement. Dropped topics in Swedish tend to be interpreted as 1st person, so example (31) would typically be interpreted as 'I am just lying on the beach', but in the context of a question like *where is Anna?*, the interpretation would be 'she is just lying on the beach'.

(31)   Ligger bara på stranden.   (Swedish)
        lie   just on beach.the
        'Just lying on the beach.'   (from Sigurðsson, 2011, 280, ex. 23a)

By contrast to Swedish, the Icelandic examples in (32) allow for a dropped subject, but their interpretation is constrained by the morphology on the verb, so that (32a) can only be interpreted as 'I' because *ligg* is 1st person, and the same holds for the other examples.

(32) a. Ligg   bara á   ströndinni.   (Icelandic)
       lie.1.SG just on beach.the
       'I am just lying on the beach.'
    b. Ligg-ur bara á   ströndinni.
       lie-3.SG just on beach.the
       'S/he is just lying on the beach.'
    c. Liggj-um bara á   ströndinni.
       lie-1.PL   just on beach.the
       'We are just lying on the beach.'
    d. Liggj-a bara á   ströndinni.
       lie-3.PL just on beach.the
       'They are just lying on the beach.'   (from Sigurðsson, 2011, 280, ex. 25)

In Sigurðsson's analysis, topic drop is possible because the null category raises to the CP area where it is "C/Edge linked" either by a topic operator or by a 1st/2nd person logophoric operator, or perhaps by both.[3]

In the current analysis, topic drop can also be treated as a case of discourse identification, although the contrast between Icelandic and Swedish follows from the fact that inflection values the NS in Icelandic but not in Swedish. Nevertheless, the MMT in both languages implies that valuation is not enough to license NSs. As a result, both NSs must be discourse-linked, but only Icelandic constrains the null topic depending on verbal agreement.[4]

6.3.5 Constraining the system

One immediate concern that arises with the proposed system is how to constrain the availability of NSs. First, if discourse-linking can supersede lack of agreement valuation, then why isn't this option generally available in all languages? Second, what are the locality restrictions that regulate discourse-linking? I believe the answers to both questions are related, so that the availability of discourse-linked NSs is constrained by locality considerations. Let us start by documenting the observation that some antecedent–*pro* relations are restricted to the immediate adjacent clause (what I will call mid-range locality), and that frequently those instances involve an impoverished inflectional paradigm.

---

[3] Although Sigurðsson assumes that agreement constraints topic drop, as noted above, it is not clear how this is formally done, given that the weight of the 1st/2nd person interpretation is carried by the logophoric operator. Presumably, a NS linked to a 1st person operator must also match the verb's morphology (if it has any).

[4] The fact that the Spec, CP must be null can follow if the null category must be moved to that position.

160 *Discourse identification*

Agreement valuation (by a morphologically rich inflectional head) is always local, i.e. it is constrained to the clause containing the subject and Infl. By contrast, discourse-linking is typically extra-clausal. However, a subtype of discourse-linking is local, so for example, absolute clauses in Spanish and Hebrew non-standard control have mid-range locality, i.e. the antecedent is typically in the adjacent clause, but not any further.

Mid-range locality seems to be quite pervasive in several syntactic and referential phenomena, constraining obligatorily controlled *PRO*, shifted pronominal readings in several languages, switch-reference, sequence of tense phenomena and cross-clausal valency concord, as I will illustrate.

The locality conditions for obligatory control are a well-known phenomenon and the locality of antecedent choice in absolute clauses has also been described for Spanish (see Camacho, 2011), so in (33), the subject of the absolute clause (*pro*) cannot be interpreted as *Marta*, because it is located too far away.

(33)   ?? Durante la recepción, primero entró   Marta$_i$, inmediatamente después
       during the reception   first   entered Marta$_i$ immediately   after
       empezó a llover. Saludad-a   *pro$_i$*, el presidente continuó con el
       started to rain   greeted-FEM.SG *pro* the president continued with the
       evento.   (Spanish)
       event
       'During the reception, first Marta entered, immediately after, it started to rain. (Having) greeted (her), the president continued with the event.'
                                                           (from Camacho, 2011, 991)

As we have already seen in Section 5.5.2, Slave and many other languages have logophoric pronouns. Baker (2008b, 132) quotes Rice's (1989, 1289) observation that shifted interpretations are local, so that in (34a), the most embedded subject, marked as 1st person on the verb, can only be coreferential with the immediately dominating subject (*Susan*), not the more distant one (*John*) or even the speaker of the sentence. In Baker's analysis, this follows from his proposal that 1st person readings arise under c-command by a S(peaker) operator. In his representation, the closest S operator to the embedded subject is distinct from the S operator in the matrix clause, as seen in (34b).

(34)   a. John   Susan   tle   gǫlį́   ʔaohde   en   wę
          John   Susan   Norman   Wells   1.SG.S.OPT.go   2.SG.S   want
          ʔadi.   (Slave)
          3.SG.S.say
          'John said that Susan wants {Susan/*John/*me} to go Norman Wells.'

6.3 Topic identification in an inflection-rich null subject language 161

b. [S$_i$ John$_k$ said [S$_k$ Susan$_n$ wants [S$_n$ I$_{n,*k,*i}$ go to Norman Wells]]]

(from Baker, 2008b, 133)

As I pointed out in Section 3.6.2, Shipibo requires at least one overt subject per combination of matrix and adjunct switch-reference clause, suggesting that the matrix clause defines the mid-range in this language. Switch-reference in Shipibo also shows mid-range locality, both in the usual coreference relationships between arguments in two clauses, and in the more exotic valency concord phenomena described in Camacho (2010b). The mid-range locality of coreferential relationships between arguments in switch-reference contexts led Finer (1985) to analyze switch-reference as a case of binding where domains were extended beyond the minimal clause. However, as Stirling (1993) has noted, switch-reference affects not only the referential properties of arguments across clauses, but also event sequencing.

The mid-range locality of these relationships is shown in a striking feature of the Shipibo switch-reference system, illustrated in (35). In this example, the subject of *oin* 'see' and the subject of *kenai* 'call' are coreferential, but additionally, the switch-reference morpheme *şon* also encodes that the verb *kenai* 'call' in the adjacent clause must be transitive, signaling a type of cross-clausal valency concord.

(35) [Nima oin-şon]   -ra   Jose-kan ken-ai.   (Shipibo)
    Nima see-PRIOR.TR.SS -DIR.EVID Jose-ERG call-IMPERF
    'When he (Jose) saw Nima, Jose called (him).'

(from Loriot *et al.*, 1993, 55–56)

Mid-range locality also constrains tense construal in a variety of constructions. For example, embedded infinitival clauses typically define their temporal reference with respect to the immediately dominating clause, as illustrated in (36). In this sentence, the temporal interpretation of the last infinitival verb *resolver* 'to resolve' is anchored on the preceding infinitival *prometer* 'to promise', which in turn is anchored in the matrix verb.

(36)   Sandra va   a exigirle   a los ingenieros prometer resolver el
       Sandra is going to require.CL to the engineers promise resolve the
       problema.   (Spanish)
       problem
       'Sandra is going to require the engineers to promise to resolve the problem.'

In the same sense, absolute adjunct clauses in Spanish have their temporal interpretation anchored to another clause, typically the matrix clause, as seen in (37). The temporal interpretation of 'being busy with the meeting' depends on the tense of the main clause verb *dio orden* 'ordered', *está dando orden* 'is ordering', *dará* 'will order'.

(37) a. Muy ocupad-a con la reunión, la director-a {dio, está dando,
very busy-FEM with the meeting, the director-FEM gave, is giving,
dará} orden de que no le pasen llamadas. (Spanish)
will give order of that not CL put-through calls
'Very busy with the meeting, the director {ordered, is ordering, will order} not to have calls put through.'

b. Terminad-a la reunión, {salí, salimos, saldré} de viaje.
finished-FEM the meeting, left, leave, will leave for trip
'The meeting finished, {I went, I am going, I will go} on a trip.'
(from Pérez Jiménez, 2007, 249)

A third context involves embedded subjunctive clauses. In particular, the embedded verb in (38) (*venga* 'come'.1/3.SG.SUBJ 'come') can only be interpreted as a simultaneous or subsequent event to *quiero* 'want'. Additionally, the subject of the embedded clause cannot be coreferential with that of the main clause, even though the subjunctive morphology would be compatible with a 1st person interpretation. This second restriction has been analyzed as a consequence of extending the binding domain of the subjunctive clause to the matrix clause, yielding a Principle B violation in case of coreference (see Kempchinsky, 1987).

(38) *pro$_i$* quiero que *pro$_{j/*i}$* venga. (Spanish)
pro want.1.SG that *pro* come.1/3.SG.SUBJ
'I want him/her to come.'

All of these examples share an extended domain that goes up to but not beyond the adjacent clause. This mid-range locality constraint contrasts with the apparently unbounded nature of long-distance wh-extraction, so we need to account for why locality is constrained in such a way in these cases. The problem can be subdivided in two separate questions. First, why is locality extended from the lower clause, and second, why is it constrained to the mid-range?

To answer the first question, we should note that in addition to the extension of the locality domain, the functional architecture of the embedded clause (IP or CP) is impoverished in all of these examples. In cases of control and absolute clauses, inflection is non-finite, and in cases of embedded subjunctives, inflection is also arguably impoverished. For the case of Shipibo switch-reference, the verb in the adjunct clause lacks much of the inflectional morphology of a main-clause verb (see Camacho, 2010b). In the case of Slave shifted readings, verbs that shift never have overt complementizers (see Rice, 1989, quoted by Baker, 2008b, 131, fn. 11). In some sense, the impoverished functional architecture is what allows the locality to be extended to the adjacent clause. This connection is particularly clear in the movement account of obligatory control (see Hornstein, 2000, 2003): because inflection does not assign case to the embedded subject, the argument can move to the higher clause, resulting in what apparently looks like coreference, but really is the same argument moved from one position to the other. Crucially, what makes movement possible (and necessary) is the absence of nominative case in the embedded subject position, due to the non-finite nature of the verb.

Let us assume, then, that an impoverished clausal structure results in an extended domain. Specifically, we propose the following general search strategy (which is very reminiscent of Huang's (1989) proposal; see Section 6.4 below):

(39)   Expand the search space for feature x if the probe for x is unspecified.

Thus, for example, if Infl is unspecified for nominative case, the search space for nominative case can be extended beyond the minimal clause. Likewise, if Infl lacks the feature that anchors it to speech time (as in the case of absolute clauses), the search may be extended to the containing clause. If we assume Zagona's (1990) and Stowell's (1993, 1996) proposals, this feature is formalized as one of the two arguments the temporal head takes, hence for the cases where the search domain is extended, this argument will be missing and the T head that selects for it must extend its search beyond the minimal CP.

The possibility of extending the search space is constrained by intervention effects: once the search finds a category with the relevant matching feature, the search stops, explaining why extension typically stops in the immediately containing clause. However, in some instances, it can proceed further, as with successive-cyclic movement. In an example like (40), the wh-word can (and must) move to the matrix CP because none of the intervening CPs have a wh-feature that will check the wh-word's question feature.

(40)   What did Mary hear [that Bill said [that Susan bought t]]?

Feature specification is essential in constraining extending the search domain beyond its natural edge. This same property provides the necessary positive evidence for learnability: only when feature underspecification has overtly detectable consequences (either morphological or otherwise) will the domain extend.

To summarize, discourse antecedents for NSs are expected to happen in situations where the NS's clause lacks the relevant feature to identify the subject, but will be restricted to the domain where an antecedent is found.

This account of domain extension does not readily explain why English lacks NSs. It is clear that NSs in English cannot be identified through morphology, but what I have assumed so far is that a NS should be possible if the relevant antecedent is available in the adjacent clause, just as it is in the case of *PRO*. Given the assumptions I have made so far, the natural explanation for why this is not an option for NSs in finite clauses in English must be related to an intervention effect. Specifically, building on the crucial difference between finite and infinitival clauses, we can assume that Infl in English does not provide a rich enough morphology for the NS to be identified, but it does act as an intervener, blocking the potential relationship between the NS and its potential antecedent.

In the following section, we turn to cases in which identification takes place fully through discourse-linking.

6.4 Subject identification in discourse null subject languages

As mentioned in Section 2.3.2, a number of languages allow for NSs and do not have verbal morphology to identify them. For Chinese, the traditional analysis dating back to Huang (1984, 1989) assumes that NSs are identified in discourse. However, as the following example shows, topic-binding does not seem to be the right notion. In this sentence, the embedded *pro* is interpreted as coreferential with the matrix subject (*Zhangsan*), not the topic (*Lisi*).

(41) Lisi$_i$, Zhangsan$_j$ ku de [*pro*$_{*i/j}$ hen shangxin]   (Chinese)
      Lisi Zhangsan cry till   very sad
      'Lisi, Zhangsan cried until he got very sad.'
      (from Huang, 1989, 198, ex. 41b)

This type of example led Huang (1989) to propose an alternative account based on the notion of control, which he extends to Italian-type NSs. Within this alternative, a null pronominal is controlled in its domain, and if it lacks one, then it may either be identified by the closest c-commanding antecedent in a preceding clause, or be interpreted arbitrarily, or be pragmatically controlled. Technically, a control domain is the S/NP containing the null category and an accessible SUBJECT. So, for example, in (42), the control domain is the minimal

6.4 Subject identification in discourse null subject languages 165

sentence that contains the NS, because AGR acts as an accessible SUBJECT. Finally, no AGR is available in (43), therefore no accessible SUBJECT is defined, hence the minimal clause does not constitute a control domain. In (44), on the other hand, the matrix clause does contain an accessible SUBJECT (*Zhangsan*), which becomes the antecedent for *pro*.

(42) [$_S$ *pro* verr-à] (Italian)
pro come.3 FUT.SG
'S/he will come.' (from Huang, 1989, 195, ex. 29b)

(43) [$_S$ *pro* lai le] (Chinese)
pro came ASP
'He came.' (from Huang, 1989, 195, ex. 30)

(44) [Zhangsan qi ma qi de [*pro* hen le]] (Chinese)
Zhangsan ride horse ride till *pro* very tired
'Zhangsan rode a horse until he got very tired.'
(from Huang, 1989, 197, ex. 40a)

In preverbal adjunct clauses, the embedded subject need not be controlled by a matrix antecedent. In Huang's analysis, this follows because the preverbal adjunct clause lacks an accessible SUBJECT, presumably because the clause is not c-commanded by the subject position in the matrix clause.

(45) [Ruguo *pro*$_{i/j}$ bu lai], ta$_i$ keneng hui shengqi. (Chinese)
if *pro* not come he possibly will angry
'If we/you/he ... doesn't come, he will probably be angry.'
(from Huang, 1989, 198, ex. 42b)

Chinese displays a subject–object asymmetry with respect to topicalization from within an island, as noted by Huang (1982) and highlighted by Li (2007). Topicalization is generally constrained by syntactic islands, but examples like (46a) seem to be an exception because the topic *Zhangsan* is linked to a subject relative clause. By contrast, topicalization from a clause in object position is not possible, as seen in (46b).

(46) a. Zhangsan$_i$, [[Ø$_i$ xihuan de shu] hen duo]. (Chinese)
Zhangsan like de book very plenty
'Zhangsan$_i$, the books [he$_i$] likes are many.'
b. * Zhangsan$_i$, wo kan-guo [Ø$_i$ xihuan de shu].
Zhangsan I see-guo like de book
'Zhangsan$_i$, I see the books [he$_i$] likes.' (from Li, 2007, 79, exx. 5, 7)

Huang's analysis traces this asymmetry to his Generalized Control Rule (GCR). In the first example, the NS is *pro*, identified within the matrix clause by the closest c-commanding antecedent (*Zhangsan*, the topic). By contrast, the closest c-commanding antecedent in the second example is the embedded subject which cannot be a resumptive pronoun for the topic. In other words, (46a) is not an extraction across an island boundary (the null pronoun is resumptive), whereas (46b) is.

Li (2007) points out that this analysis correctly predicts the possible range of interpretations of NSs inside islands. In particular, if the NS is not coindexed with the subject of the higher clause (the closest c-commanding NP), the sentence is ungrammatical, as seen in (47).[5]

(47) Wo$_i$ yinwei [Ø$_{i/*j}$ bu xihuan Zhangsan] you diar shiwang /
    I because   not like Zhangsan have slight disappointment /
    bu-hao-yisi.   (Chinese)
    embarrassment
    'I am somewhat disappointed/embarrassed because I/*he/*she does not like Zhangsan.'   (from Li, 2007, 80, ex. 23)

By contrast to the languages we discussed in previous sections, it is clear that NSs in Chinese and Japanese are not recovered through morphology, but by coreference with the closest c-commanding antecedent in the control domain. This account readily accommodates to the framework we have been developing. Specifically, the notion of extending the search space is closely reminiscent of Huang's GCR.

The proposed analysis also accounts for an apparent counter-example to the GCR (see Huang, 1989) in a straightforward way. In (48a), the GCR predicts that the null object should seek the subject of the embedded clause as an antecedent, since it is the closest c-commanding NP. However, the null object is

---

[5] Huang's analysis has been questioned on the basis that control is not always obligatory, as shown in (i). In this example, the control domain is the main clause, but the embedded subject can have an alternative antecedent. As Audrey Li (p.c.) points out, *say*-type verbs (which can take quotations), can have the NS refer to a discourse topic if the context is very clear and strongly favors the interpretation. See also Huang (1992) for other arguments against J. T. Huang's analysis.

(i) Xiaohong de meimei   shuo Ø xihuan tan gangpin.   (Chinese)
   Xiaohong GEN younger-sister say like play piano
   'Xiaohong$_i$'s younger sister$_j$ says that (I/you/he/she$_{i/j/k}$/we/they) like(s) to play the piano.'   (from Huang 2000, quoted in Cole, 2009, 560, ex. 1)

6.4 Subject identification in discourse null subject languages   167

interpreted as coindexed with the topic, as shown in (48).[6] In order to account for this apparent bypassing of the first c-commanding antecedent, Huang proposes that the null object topicalizes within the embedded clause, as in (49). We can assume the same type of proposal, although I assume that the position to which *pro* moves is not a topic position.[7]

(48) a. Zhe-ben shu$_i$, [[Lisi kan Ø$_i$] zui heshi].   (Chinese)
          this-CL book Lisi read   most appropriate
          'This book, for Lisi to read [it] is most appropriate.'
                                                         (from Li, 2007, 79, ex. 10)
      b. Kono hon$_i$-wa Lisi-ga   pro$_i$ yom-u-no-ga itiban
          this book-TOP Lisi-NOM read-PRES-C-NOM most   appropriate
          husawasii.   (Japanese)
          'As for this book, it is most appropriate for Lisi to read.'
                                                         (from Hiroshi Aoyagi, p.c.)

(49)   Topic$_i$ [$_{CPmain}$ [$_{Island}$ *pro*$_i$ Lisi$_j$ ... t$_i$] ...]

An alternative compatible with the proposed analysis is Zushi's (2003), who suggests that Japanese and Chinese allow for a base-generated zero topic. Let us assume, then, that a null pronominal in Chinese must be identified by the first c-commanding NP (typically the subject or topic) in the minimal search domain that contains it.

6.4.1   Two types of nominals

A question that comes up at this point is whether cross-linguistic variation is simply a matter of how an NS is identified (agreement vs. discourse), or whether the structure of NSs in each language also plays a role. From the

---

[6] The Japanese example has the variant in (i), where the embedded clause is marked with dative, as opposed to nominative in (48b). According to Hiroshi Aoyagi (p.c.), in the nominative version in (48b), the predication seems to be about the event of 'Lisi's reading (the book)', whereas in (i), it seems to be about 'the book'.

  (i)   Kono hon$_i$-wa Lisi-ga pro$_i$ yom-u-no-ni itiban husawasii.   (Japanese)
        this book-TOP Lisi-NOM read-PRES-C-DAT most appropriate
        'As for this book, it is most appropriate for Lisi to read.'   (from Hiroshi Aoyagi, p.c.)

[7] The GCR applies not only to subjects, but also to null objects. In the case of objects, it predicts that they should not be possible as pronominals, since the first c-commanding antecedent in the control domain would be the subject of their clause, yielding a Principle B violation.

analysis developed so far, nothing seems to distinguish NSs across languages in a principled way. In particular, Chinese or Japanese are the way they are because they lack verbal morphology, hence NS identification can only be done through the discourse. However, as we pointed out earlier, Tomioka (2003) has advanced the idea that perhaps there is a principled distinction between null categories in both types of language, which relates to the structure we observe in overt nominals. Specifically, following Chierchia (1998), languages like Japanese have NPs, but languages like Spanish or Italian have DPs. Correspondingly, according to Tomioka, null categories in Japanese are NPs.

From a slightly different perspective, Neeleman and Szendroi (2005, 2007, 2008) propose that agglutinating morphology on pronouns is a requirement for *pro* in discourse-related languages.

While these proposals are interesting, extending them to other discourse-related languages presents a challenge. As Cole (2009, 561) points out, several languages seem to lack agglutinative pronominal morphology but can have *pro*. Examples include Lao, Aiton (a Tai language spoken in Assam) and Vietnamese. Li (1999, 2007), on the other hand, points out that the distribution and interpretation of null categories in Japanese and Chinese differ substantially. Specifically, she argues that overt nominals in Chinese show properties typical of DPs, unlike in Japanese. Among them are certain distributional restrictions and interpretive asymmetries. For example, she notes that nominals with number expressions can have a truly quantitative interpretation or an individual-denoting interpretation that depends on the position they take in the clause. This asymmetry can be best explained if they have distinct structures (NumP and DP respectively), which also correlate with a host of other differences, like coreferential possibilities, scope properties, etc. Additionally, nominals in Chinese exhibit a fixed word order [Demonstrative + Number + Classifier + N] without the modification marker *de*, as illustrated in (50a) and (51a) whereas all other modifiers have quite free word order and are followed by *de*. In contrast, Japanese demonstratives and modifiers have a similar distribution as other modifiers in the sense that the Japanese counterpart of *de* must occur with demonstratives and classifier phrases (cf. *no* in (50b) and (51b)):

(50)   a. * san-ben-de shu / san-ge-de xuesheng   (Chinese)
three-CL-de book / three-CL-de student

b. san-satu-no hon / san-nin-no gakusei   (Japanese)
three-CL-NO book / three-CL-NO student   (from Li, 2007, 80, ex. 43)

(51) a. * zhe-de / na-de   (Chinese)
          this-de / that-de
      b. ko-no / so-no / a-no   (Japanese)
          this-NO/ that-NO/ that-NO   (from Li, 2007, 80, ex. 43)

For Li, this suggests that nominals have a DP-like structure in Chinese but not in Japanese (see Tomioka, 1999, 2003). Assuming that the typology of null categories is the same as that of overt ones in any given language, this means that the corresponding null categories would presumably be D and N respectively (see Fukui, 1988; Noguchi, 1997; Hoji, 1998; Tomioka, 2003).

The different nature of *pro* in Chinese and Japanese suggests an explanation for another difference between both languages. Li (2007) points out that Japanese lacks true sloppy interpretations in ellipsis (see Hoji, 1998), whereas Chinese has them: if the null category in ellipsis is pronominal in both of these languages (as argued for by Hoji (1998) for Japanese), then the sloppy reading asymmetry can follow from *pro*'s different category in each language.

Assuming that this analysis is correct, the representation of pronouns would be the ones in (52). However, this means that Japanese pronouns (and nominals in general) are not referential in the sense of (8), repeated in (53), rather their reference is achieved through a different mechanism (along the lines of Chierchia, 1998).[8]

(52)   Chinese null pronouns   Japanese null pronouns

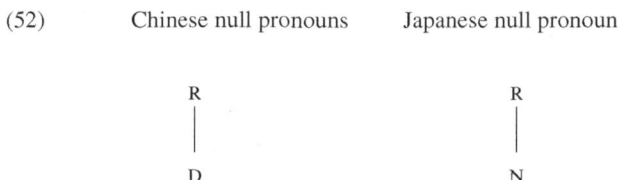

(53)   Conditions on referential categories
       a. Referential categories must be contentful.
       b. Referential categories must be discourse-linked.

One final consequence of this parametric difference, according to Li (2007), is that while Chinese null categories are regulated by the GCR, Japanese ones are not. For example, NSs need not be bound by the first c-commanding antecedent, as illustrated in (54a). By contrast, the NS in Chinese in (54b) cannot skip the subject to seek the topic.

---

[8] Chierchia actually treats Chinese and Japanese as belonging to the NP language-type.

(54) a. Bush-wa,   maikeru   muua-ga   senkyo-ni   katta   node
         Bush-TOP   Michael   Moore-NOM   election-DAT won   because
         gakkari siteita.   (Japanese)
         disappointed
         'Bush, Michael Moore was disappointed because (he) won the election.'
                                                    (from Li, 2007, 80, ex. 40)

     b. *(Lisi$_1$,) wo yinwei [e$_1$ hai bu renshi naxie ren]   hen danxin.
         Lisi   I because   still not know those people   very concerned
                                                                     (Chinese)
         '(Lisi,) I am very concerned because Lisi still does not know those
         people.'   (from Li, 2007, 80, ex. 41b)

These proposals entail that Japanese *pro*$_N$ is not subject to valuation or agreement, since it lacks the node that triggers such mechanisms, whereas Chinese *pro*$_D$ is. However, Chinese differs from Spanish or Italian in one crucial respect, the availability of another type of null category in Chinese. If Huang's analysis is correct, Chinese null objects cannot be pronominal because they would be subject to the GCR and they would be c-commanded by the subject in their clause, so they would have to be anaphoric to the subject. Given that they need not always be interpreted as anaphors, then they must either be some other category or be interpreted by some other mechanism. Li (2007) argues for the former option, suggesting that the null objects in Chinese are a type of True Empty Position (TEP), which is a last-resort empty element necessary for subcategorization purposes, but devoid of any content and whose interpretation is done by purely pragmatic means. TEPs can be interpreted as pronouns but also as other categories, for example in the context of ellipsis. This is possible because they lack content, and in terms of our analysis, they would correspond to a feature geometry that only has an [R] node. In languages like Spanish, however, these categories do not seem to be available.

6.4.2   Shipibo and Capanawa

Shipibo is a particularly interesting language from our perspective, because it displays person asymmetries but lacks morphological agreement, as we already described in Section 3.6. To summarize again, 1st and 2nd person subjects are obligatorily overt, but 3rd person ones are optional in main clauses. In embedded switch-reference clauses, both are optional, as illustrated in the paradigm in (55), where the switch-reference clause appears in first position and is enclosed by brackets. As these examples show, a 1st person subject can be overt in both clauses (cf. *en* 'I' in (55a)), null in the main clause (cf. (55b)) or null in the switch-reference clause (cf. (55c)), but if no overt subject appears in either case, as in (55d), the sentence cannot be interpreted as having null 1st/2nd person subjects. However, this example can be interpreted as having 3rd person subjects.

(55) a. [En westiora ipo   chachi-şon]   -ra   en Quique kena-ke.
        IP a   carachama catch-PRIOR.SS.TR -EVID IP Quique call-PERF
        (Shipibo)
        'I caught a carachama (type of fish) and called Quique.'
    b. [En westiora ipo   chachi-şon]   -ra   Quique kena -ke.
        IP a   carachama catch-PRIOR.SS.TR -EVID Quique call -PERF
        'I caught a carachama (type of fish) and called Quique.'
    c. [Westiora ipo   chachi-şon]   -ra   en Quique kena -ke.
           a   carachama catch-PRIOR.SS.TR -EVID IP Quique call -PERF
        'I caught a carachama (type of fish) and called Quique.'
    d. #[Westiora ipo   chachi-şon]   -ra   Quique kena -ke.
           a   carachama catch-PRIOR.SS.TR -EVID Quique call -PERF
        'He/she/*I/*you caught a carachama (type of fish) and called Quique.'

The first question is whether *pro* in Shipibo is N (as in Japanese) or D (as in Chinese). We find two partially contradictory classifications of whether a language is NP-like or DP-like. Chierchia (1998, 354) proposes four criteria to determine whether a language has NPs or DPs: NP languages have generalized bare arguments, they lack plurals, the extension of all nouns is mass and they have a generalized classifier system. By these criteria, Shipibo shows a mixed or perhaps undetermined pattern. First, it has fairly generalized bare arguments, in particular, bare nominals can appear in subject and object position and be interpreted as definite, as seen in (56). Second, plurals are optionally marked either on the nominal (cf. (57a), on on the verb (cf. (57b)), or on both (cf. (57c)). If plurality is not marked on either category, the interpretation is obligatorily singular, as in (57d).[9]

(56)   Bake-n   -ra   kinan-ke   atsa-n   tita.   (Shipibo)
        child-ERG -EVID vomit-PERF yuca-GEN mother.ABS
        'The child vomited the *atsan tita* (lit. 'yuca's mother;' i.e., a beverage given to children in order to make them become fatter).'
                                            (from Valenzuela, 2003b, 579, ex. 29)

(57)   a. Isa-bo   -ra   noya-[a]i.   (Shipibo)
           bird-PL.ABS -EVID fly-INC
           '(The) birds are flying.'

[9] The initial vowel in the suffix *ai* INC is fused to the preceding vowel in (57a, d).

b. Isa   -ra   noya-kan-ai.
   bird.ABS -EVID fly-PL.INC
   'The birds are flying.'

c. Isa-bo   -ra   noya-kan-ai.
   bird-PL.ABS -EVID fly-PL-INC
   'The birds are flying.'

d. Isa   -ra   noya-[a]i.
   bird.ABS -EVID fly-INC
   'The / a bird is flying.'   (from Valenzuela, 2003b, 203, ex. 61)

Third, the language distinguishes between mass and count nouns. Thus, according to Valenzuela (2003b, 204), "[n]on-count nouns do not combine with numerals and cannot take the plural *-bo*." Finally, Shipibo lacks a classifier system. The first property would group it with NP languages, but the other three would suggest it is a DP-like language. Additionally, demonstratives seem to be able to function as a definite article in certain cases, as illustrated in (58a), and the numeral *westiora* 'one' can function as an indefinite determiner, as seen in (58b) (see Loriot et al., 1993, 43).

(58)   a. Ja oi   beain-bira,   ea k-ai.   (Shipibo)
           this rain come-despite, I leave.INC
           'Even if the rain comes, I am leaving.'

        b. Moatian-ronki   ipaoni-ke westiora joni kikin-bires   koshi.
           long ago-HRSAY was-INC   one   man extremely-INTEN strong
           'In the old days (they say) there was a very strong man.'
                                        (from Loriot et al., 1993, 43, my glosses)

Within the switch-reference clause, a NS will remain unvalued, because inflection lacks the relevant specification required, as in Chinese (cf. (59)). In this representation, each subject agrees with its own Infl (as noted by the lower arrows), but in the case of the switch-reference clause, Infl is underspecified, hence *pro* remains partially unvalued. Following the assumptions we made earlier, the search domain is extended to the main clause, where one of two things can happen: either the higher-clause subject is overtly marked for 1st and 2nd person (in (59), I have illustrated the latter case with the feature SPKR copied from the DP to *pro*, as signaled by the upper arrow), or the embedded *pro* encounters another *pro* that lacks the relevant values, as in (60), and they are interpreted as 3rd person by a default mechanism.

(59) [... DP$_i$ I ... [$_{CP}$ pro$_i$ I ...]] $\longrightarrow$ [... DP$_i$ I ... [$_{CP}$ pro$_i$ I ...]]
       [SPKR]   [R]   [SPKR]   [SPKR]

(60) [... pro$_i$ I ... [$_{CP}$ pro$_i$ I ...]]
       [R]   [R]

6.5 Chapter summary

In this chapter, I have explored how the theory of NS identification extends discourse identification. First, I have shown that discourse identification is required even in languages with strong agreement, involving absolute clauses in Spanish, adjunct clauses in Hebrew and subjunctive in Spanish/Italian. I have then explored discourse identification in languages where it is the only available mechanism, including Germanic topic drop, Japanese, Chinese and Shipibo. One of the resulting proposals is that a search can be extended beyond its minimal domain if the probe is unspecified for the relevant value, resulting in what I have called mid-range binding/control of NSs, a set of phenomena that include adjuncts in Spanish and Hebrew, as well as control in Chinese.

7 Null/overt subject contrasts

The proposed analysis of NSLs in terms of valuation of *pro* by a morphologically specified inflection and by a discourse antecedent raises the issue of what happens in agreement-rich NSLs when subjects are overt. To frame the discussion, consider the Quechua examples from Section 2.1.1, repeated below. Whereas in (1a), *pro* is valued as 3.SG. by the probe, (1b) has an overt subject *Huwan* with an inherent value, so VALUATION would imply erasing the existing values of one of the elements.

(1)   a. Papa-ta   mikhu-n-mi.   (Quechua)
   potato-ACC eat-3.SG-FOC/EVID
   'S/he eats potatoes.'

        b. Huwan-mi   papa-ta   mikhu-n.
   Huwan-FOC/EVID potato-ACC eat-3.SG
   'Huwan eats potatoes (attested).'

Consider more closely the logical possibilities that VALUATION entails within the model I have proposed. When two categories agree, either only one of them has values (as in (2a)), or both do. In this second case, the values can be identical (as in (2b)) or different (as in (2c)). If valuation involves sharing of a terminal node by the root, then the outcomes (presented at the right-hand side of the arrows in (2)) would yield a non-contradictory result in (2a–b) but not in (2c)), where each node must be interpreted as simultaneously having the values A and B. We can therefore assume that VALUATION involves terminal node sharing, with the proviso that the resulting structure must be interpretable and hence cannot contain contradictory information.

(2)   a.

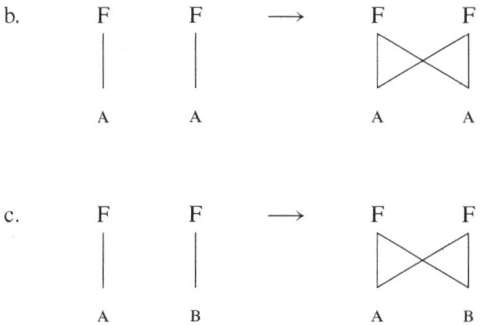

Thus, although agreement between an overt subject and inflection can be subsumed under the proposed mechanism, the question remains as to whether an overt subject always has the representation in (3a), or whether the structure in (3b) is also possible. In the first representation, the overt subject has some kind of direct agreement with inflection, whereas in the second one, T values *pro*, and the overt subject is dislocated.

(3)   a.   [DP   T]   b.   [DP$_i$ [*pro*$_i$ T]]
              [3SG]   [3SG]   [3SG]   [3SG] ← [3SG]

In this chapter, I review existing arguments in the literature for a principled distinction between NSs and overt pronominals, and in Chapter 8, I turn to the nature and position of overt DPs. After reviewing the evidence, I will argue that overt subjects have the representation in (3b).

7.1   *Pro* as a weak pronoun

Cardinaletti (1997) and many others assume that *pro* is a weak pronoun. In Section 4.3.3, I already introduced the properties ascribed to weak pronouns, which I briefly review here. According to Cardinaletti and Starke (1999), weak pronouns must occupy a dedicated position, although this property is not directly observable in the case of *pro*. They generally cannot be coordinated, as seen in the Spanish examples in (4a). In the first example, an NS cannot appear as a conjunct, as opposed to an overt pronoun in the second example. Recall, however, that in languages like Irish, an NS can be coordinated if it is interpreted contrastively, as shown in (5).

(4) a. *Pedro / ella y salimos a la calle. (Spanish)
         Pedro / she and went-out to the street.

     b. Pedro / ella y yo salimos a la calle.
        Pedro / she and I went-out to the street.
        'Pedro and I went out on the street.'

(5) da mbeinn   -se   agus tusa ann.   (Irish)
     if be.COND.1.SG -CONTR and you there
     'If you and I were there.'   (from McCloskey and Hale, 1984, 501, ex. 31a)

Additionally, weak pronouns cannot acquire their reference through ostention (pointing), so (6a) is not acceptable when one points to some overt referent, as opposed to (6b). Weak pronouns can also refer to a [–human] referents, so that (7a) is ambiguous between a [+human] and [–human] interpretation, whereas (7b) can only refer to a [+human] one.

(6) a. # *Pro* è veramente bello.   (Italian)
        pro is truly   beautiful
        'He (over there) is truly beautiful.'

     b. Lui è veramente bello.
        he is truly   beautiful
        'He (over there) is truly beautiful.'   (from Roberts, 2010a, 71, ex. 17d)

(7) a. *Pro* se cayó.   (Spanish)
        pro CL fell
        'It / he / she fell.'

     b. Él / ella se cayó.
        he / she CL fell
        'He / she / *it fell.'

Weak pronouns cannot be modified, so that (8a) cannot mean the same thing as (8b). Once again, Irish is also an exception to this property, as already seen in (5). Finally, weak pronouns (as instantiated by *pro*) can appear in impersonal clauses, so that (9a) can be interpreted impersonally (as the translation implies), but the overt counterpart can only have a referential reading, as in (9b).

(8) a. # Solo *pro* saben la respuesta.   (Spanish)
        only *pro* know the answer

     b. Solo ellas   saben la respuesta.
        only they.FEM know the answer
        'Only they know the answer.'

(9) a. *Pro* me vendieron un aguacate dañado. (Spanish)
    pro CL sold.3.PL an avocado damaged
    'I was sold a damaged avocado.'

b. Ellos me vendieron un aguacate dañado.
   they CL sold.3.PL an avocado damaged
   'They sold me a damaged avocado.'

Cardinaletti and Starke (1999) derive the difference between strong/weak pronouns from distinct syntactic structures. In particular, strong elements have a CP, but weak ones do not. The CP category, in turn, has a referential index, which derives some of the referential asymmetries observed above.

7.2 On the difference between null and overt pronouns

We can translate Cardinaletti and Starke's assumption that strong pronouns have a referential index in the following way: by virtue of being unspecified, *pro* lacks any of the referential nodes that an overt category has by default (D, SPECIFIC, DEFINITE, DEICTIC). Even after VALUATION, *pro* will not have reference because inflection does not have interpretable features. Thus, assuming the representations in (10) for an overt 3rd person pronominal, a null pronominal and 3rd person inflection, the crucial difference between an overt pronoun and inflection is that inflection has uninterpretable D/π (signaled by *u*).

(10) Overt pronominals, null pronominals and inflection

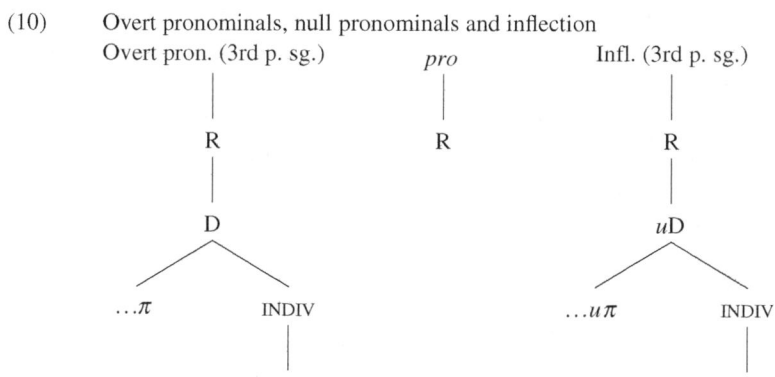

After VALUATION, *pro* will have an uninterpretable D/π feature, so if nothing else happens, it will not receive a referential interpretation. One source for

178 *Null/overt subject contrasts*

the referential content for D/π is discourse linking, as discussed in Chapter 6. Thus, the referentially defective nature of null pronouns provides us with a unified theme for the two major strands of analysis of NSs. On the one hand, Rizzi (1986a) argues that *pro* needs to be identified by copying rich agreement. On the other hand, Frascarelli (2007) argues that *pro* is always identified by a topic, even in a language like Italian. Assuming Rizzi's perspective, one might wonder why topic identification is needed, given that morphology already values *pro*. Conversely, if topic identification is always obligatory, as Frascarelli proposes, what is the purpose of having verbal person/number/gender morphology? The proposed answer is that both types of identification are needed. Throughout this book, we have seen examples that each type of identification is attested in different languages and even within a single language. Within the perspective adopted in this chapter, morphological identification does value *pro*, but not sufficiently for it to have referential properties. Thus, it is possible to have an expletive *pro* without discourse identification, but in order to have a referential interpretation, discourse-linking becomes critical.[1]

Note that this conception departs somewhat from the traditional distinction between interpretable and uninterpretable features. In particular, *pro* can be filled by the uninterpretable features in Infl, which then must be rendered referential by a discourse antecedent. In this sense, uninterpretability is not an absolute property, but rather a property that requires some additional mechanism to become interpretable.

7.2.1   Binding effects

Recall from Section 2.2.3 that for some speakers of NSLs, overt pronouns cannot be bound by a quantifier (Montalbetti, 1984). This effect happens both in languages with rich morphological agreement and no morphological agreement, as illustrated in (11)–(13), for Spanish, Chinese and Japanese respectively. In each of these pairs, the overt pronoun cannot be bound by a quantifier, so for example, (11b) cannot be interpreted as 'each student thinks that that student is intelligent'.

(11) a. Todo estudiante$_i$ cree   que *pro$_i$* es inteligente.   (Spanish)
         every student   thinks that *pro* is intelligent
         'Every student$_i$ thinks that he$_i$ is intelligent.'

---

[1] In the proposed analysis, I do not assume a unified concept of weak pronouns, but rather I assume that the properties described by Cardinaletti and Starke (1999) are derived from separate principles: lack of overt content and possibly reduced structure. The semantic effects observed for weak pronouns stem from reduced structure (lack of D), but lack of conjoinability derives from prosodic conditions on coordination.

b. Todo estudiante_i cree que él_{*i/j} es inteligente.
every student thinks that he is intelligent
'Every student_i thinks that he_j is intelligent.'

(12) a. Meige ren_i xihuan Ø_i neng xingfu.   (Chinese)
every man wish   can happy
'Everybody wishes that s/he can be happy.'

b. * Meige ren_i xihuan ta_i neng xingfu.
every man wish he can happy
'Everybody wishes that s/he can be happy.'
(from Montalbetti, 1984, 187–188, exx. 13b, 14b)

(13) a. Dare_i-ga [Ø_i sore-o mita to] itta no.   (Japanese)
who-NOM   that-ACC saw that said Q
'Who_i said that (he_i) saw that?'

b. * Dare_i-ga [kare_i-ga sore-o mita to] itta no.
who-NOM he-NOM that-ACC saw that said Q
'Who_i said that (he_i) saw that?'   (from Kanno, 1997, 266, ex. 3)

For languages like Japanese, experimental data from Kanno (1997) suggest that native speakers unanimously disallow bound readings with overt pronouns like *kare*. Lozano (2002) found the same results for Spanish and Greek natives, but some speakers of Spanish seem to lack OPC effects.

Under the assumptions I have been making, *pro* lacks a valued D in both Chinese and Italian/Spanish, and in examples like (11a)–(13a), the quantifier serves as the antecedent that values D.[2] One can see the quantifier as valuing *pro*'s referential value through quantification, as in (14).

(14)   QP_i ... [[R[D_i]] VP]

If, on the other hand, the overt pronoun has a valued referential D as part of its lexical entry, then the quantifier does not directly value the pronoun's [D] node, so a bound interpretation requires some independent mechanism. We can speculate that this alternative mechanism is less economical if valuation is available, hence a preference for the null pronoun counterpart.

This analysis does not entail that overt pronouns can never be bound. For example, certain overt pronouns can be interpreted as generic in Spanish. Specifically, a 2nd person can be used to denote a generic reading, as in (15a), even if the pronoun is overt as in (15b). Notice, however, that if one takes

---

[2] The quantifier must do something else, given that the interpretation in all three cases is quantificationally bound. I leave that aside.

valuation at face value, the morphological representation for the pronouns in (15) must be independent of the semantic interpretation, which does not necessarily include the addressee.

(15) a. Cuando visitas una bodega, normalmente te dejan probar los vinos. (Spanish)
 when visit.2.SG a winery, normally CL.2.SG let try the wines
 'When you visit a winery, they normally let you try the wines.'
 b. Cuando visitas una bodega, tú no sabes si te van a cobrar por probar.
 when visit.2.SG a winery, you not know if CL.2.SG are-going to charge for taste
 'When you visit a winery, you don't know if they are going to charge you for tasting.'

It follows that even pronouns that have an overt D can treat it as non-referential (see Vergnaud and Zubizarreta, 1992). Perhaps this alternative semantic interpretation of D is also more generally available for speakers that do show OPC effects in NSLs.

7.2.2 Backwards coreference in temporal adjunct clauses

The overt/null contrast surfaces again in cases of backwards anaphora in temporal clauses. Larson and Luján (1989, 1) point out that an overt pronoun cannot be coreferent with the main-clause subject in (16a), but its null counterpart can in (16b) in Spanish. Comínguez (2011) conducted an experimental study of binding possibilities for L2 speakers in this context and found that only 15.7% of native Spanish control speakers picked coreference between the two subjects if the first one was an overt pronoun, but up to 80% did if it was null. Italian seems to pattern in the same way as Spanish (thanks to Vieri Samek-Lodovici (p.c) for judgements).[3]

(16) a. Cuando él$_{*i/j}$ trabaja, Juan$_i$ no bebe. (Spanish)
 when he work.3.SG Juan not drink.3.SG
 'When he (someone else) works, Juan doesn't drink.'

---

[3] Larson and Luján (1989, 4) note that the contrasts in (16) can be reproduced in English with unstressed and stressed pronouns, as in (i)–(ii).

(i) * When HE$_i$ works, John$_i$ doesn't drink.
(ii) When he$_i$ works, John$_i$ doesn't drink. (from Larson and Luján, 1989, 4, ex. 14)

b. Cuando pro$_{i/j}$ trabaja,   Juan$_i$ no bebe.
   when   pro   work.3.SG Juan not drink.3.SG
   'When he works, Juan doesn't drink.'
                                    (from Larson and Luján, 1989, 1, ex. 1)

In their analysis, this follows from the fact that the overt pronoun/emphatic pronoun is focused and occupies a higher position than the null one, as in (17), from which the focused pronoun can c-command the R-expression, yielding a Principle C violation of the Binding Theory.

(17)   a. [... pro ...]

        b. [él]$_i$ [... t$_i$ ...]   (from Larson and Luján, 1989, 1, ex. 2)

As expected, when the emphatic pronoun does not c-command the R-expression, the contrast disappears, as seen in (18). Assuming that the temporal clause is higher than the main clause, even if the overt pronoun in (18b) is raised outside of its base position in the matrix clause, it will not c-command the DP *Juan*.

(18)   a. Cuando Juan$_i$ trabaja,   pro$_{i/j}$ no bebe.   (Spanish)
           when   Juan work.3.SG   not drink.3.SG
           'When Juan works, he doesn't drink.'

        b. Cuando Juan$_i$ trabaja,   él$_{i/j}$ no bebe.
           when   Juan work.3.SG   he not drink.3.SG
           'When Juan works, he doesn't drink.'
                                    (from Larson and Luján, 1989, 3, ex. 7)

Larson and Luján's pronominal typology includes two types of pronouns: emphatic and non-emphatic. However, Sánchez (1994, 489) suggests that Larson and Luján's contrasts disappear when the pronoun is stressed (cf. also Luján, 1987). However, for other speakers focus on the pronoun only improves these examples marginally. To the extent that I have been able to identify the dialectal differences, speakers who do not find improvement with focus belong to the Porteño dialect of Spanish, spoken in Buenos Aires, whereas speakers of other varieties (including from other areas of Argentina, Lima and Spain) do find a significant improvement.

(19)   Cuando ÉL$_i$ trabaja, Juan$_i$ no bebe.   (Spanish)
        when   HE works, Juan not drinks.
        'When HE works, Juan doesn't drink.'   (from Sánchez, 1994, 489, ex. 41)

Italian also shows improved coreferential possibilities when the pronoun is stressed, as in (19). As Samek-Lodovici (p.c.) points out, extending the anti-c-command analysis for the pattern in (20), requires that the focused pronoun does not move, or that it moves to a position that is lower than the unstressed pronoun counterpart of (16b) above.

(20) Quando guida LUI$_i$, Gianni$_i$ non beve.   (Italian)
      when   drives HE   Gianni   not drinks
      'When HE drives, Gianni doesn't drink.'   (from Vieri Samek-Lodovici, p.c)

An alternative account more consistent with the analysis developed here would be the following: the crucial difference between the null and overt pronoun is that the former requires a topic antecedent to provide interpretable content to the D feature, whereas the latter does not. Consider the topic structure for the different examples.

(21) a. Top$_i$ [cuando   pro$_i$ ...] [DP$_i$ ...]
                             [uD]

      b. Top$_i$ [cuando   él$_i$ ...] [DP$_i$ ...]
                             [iD]

      c. Top$_i$ [cuando   ÉL$_j$ ...] [DP$_j$ ...]
                             [iD]

In (21a), the topic provides an interpretable value to *pro*'s [D], and also acts as a topic for the following DP. On the other hand, if the topic is coindexed with the overt pronoun (as in (21b)), the resulting structure involves two independently valued but coreferential D features, but as suggested in the previous section, valuation of the null option is preferred (over independent values that result in coreference). On the other hand, (21b) is fine with a disjoint reading, because no alternative option based on valuation is available. Finally, the stressed pronoun is interpreted as a contrastive topic in (21c), which makes it possible for it to be indexed differently from the preceding topic.

7.2.3 Backwards anaphora in conditional sentences

Frascarelli (2007) quotes patterns for Italian conditional clauses that are reminiscent of the ones just seen in the preceding section for Spanish. The overt pronoun cannot serve as an antecedent to an overt DP as in Spanish temporal adjunct clauses. However, unlike in the Spanish case, the overt pronominal can never be coreferential with a DP, regardless of which position each one occupies, as seen in (22a)–(24a). Conversely, a null subject can be coreferential in most instances (with one exception I will return to below), as seen in (22b)–(24b).

(22) a. * Se lui$_i$ si sentirà bene Jim$_i$ andrà. (Italian)
          if he CL will feel well Jim will leave
          'If he feels well, Jim will go.'

      b. Se *pro*$_i$ si sentirà bene Jim$_i$ andrà.
          if *pro* CL will feel well Jim will leave
          'If he feels well, Jim will go.'   (from Frascarelli, 2007, 695, ex. 6b)

(23) a. * Jim$_i$ andrà se lui$_i$ si sentirà bene. (Italian)
          Jim will go if he CL will feel well
          'Jim will go if he feels well.'

      b. Jim$_i$ andrà se *pro*$_i$ si sentirà bene.
          Jim will go if *pro* CL will feel well
          'Jim will go if he feels well.'   (from Frascarelli, 2007, 695, ex. 6a)

(24) a. * Se Jim$_i$ si sentirà bene lui$_i$ andrà. (Italian)
          if Jim CL will feel well he will go
          'He will go if Jim feels well.'

      b. Se Jim$_i$ si sentirà bene *pro*$_i$ andrà.
          if Jim CL will feel well   will go
          'If Jim feels well, he will go.'   (from Frascarelli, 2007, 695, ex. 6d)

These patterns are identical in Spanish, so conditionals seem to have a different distribution with respect to the null/overt pronoun contrast in both languages than temporal adjunct clauses.[4] These constructions raise a challenge for a Larson and Luján-type of account, because that analysis is crucially based on whether the overt pronoun c-commands the DP, and c-command obtains in certain contexts but not others (cf. (16b) vs. (18b) above). If that analysis were to apply to the conditional cases, one would have to show that the overt pronoun c-commands the DP in all of the relevant examples, regardless

---

[4] Example (24b) above minimally contrasts with (i) below, which is ungrammatical, for reasons that are not clear to me.

  (i)   * *Pro*$_i$ andrà se Jim$_i$ si sentirà bene. (Italian)
          will go if Jim CL will feel well
          'If Jim feels well, he will go.'   (from Frascarelli, 2007, 695, ex. 6c)

of whether the pronoun appears in the *if*-clause or the consequence clause, as in (25).

(25) a. *Lui$_i$ [$_{CP1}$ si/se t$_i$ ...] [$_{CP2}$ DP$_i$ ...]
 b. *Lui$_i$ [$_{CP1}$ t$_i$ ...] [$_{CP2}$ si/se DP$_i$ ...]

However, extraction facts suggest that the symmetric structures in (25) cannot be right, because extraction from both clauses is not equally possible in conditional constructions. In Spanish, for example, wh-extraction is possible from the consequence-clause (cf. (26b)), but not from the *if*-clause (cf. (26c)).

(26) a. Si Ana organiza la fiesta, Blanca va a traer la comida.
 if Ana organizes the party Blanca goes to bring the food
 (Spanish)
 'If Ana organizes the party, Blanca is going to bring the food.'
 b. ¿Qué va a traer Blanca t [si Ana organiza la fiesta]?
 what go to bring Blanca if Ana organizes the party
 'What is Blanca going to bring if Ana organizes the party?'
 c. *¿[Qué si Ana trae t] Blanca va a organizar la fiesta?
 what if Ana brings Blanca goes to organize the party
 'What if Ana brings is Blanca going to organize the party?'

If pronoun raising and wh-extraction are subject to the same locality constraints, then one would expect coreference to be impossible when the pronoun is in the consequence clause but not in the *if*-clause, because wh-movement is not possible from the *if*-clause (cf. (26c)).

Note, furthermore, that the two clauses are not completely symmetric. Rather, it seems that the *if*-clause occupies the same position as a clitic left-dislocated phrase, that is, to the left of a wh-word. Consider, for example, the paradigms in (27). In the most natural order, the wh-word appears adjacent to its own condition clause (cf. (27a–b)), but as (27c) shows, a wh-word to the left of the *if*-clause is fairly marginal, and only improves with a rhetorical question flavor. This is similar to the distribution of clitic left-dislocated phrases, as seen in (28).

(27) a. [Si Ana trae el pastel] ¿quién va a organizar la fiesta?
 if Ana brings the cake who is going to organize the party
 (Spanish)
 'If Ana brings the cake, who is going to organize the party?'
 b. ¿Quién va a organizar la fiesta [si Ana trae el pastel]?
 who goes to organize the party if Ana brings the cake
 'Who is going to organize the party if Ana brings the cake?'

c. ?? ¿Quién [si Ana trae el pastel] va a organizar la fiesta?
   who   if Ana brings the cake is going to organize the party
   'Who, if Ana brings the cake, is going to organize the party?'

(28) a. A la hermana de Ana, ¿quién la va a invitar a la fiesta?
        to the sister of Ana, who CL is going to invite to the party
                                                                (Spanish)
     'Ana's sister, who is going to invite her to the party?'
   b. *? ¿Quién a la hermana de Ana la va a invitar a la fiesta?
        who to the sister of Ana CL is going to invite to the party
     'Who, Ana's sister, is going to invite (her) to the party?'

This parallelism between CLLD phrases and conditionals suggests a structure like (29) for conditionals, assuming an extended version of CP. In this structure, the *if*-clause is in a specifier of a left-peripheral position of the consequent clause. This derives why extraction from the *if*-clause is not possible (cf. (26c)).

(29)   [$_{XP1}$ [$_{CP2}$ si ...] [$_{X1}$ [$_{CP1}$ quién [$_{IP1}$ va a ...]]]]

These facts argue against a symmetric analysis of the coreferential facts along the lines of (25). Rather, extending the alternative analysis proposed for adjunct temporal clauses, let us assume that a topic is present in all configurations, yielding the structures in (30)–(32). In (30a)–(32a), the topic can identify *pro*, which in turn can be coindexed with the DP. In (30b)–(32b), the overt pronoun should indicate a change of topic, hence it would be marked with a different index, leading to a clash in indices between the topic and the subsequent DP.[5]

(30) a. Top$_i$ [si/se *pro$_i$* ...] [DP$_i$ ...]
                      [uD]

     b. *Top$_i$ [si/se él/lui$_i$ ...] [DP$_i$ ...]
                       [iD]

---

[5] I am abstracting away from the sentence-internal structure of the sequence in (32). Since the *if*-clause follows the consequence clause, there must be some additional movement of that clause to a left-peripheral position higher than the *if*-clause.

(31) a. Top$_i$ [si/se DP$_i$ ...] [pro$_i$ ...]
         [uD]

b. *Top$_i$ [si/se DP$_i$ ...] [él/lui$_i$ ...]
                                  [iD]

(32) a. Top$_i$ [pro$_i$ ...] [si/se DP$_i$ ...]
              [uD]

b. *Top$_i$ [él/lui$_i$ ...] [si/se DP$_i$ ...]
           [iD]

To summarize, the evidence from backwards pronominalization better supports the analysis based on topic binding of *pro* than the alternative based on the anti-c-command condition.

7.3 Deriving expletives

In Section 4.4, I suggested that NSLs may lack expletives altogether; however, the proposed analysis could allow for a null expletive, as I will show in this section. One of the most notable features of expletives is that the verb appears in 3rd person singular, and it would be an added value if the theory could derive this restriction. It seems reasonable to relate this property to the the fact that expletive constructions do not assign a regular theta role.

Svenonius (2002, 6) notes that several researchers have ascribed semantic content to certain expletives, as already noted in Section 2.1.2. In support for this contention, Chomsky (1981, 323–5) points to examples of alleged control by weather-verb expletives (cf. (33)). Additionally, Hoekstra (1983) argues that extraposition *it* is referential, because it is always coindexed with a CP (cf. (34)). However, it is not clear that coindexing here means the same as coreferential, just as agreement involves some notion of matching that does not imply coreference.

(33) a. It often clears up here right after snowing heavily.
                                           (from Svenonius, 2002, 6, ex. 5a)
b. Korai szürkületet okozva befelhösödött.   (Hungarian)
   early twilight.ACC causing clouded
   'It clouded, causing early twilight.'   (from Kiss, 2002, 119, ex. 39a)

(34) It is obvious where you got that hickey. (from Svenonius, 2002, 5, ex. 4a)

A slightly different argument for the semantic content of expletives comes from the fact that extraposition pronouns can be focused in Hungarian (cf. (35)), as noted by Kiss (2002).[6]

(35) Számomra   csak   az   volt   nyilvánvaló   hogy   Éva
     for.me   only   that.NOM   was   obvious   that   Eve
     megbukik.   (Hungarian)
     fails
     'Only that was obvious for me that Eve would fail.'
                                              (from Kiss, 2002, 112, ex. 17b)

Assuming for the sake of argument that some expletives are not semantically vacuous, it is clear that their content is not fully referential, and that if they receive a theta role, it is not one of the usual ones.[7] Consider an expletive construction in Spanish, such as (36). Suppose that *pro* appears as the subject of this construction, being valued by inflection and inheriting the uninterpreted D feature. By assumption, this feature must be recovered in discourse. If a topic were to value it, then the resulting structure would have a topic with no semantic connection to the clause, something like 'as for x, x is obvious that s/he didn't come', because nothing in that clause assigns a theta role to *pro*. Thus, the only possible interpretation would entail a non-canonical theta role (if Chomsky is right).

(36) Es obvio   que no vino.
     is obvious that not come.PAST
     'It is obvious that s/he didn't come.'

If there is no topic, then *pro*'s uninterpreted D feature would receive no reference. If a default mechanism exists, it would apply to it, yielding the

---

[6] Note that the kind of expletive illustrated in (35) is only possible in an NSL like Spanish with an overt demonstrative, as shown in (i). This is expected if elements modified by *solo* must be focused and focus is typically associated with stress in these languages. But this also means that strictly speaking, one cannot test whether a null expletive can be focused.

  (i) Solo ESO es obvio   que Eva va a fracasar.   (Spanish)
      only that is obvious that Eva will fail
      'Only that was obvious that Eva would fail.'

[7] Some varieties allow for expletives to agree with 1st–2nd person constructions, as discussed in Manzini and Savoia (2002) for several Italian dialects. However, this possibility is independent of whether the variety has NSs or not, and is subject to several other restrictions.

188 *Null/overt subject contrasts*

quasi-expletive effect. Presumably, this mechanism applies only to the least specified feature-representation, namely the 3rd person.[8]

7.3.1 Reference to clauses

Recall the observations from Iatridou and Embick (1997) reported in Section 2.2.2 that a thematic *pro* cannot refer to an IP/CP projection, as illustrated in (37). On the other hand, an expletive can appear with an extraposed clause, as in (38).

(37) a. O Kostas ine panda argoporimenos. (Greek)
 the Kostas is always delayed
 'Kostas is always delayed.'

 b. Pragmatika. *ke *pro* epise ton patera tu na tu agorasi aftokinito.
 indeed and convinced the father his MOD him buy car
 'Indeed, and he convinced his father to buy him a car.'
 (from Iatridou and Embick, 1997, 58, ex. 2)

(38) a. An o Kostas argisi *pro* tha ine dropi. (Greek)
 if the Kostas is late *pro* FUT be shame
 'If Kostas arrives late, it will be a shame.'

 b. *pro* ine dropi pu o Kostas tha figi.
 pro be shame that the Kostas FUT leave
 'It is a shame that Kostas will leave.'
 (from Iatridou and Embick, 1997, 60, ex. 6)

Why is coreference possible in (38) and not in (37b)? Iatridou and Embick (1997) suggest that the ungrammaticality of (37b) stems from a feature mismatch between thematic *pro* and IP/CP. Thematic *pro* must match number, gender and possibly person, but IP/CP lacks those features. In the current framework, this means that the *pro* in (37b) must include at least π, whereas the one in (38) does not.

---

[8] The default 1st person assignment we discussed earlier will be unavailable precisely because there is no theta role assignment: it makes little sense to assign a speaker role to a situation in which no theta roles are defined. One could assign such an interpretation to an evidential, but in such case the constant function does not apply to the subject of the clause, but to a separate layer that contains evidential heads, as illustrated by the following Quechua example provided by Liliana Sánchez (p.c.).

(i) Paramu-chkan-mi. (Quechua)
 rain-PROG-EVID
 '(I have direct evidence that) It is raining.'

7.4 Chapter summary

In this chapter, I have reviewed interpretive contrasts between overt and null subjects. I adapted Cardinaletti and Starke's (1999) proposal that strong pronouns have a referential index to the proposed analysis by suggesting that null pronouns have an uninterpretable D/π feature that requires anchoring in discourse, a process that is achieved through topic identification. In this sense, most languages with NSs require both morphological valuation and topic identification. From this assumption, I attempted to derive binding effects asymmetries (essentially Chomsky's Avoid Pronoun Constraint): It is more economical to value the unvalued features of *pro* than to match the features of two categories that are independently valued. This idea also extends to backwards anaphora. Finally, I have argued that the proposed analysis can shed light on why expletives are generally 3rd person and why they are null in NSLs. An NS will lack referential content, so in the context of an expletive verb, it will not receive a topic interpretation, and a default mechanism will allow for expletive interpretation.

8 The status of preverbal subjects in null subject languages

As mentioned in Section 4.2, treating verbal morphology as pronominal means that overt preverbal subjects (PSs) are not the 'real' subject of a clause in an NSL, but perhaps a dislocated or A′ constituent. Even if one does not accept the pronominal agreement hypothesis, the distribution of PSs seems to be substantially different from that of overt subjects in languages like English. For these reasons, much of the debate over the past 30 years has centered on the status of PSs (see Rizzi, 1982; Rigau, 1988; Contreras, 1991; Koopman and Sportiche, 1991; Solà, 1992; Zubizarreta, 1994; Cardinaletti, 1997, 2004; Alexiadou and Anagnostopoulou, 1998; Goodall, 1999; Ordóñez and Treviño, 1999; Suñer, 2003; Camacho, 2006; Frascarelli, 2007; Sheehan, 2007, among others). This debate usually conflates logically independent notions: first, whether PSs occupy an A or A′-position, second, whether PSs have the properties of clitic left-dislocated (CLLD) phrases, and third, whether they are interpreted as topics or not.

These notions overlap in many ways, but they are not completely identical. For example, some researchers argue that PSs are CLLD phrases based on similarities with respect to reconstruction and scope, following Cinque (1990, 66). Thus, according to Cinque, sentences like (1a) and (2a) differ with respect to the possibility of interpreting the first constituent in its base position: The former can be interpreted as its counterpart in (1b), without displacement, whereas the latter cannot. These interpretive differences correlate with the fact that (2a) is a CLLD construction (with a null clitic, as in (2b)), but (1a) is not.[1]

(1) a. PER QUESTA RAGIONE$_i$, ha detto che se ne andrà t_i. (Italian)
         for this   reason   has said that CL CL will leave
     'FOR THIS REASON he said that he would leave.'

---

[1] In Cinque's analysis, CLLD does not involve movement, but focalization or wh-questions do.

b. Ha detto che se ne andrà   per questa ragione.
has said that CL CL will leave for this   reason
'S/he said that s/he will leave for this reason.'
(from Cinque, 1990, 64, ex. 13)

(2)   a. * Per questa ragione$_i$, ha detto che se ne andrà t_i.   (Italian)
for this   reason   has said that CL CL will leave
'For this reason, he said that he would leave.'
(from Cinque, 1990, 66, ex. 14)
b. [$_{PP}$ Per questa ragione]$_i$ [ha detto [$_{CP}$ che [CL$_{\emptyset-i}$ se ne andrà]]]

Based on the idea that CLLD phrases do not reconstruct, Alexiadou and Anagnostopoulou (1998) argue that PSs are also left-dislocated, since they do not reconstruct either (see below). However, it is logically possible that PSs and CLLD phrases do not reconstruct for independent reasons. For example, PSs could fail to reconstruct because they are A′-moved, whereas CLLD phrases do not reconstruct because they are base-generated in their peripheral positions. On the other hand, one could argue that both are base-generated in peripheral positions, but the nature of those positions is different.

Clitic left-dislocated phrases are usually interpreted as topics, and PSs are as well, although not always, but once again, these are two potentially independent properties: topichood is a discourse-related property that does not correlate one-to-one with any given syntactic position (even in proposals that assume a highly articulated structure of the left periphery, cf. Rizzi, 1997). As is well known, so-called hanging topics (cf. (3)) are semantic topics but have distinct syntactic properties from CLLD phrases or topicalization. For example, the hanging topic in (3a) has no syntactic connection with the embedded verb *seguir* 'continue', whereas dislocated phrase and the clitic *la* 'it' in (3b) do. In fact, as we saw in Section 6.2, there may be several syntactic topic positions within the clause.

(3)   a. En cuanto a   la   decisión,   tenemos   que   seguir   la
with respect to   the   decision,   have   to   continue   the
discusión.   (Spanish)
discussion
'With respect to the decision, we have to continue the discussion.'
b. La decisión, tenemos que continuar discutiendo-la.
the decision, have   to   continue discussing-CL.FEM.ACC
'The decision, we have to continue discussing it.'

The strongest version of the PS-as-CLLD proposals assumes that **all** preverbal subjects should be in an A′ position and that PSs have exactly the same properties instantiated in CLLD phrases, i.e. as topics (among other things). A weakened version would argue that some subjects may be in A′, while others are in A-position (Goodall, 1999; Suñer, 2003; Camacho, 2006; Sheehan, 2007). I will briefly discuss the main points of the debate, following Sheehan's (2007, 50–89) and Camacho's (2006) discussion.

8.1   Preverbal subjects as CLLD phrases

8.1.1   Scope asymmetries

Alexiadou and Anagnostopoulou (1998, 504) argue that PSs have the same scope properties as CLLD constituents, and these are reflected in two specific areas: their scope interactions with other quantifiers, and with sentential modals and negation. According to them, quantified and indefinite PSs in Greek and Spanish only take wide scope with respect to other quantifiers in the clause.

(4) a. Kapios fititis   stihiothetise kathe arthro.   (Greek)
       some   student filed   every article
       'Some student filed every article.' (not 'For every article there was a student who filed it.')

   b. Algún/un estudiante archivó todos los artículos.   (Spanish)
       some/a   student   filed   every the articles
       'Some student filed every article.'(not 'For every article there was a student who filed it.'

This follows if they do not reconstruct, like CLLD phrases (cf. the discussion of (1)–(2) above). However, quantifier scope facts are more complex than example (4) would suggest. Suñer (2003, 344) points out that PSs can have narrow scope, as shown in the interpretation in (5b) for (5a), and in fact she argues that this is the preferred interpretation for that example. As Sheehan (2007, 57–58) notes, PSs can have narrow scope in European Portuguese, Romanian and Italian in addition to Spanish.

(5) a. En la   biblioteca departamental, algún estudiante sacó prestado cada libro.
       in the library   departmental, some student   took loaned   each book
                                                                        (Spanish)

   b. 'In the departmental library, each book was taken out by some student.'
       (narrow scope subject)

   c. 'In the departmental library, some (specific) student took out each book.'
       (wide scope subject, dispreferred)

8.1 Preverbal subjects as CLLD phrases   193

A slightly different version of the scope argument is presented by Barbosa (1995, 36–37), as noted by Sheehan (2007, 58–61). Barbosa argues that indefinite subjects always take wide scope over other scope-bearing elements, unlike in English or French. Thus, she points out that in a context where I am being reminded of the items that are necessary in order to apply to a certain job, English (6a) and French (6b) are both grammatical, but (7a)–(10a) are not. By contrast, (7b)–(10b) are (her judgements).[2]

(6)   a. A letter of recommendation is required.
      b. Une lettre de recommendation est requise.   (French)
         a   letter of recommendation is   required
         'A letter of recommendation is necessary.'
                              (from Barbosa, 1995, 35, exx. 61–62)

(7)   a. ??? Una carta de recomanació   es necessaria.   (Catalan)
         a   letter of recommendation is necessary
         'A letter of recommendation is necessary.'
      b. Es necessaria una carta de recomanació.
         is necessary a   letter of recommendation
         'A letter of recommendation is necessary.'
                              (from Barbosa, 1995, 36, ex. 63)

(8)   a. ??? Una carta de recomendación   es necesaria.   (Spanish)
         a   letter of recommendation is necessary
         'A letter of recommendation is necessary.'
      b. Es necesaria una carta de recomendación.
         is necessary a   letter of recommendation
         'A letter of recommendation is necessary.'
                              (from Barbosa, 1995, 36, ex. 64)

(9)   a. ??? Una lettera di raccomandazione é necessaria.   (Italian)
         a   letter of recommendation is necessary
         'A letter of recommendation is necessary.'
      b. E necessaria una lettera di racomandazzione.
         is necessary a   letter of recommendation
         'A letter of recommendation is necessary.'
                              (from Barbosa, 1995, 36, ex. 65)

(10) a. ??? Uma carta de recomendação   é necessaria.   (EP)
         a   letter of recommendation is necessary
         'A letter of recommendation is necessary.'

---

[2] The (a) versions of (7)–(10) are appropriate if the letter is interpreted as a specific indefinite ('one of the letters').

b. É necessaria uma carta de recomendação.
   is necessary a   letter of recommendation
   'A letter of recommendation is necessary.'

(from Barbosa, 1995, 36, ex. 66)

According to Barbosa, the deviant examples are inadequate because the context is set up for a wide-scope reading of the modal, but given the wide-scope requirements of the indefinite, the modal cannot take wide scope. If both English subjects and NSL PSs are derived by A-movement, Barbosa points out, then one needs to suggest some extra machinery to account for the contrast between English/French and the other languages, whereas if PS subjects are left-dislocated, all that remains to be added is an independent theory of why dislocated indefinites take wide scope.

I think both Alexiadou and Anagnostopoulou's and Barbosa's contrasts can be subsumed under the criterial freezing account adopted earlier (see Section 4.4.3). The relevant generalization from these examples is that indefinite subjects in NSLs take the widest scope possible. This suggests that the subject is not frozen in Spec, TP in these languages, as the Subject Criterion analysis correctly predicts. In English and French, on the other hand, subjects are frozen in Spec, TP so their scope possibilities are limited to that position. If the modal (or another quantifier) can raise to a higher scope position, then the attested scope relations obtain. The difference between Alexiadou and Anagnostopoulou's examples (where the subject takes wide scope over the object) and Suñer's examples (where the object can have wider scope) has to do in part with the fact that distributive quantifiers like *cada* 'each' favor widest scope.

From another perspective, Zubizarreta (1994, 1998) shows that CLLD constituents and PSs do not pattern uniformly with respect to reconstruction, and CLLD phrases themselves vary depending on whether they are accusative or dative. First, a quantified DP subject can bind a pronoun inside an accusative CLLD phrase if the subject is preverbal, not if it is postverbal (cf. (11a vs. b) and also Suñer, 2003). According to Zubizarreta (1998, 114–15), this is evidence for an intermediate projection for the clitic, above VP but below TP, to which the CLLD phrase can reconstruct, as in (12). Since postverbal subjects are inside VP, the reconstructed phrase will always be higher.

(11) a. A su hijo$_i$, cada madre$_j$ deberá acompañar-lo$_i$ el primer día
       to her son, each mother   must   accompany-CL.ACC.3.SG the first day
       de escuela.   (Spanish)
       of school
       'Each mother must accompany her child on the first day of school.'

b. * El primer día de escuela, a su hijo₍ᵢ₎ deberá acompañar-lo
'the first day of school, to her son must accompany-CL.ACC.3.SG
cada madre₍ⱼ₎. (Spanish)
each mother
'Each mother must accompany her child on the first day of school.'
(from Zubizarreta, 1998, 114, ex. 38)

(12) a. [~~su hijo~~   [TP cada madre₍ᵢ₎ T   [ClP su hijo₍ᵢ₎ [VP ...]]]]
         └─────────────────────↑

     b. *[~~su hijo~~   [TP T   [ClP su hijo₍ᵢ₎   [VP cada madre₍ᵢ₎ ...]]]]
          ↑───────────────────────┘

Second, the contrast observed in (11) does not extend to dative CLLD phrases, as seen in (13). Zubizarreta derives the difference between datives and accusatives from distinct structural configurations, where the dative ClP is lower than the VP projection that hosts the postverbal subject, as in (14).

(13) a. A su₍ᵢ₎ editor, cada autor₍ᵢ₎ le₍ᵢ₎   envió un manuscrito.   (Spanish)
        to his editor, each author CL.3.DAT sent a manuscript
        'Each author sent a manuscript to his editor.'

     b. A su₍ᵢ₎ editor, le₍ᵢ₎   envió cada autor₍ᵢ₎ un manuscrito.
        to his editor, CL.3.DAT sent each author a manuscript
        'Each author sent a manuscript to his editor.'
        (from Zubizarreta, 1998, 115, ex. 41)

(14) a. [~~su hijo~~   [TP cada madre₍ᵢ₎ T   [VP1 V1 [ClP su hijo₍ᵢ₎ [VP2 ...]]]]]
         └────────────────────────────↑

     b. *[~~su hijo~~   [TP T   [VP1 cada madre₍ᵢ₎ V1   [ClP su hijo₍ᵢ₎ [VP2 ...]]]]]
          ↑─────────────────────────┘

Note that unlike Alexiadou and Anagnostopoulou's examples, these cases do not involve quantificational scope interactions, but quantifier binding, so the notion that the distributive quantifier takes widest scope no longer applies.

We can conclude from these examples that CLLD phrases do not show uniform behavior with respect to the possibility and locus of reconstruction. Thus, the idea that PSs cannot reconstruct because they are CLLD phrases cannot be maintained, because when CLLD phrases reconstruct, they do so to different positions.

8.1.2 Extraction facts

Ordóñez and Treviño (1999) present certain extraction asymmetries as evidence in favor of the PS-as-CLLD analysis. Jaeggli (1987) noted that fronting a wh-word over a preverbal wh-subject is ungrammatical, whereas fronting over a postverbal wh-subject is not, as seen in (15).

(15)   a.   * ¿Qué dijiste que quién compró el otro día?   (Spanish)
what said that who bought the other day
'Who did you say bought what the other day?'

     b.   ¿Qué dijiste que compró quién el otro día?
what said that bought who the other day
'What did you say who bought the other day?'

(from Ordóñez and Treviño, 1999, 51, ex. 50)

Ordóñez and Treviño argue that this same pattern obtains with respect to CLLD wh-objects and wh-indirect objects as well. Thus, in (16), the subject can be extracted if the wh-indirect object is postverbal but not if it is preverbal (cf. 16a vs. b). Since non-wh CLLD indirect objects do not induce the same effect, as seen in (16c), they suggest that the explanation cannot be due to whether the Spec, IP position is properly governed or not.

(16)   a.   ¿Quién crees que le va a dar eso a quién?   (Spanish)
who think that CL.3.SG will give that to whom
'Who do you think will give that to whom?'

     b.   * ¿Quién crees que a quién le va a dar eso?
who think that to whom CL.3.SG will give that
'Who do you think that to whom will give that?'

     c.   ¿Quién crees que a ti te va a dar eso?
who think that to you CL.2.SG will give that
'Who do you think that will give that to you?'

(from Ordóñez and Treviño, 1999, 50, ex. 52)

Rather, they connect this difference with the scope possibilities found in examples like (17). In (17a), the quantified DP *cada senador* 'each senator' only has narrow scope with respect to the wh-phrase, i.e. it is not possible to interpret it as each senator loves a different person, but in (17b), with a postverbal subject, the scope ambiguity reappears.

(17)   a.   ¿A quién dices que cada senador amaba?   (Spanish)
to who say that each senator loved
'Who do you say that each senator loved?'

b. ¿A quién dices que amaba cada senador?
   to who say that loved each senator
   'Who do you say that each senator loved?'
   (from Ordóñez and Treviño, 1999, 52, exx. 53–54)

Ordóñez and Treviño propose that freezing of the quantified subject in (17) would follow if it already occupies a topicalized, A'-position, as it would if it were CLLD. However, this logic leads to analyzing (16c) as involving non-cyclic movement of the subject from a postverbal position, otherwise we would predict that it should be ungrammatical if the wh-subject is moved from the pre-verbal A' position. This contrast between (16a) and (16c) suggests that the effect is not due to being frozen in an A' position. Rather, a general property of Spanish is that it does not allow wh-words to appear in embedded position with verbs that do not select for wh-questions. Thus, (18) shows the same contrast as (15), but with a single wh-word.

(18) a. *¿Pedro dijo que quién compró una casa el otro día?
       Pedro said that who bought a house the other day
       (Spanish)

   b. ¿Pedro dijo que compró una casa el otro día quién?
      Pedro said that bought a house the other day who
      'Who is it that Pedro said that bought a house the other day?'

8.1.3 Adverb intervention effects

Alexiadou and Anagnostopoulou (1998, 502) point out that in Spanish and Greek an adverb can follow a PS (cf. (19a)), whereas they cannot in French and Italian (cf. (19b)). Assuming that adverbs adjoin to a maximal projection, the subject and the verb cannot be in the same maximal projection in Spanish and that the verb is in I, it follows that the subject must be higher. In French and Italian, on the other hand, the subject could be in Spec, IP.

(19) a. Juan ya se fue. (Spanish)
       Juan already CL left
       'Juan has already left.' (from Sheehan, 2007, 51, ex. 48)

   b. Jean (*déjà) veux (déjà) s'en aller. (French)
      Jean already wants already CL-of go
      'Jean already wants to leave.' (from Sheehan, 2007, 51, ex. 50)

   c. Maria (*già) parlava già di lui. (Italian)
      Maria already was-speaking already of him
      'Maria was already speaking about him.'
      (from Sheehan, 2007, 52, ex. 51)

However, as Sheehan (2007, 52) points out, the corresponding adverb in Italian patterns with the French one, suggesting that the test does not give similar results for Italian and Spanish, although they both are NSLs. Rather than follow from the NSL status, the contrasts in (19) would follow if the verb in Italian and French raises to a higher position than in Spanish.

The strong PS-as-CLLD hypothesis cannot readily explain why the adverb *probabilmente* 'probably' in Italian cannot intervene between the negative quantifier *nessuno* 'nobody' and the verb, as seen in (20a). If PSs uniformly occupy the same A'-position, this is somewhat unexpected. Notice that if *nessuno* is contrastively focalized, then the sequence becomes acceptable (cf. (20b)). Recall that contrastive focus is analyzed by Cinque (1990, 66) as movement, but this would suggest that the ungrammaticality of (20a) follows from a requirement that the quantifier be in the Spec of IP, rather than in the CLLD position (cf. Belletti, 1990, quoted in Sheehan, 2007, 52).

(20)   a. * Nessuno probabilmente telefonerà alle 5.   (Italian)
nobody probably will-phone at-the 5
'Nobody will probably phone at 5 o'clock.'

b. NESSUNO probabilmente telefonerà alle 5.
nobody probably will-phone at-the 5
'NOBODY will probably phone at 5 o'clock.'

A similar state of affairs holds in Spanish with respect to negative quantifiers, the adverb *casi* 'almost' and a modal (see Camacho, 2006). As (21) shows, a negative quantifier in PS position cannot precede a modal when the adverb *casi* 'almost' intervenes, contrasting with a non-quantified DP (cf. (21b) vs. (22a)) and with one in postverbal position (cf. (21b) vs. (22b)). Finally, the PS negative quantifier also contrasts with a CLLD negative quantifier (cf. (21b) vs. (22c)).

(21)   a. Nadie pudo avanzar 3 metros.   (Spanish)
no one could advance 3 meters
'No one could advance 3 meters.'

b. * Nadie casi pudo avanzar 3 metros.
no one almost could advance 3 meters

c. * Ninguno de ellos casi pudo avanzar 3 metros.
none of them almost could advance 3 meters

(22)   a. La tortuga casi pudo avanzar 3 metros.   (Spanish)
the turtle almost could advance 3 meters
'The turtle could almost advance 3 meters.'

b. Casi no pudo avanzar 3 metros nadie.
   almost not could advance 3 meters no-one
   'No one could almost advance 3 meters.'

c. A ninguno de los culpables casi lo descubrieron.
   to none of the guilty almost CL discovered
   'None of the guilty were almost discovered.'

These contrasts suggest that a unified account of PSs as A′ CLLD constituents is not fine-grained enough to account for the distributional complexities.

8.1.4 PS incompatibility with quantified CLLD phrases

Ordóñez and Treviño (1999, 45) note that although quantified DPs can appear as CLLD phrases (cf. (23a)), an overt PS intervening between the quantified phrase and the verb makes the sequence ungrammatical (cf. (23b–c)). As the example in (24) shows, this same pattern exists when the PS is quantified and the CLLD phrase is not.

These patterns would be unexpected if *pro* and the overt PS occupy the same position in each of those examples. According to Ordóñez and Treviño, if PSs and CLLD phrases occupy a similar position, the contrast follows: in (23b–c), the non-quantified phrase blocks the relationship between the quantifier and inflection. Furthermore, this contrast can be taken as evidence in favor of treating inflection as pronominal, if one assumes that bound morphemes do not block relationships between heads and maximal projections, the contrast between (23a) and (23b) follows.

(23) a. Nada le debe a sus amigos. (Spanish)
        nothing CL.3SG owes.3.SG to his/her friends
        'He/she owes nothing to his/her friends.'
                                        (from Ordóñez and Treviño, 1999, 44, ex. 25)

     b. *Nada Juan le debe a sus amigos.
        nothing Juan CL.3.SG owes.3.SG to his/her friends
        'Juan owes nothing to his/her friends.'
                                        (from Ordóñez and Treviño, 1999, 45, ex. 29)

     c. *A nadie Juan le debe la renta.
        to nobody Juan CL.3.SG owes.3.SG the rent
        'Juan owes the rent to nobody.'
                                        (from Ordóñez and Treviño, 1999, 45, ex. 30)

(24) a. *Nadie el libro se lo regaló a Marta. (Spanish)
        no one the book CL.3.DAT CL.3.ACC gave to Marta
        'The book, nobody gave it to Marta.'

b. El libro, nadie se lo regaló a Marta.
the book, no one CL.3.DAT CL.3.ACC gave to Marta
'The book, nobody gave it to Marta.'

Notice that these facts are very similar to (21), where the adverb *casi* cannot intervene between the negative quantifier and a modal. These two sets of facts suggest that the negative quantifier must be adjacent to an inflectional projection, and that nothing can block that relationship, as Ordóñez and Treviño suggest. Since the effect is limited to negative quantifiers, and we know independently that negation must be adjacent to Infl (cf. (25)), we can assume with Bosque (1980) and Laka (1990) that the NPIs must be adjacent to NegP.[3]

(25) a. Alfonso casi no sobrevivió al accidente. (Spanish)
Alfonso almost not survived to-the accident
'Alfonso almost didn't survive the accident.'
b. *Alfonso no casi sobrevivió al accidente.
Alfonso not almost survived to-the accident

In any case, given the fact that the content of the quantifier drives the restrictions above, it seems that one cannot generalize from these data that PS are always dislocated, but rather that negative quantifiers in preverbal position must be adjacent to an inflectional projection.

8.1.5 The distribution of bare NPs

One final argument in favor of the PS-as-CLLD analysis relates to the impossibility of having bare NPs as PS or as CLLD phrases, as seen in (26a)–(27). Both bare PS NPs and bare CLLD phrases are ungrammatical. Once again, this would be an expected consequence if PSs are CLLD phrases.

(26) a. *Niños no llegaron esta mañana. (Spanish)
children not arrived this morning
'Children didn't arrive this morning.'
b. No llegaron niños esta mañana.
not arrived children this morning
'Children didn't arrive this morning.'

(27) a. *Niños, no los vi esta mañana. (Spanish)
children not CL.3.PL saw this morning
b. *A niños, no los vi esta mañana.
to children not CL saw this morning

---

[3] It is possible that the effects described by Ordóñez and Treviño extend to other categories associated with Laka's (1990) ΣP.

8.1 Preverbal subjects as CLLD phrases 201

However, the grammaticality of (28a) complicates the picture, since that example can be analyzed as having a null clitic, as in (28b). In fact, an overt partitive clitic appears in these constructions in languages like Catalan (cf. (29)). If this is correct, then the contrast between (26a) and (28a) would follow from the distinct specifications of the agreement clitic, on the one hand, and the null clitic on the other.

(28)   a. Niños, no vi esta mañana.   (Spanish)
    children not saw this morning
    'Children I didn't see this morning.'
  b. [NP$_i$ [IP $\emptyset_{CL-i}$ V ...]]

(29)   a. Nens, no n' he vist al parc.   (Catalan)
    children, not CL have seen at-the park
    'Children, I haven't seen (any) at the park.'
  b. Llibres, no en tinc.
    books, not CL have
    'Books, I don't have (any).'   (from Francisco Ordóñez, p.c.)

Note also that the counterpart of (26b) with a clitic is not grammatical, perhaps because of the definite/specific nature of the clitic, as seen in (30). However, this same explanation does not extend to the ungrammaticality of (26a), since (26b) is grammatical and the counterpart of the clitic (inflection) remains constant.

(30)   * No los vi (a) niños esta mañana.   (Spanish)
    not CL saw to children this morning
    'I didn't see children this morning.'

In conclusion, the distribution of bare NP CLLD phrases does not seem completely parallel to that of PSs, and so the stronger version of the PS-as-CLLD hypothesis is somewhat weakened.

8.1.6   Section summary

This section has reviewed several types of arguments in favor of considering PSs as CLLD phrases, including their similar scope properties, extraction asymmetries, adverb intervention facts and behavior of bare NPs and quantified CLLD phrases. Like CLLD phrases, PSs have been proposed not to reconstruct and to have wide scope, although evidence from Zubizarreta and Suñer suggest that this is not accurate for Spanish.

Regarding extraction asymmetries, wh-subjects, wh-direct objects and wh-indirect objects block extraction of another wh-phrase if they are preverbal, and PS quantified subjects have narrow scope with respect to a matrix wh-phrase. All of these facts are taken as evidence that preverbal arguments (PSs, CLLD objects and indirect objects) occupy a similar, A′-position. However, as noted, scope facts are not consistent for all quantifiers, and wh-extraction facts may be due to a different reason, namely the generalized impossibility to have embedded wh-words with verbs that do not select for questions. With respect to adverb intervention effects, an adverb can intervene between the PS and the verb in Greek and Spanish but not in French. However, it was argued that this is not a consistent behavior of all adverbs and all PSs, suggesting that at least certain PSs are not left-dislocated.

Negative quantified phrases are ungrammatical when some constituent (a CLLD phrase, a PS or certain adverbs) intervenes between them and inflection. We argued that this distribution effectively groups CLLD phrases and PSs, but only when they are negative quantifiers, hence these data do not allow us to generalize to all types of CLLD phrases and subjects.

Finally, neither bare NP can be used as a CLLD phrase or PS, but as noted, for the case of CLLD phrases, this may be due to the nature of the clitic, since dislocations that have a partitive clitic in Catalan can be bare in Spanish.

8.2   Against PS-as-CLLD

Several researchers have pointed out a number of areas in which PSs do not pattern like CLLD phrases. In this section, we will review a few of the arguments that have been given against equating both types of elements.

8.2.1   Quantified PS and CLLD phrases

Rizzi (1986b, 395) points out the following contrasts in Italian: in (31), *nessuno* 'nobody' can appear as a PS but not as a CLLD element, and the same holds of *tutto* 'everything'. Ordóñez and Treviño (1999, 52, fn. 16) argue that this contrast is a matter of incompatibility between the accusative clitic *lo* and the quantifier. They point out that dative clitics do not have this kind of restriction in Spanish, as seen in (32a). The fact that the equivalent of *tutto* 'everything' can be a CLLD phrase in Spanish (cf. (32b–c)) also suggests that each clitic's specification may be different, and this specification may constrain what can be dislocated.

(31)   a. Nessuno è   venuto.   (Italian)
           nobody has come
           'Nobody came.'

b. *Nessuno, l' ho visto.
    nobody CL have seen
    'Nobody, I've seen (him).'

c. *Tutto, lo dirò alla polizia.
    everything CL.3.SG will say to-the police
    'Everything, I will tell (it) to the police.'

(32) a. A nadie le han avisado todavía el resultado.   (Spanish)
    to nobody CL.3.SG have notified yet the result
    'They haven't notified the result to anybody.'

b. Todo lo he estudiado.'
    everything CL.3.SG have studied
    'I've studied everything.'

c. A todos los saludé ya.
    to everybody.PL CL.3.PL greeted already
    'I greeted everybody already.'

8.2.2 Discourse status of PS and CLLD phrases

Sheehan (2007, 74–77) points out that if PSs are CLLD phrases, they should have the same informational status as other CLLD phrases, but they pattern differently as possible answers to a question like *what happened?* The answer to this type of question is usually assumed to have wide focus (i.e. to be non-presupposed) (see Zubizarreta, 1998, 1–2). In European Portuguese, the answer to that question is obligatorily SV(O), according to Costa (2001), as seen in (33), and left-dislocation is not possible (cf. Rizzi, 2006, 122 for Italian).

(33) a. O que é que aconteceu?   (EP)
    the what is that happened
    'What is it that happened?'

b. O Pedro partiu o braço.
    the Pedro broke the arm
    'Pedro broke his arm.'

c. #Partiu o Pedro o braço.
    broke the Pedro the arm

d. #O braço, o Pedro partiu-o.
    the arm the Pedro broke-CL.3.SG

As Pilar Barbosa (p.c.) points out, topicalized subjects in European Portuguese can appear in a wide focus context, as illustrated in (34). The question in (34a), uttered in a context in which a mother is making a fuss about unexpected news, can be answered with (34b). Note that in this sentence, *seem* is singular, and *as crianças* 'the children' does not agree with it, so it is a topic. The contrasts between the possibility of subjects, topicalized subjects and CLLD phrases in wide focus contexts (cf. (33) vs. (34)) are somewhat surprising if subjects are CLLD phrases (and CLLD phrases all have the same interpretation).

(34)   a. O que é que aconteceu?   (EP)
          the what is that happened
          'What happened?'
        b. As crianças parece   que afinal vêm hoje.
          the children, seems.3.SG that after all come today
          'The children, it seems that they are coming today, after all.'

In Spanish and Catalan, the typical answer to wide-focus questions is also SV(O). Regarding dislocated phrases, both languages show a contrast between animate and inanimate DPs. Inanimate ones (which tend to be accusative) pattern like the EP example in (33d), but animate dative dislocations do allow for a wide focus reading, as seen in (35). So suppose that I hear a sudden scream in the next room and I ask (35a). In that context, the answers in (35b–c) with a dislocated animate phrase (dative or accusative) is perfectly acceptable, just as the non-dislocated counterparts are. However, in this same context, an inanimate accusative left-dislocated phrase is not possible, as seen in (35d).

(35)   a. ¿Qué pasó?   (Spanish)
          what happened
          'What happened?'
        b. A Marta le   dieron la noticia de su premio.
          to Marta CL.3.DAT gave   the news of her prize
          'They gave Marta the news about her prize.'
        c. A Marta la   saludó Clooney por la calle.
          to Marta CL.3.FEM.ACC greeted Clooney on the street
          'Clooney greeted Marta on the street.'
        d. #La noticia de su premio, se la   dieron a Marta.
            the news of her prize,   CL CL.3.FEM.ACC gave to Marta

In EP the corresponding examples also show an asymmetry (thanks to Pilar Barbosa, p.c.): The one corresponding to (35b) is more acceptable than the one corresponding to (35d), although neither is very good. Dislocated experiencers, on the other hand, are appropriate in this context, so (36b) is a good answer to a question like (36a) in a context in which *Maria* is yelling on the phone:

(36)   a. O que aconteceu?   (EP)
          the what happened
          'What happened?'

b. A Maria não lhe convêm que as crianças venham hoje.
the Mary not CL is convenient that the children come today
'It's not convenient for Maria that the children come today.'

Catalan seems to have a pattern similar to the one quoted for Spanish, according to Solà (1992, quoted in Barbosa, 1995, 26). Thus, both examples in (37) are possible responses to a question like *What is happening?* (thanks to Francisco Ordóñez for discussing the Catalan data).

(37)   a. A en Joan li han robat la cartera.   (Catalan)
to the Joan CL have robbed the wallet
'They have stolen Joan's wallet.'

b. Al nen l' ha mossegat una rata.
to-the child CL has bitten a rat
'A rat has bitten the child.'   (from Barbosa, 1995, 26)

These examples from Spanish, Catalan and EP suggest that animate CLLD phrases (including subjects, overtly topicalized subjects and experiencers) are compatible with a clause-wide non-presupposed interpretation, whereas inanimate CLLD phrases are not. One logical possibility would be that the incompatibility of inanimate CLLD phrases with a clause-wide non-presupposed interpretation follows from the fact that they must be necessarily presupposed, whereas the other three elements (subjects, overtly topicalized subjects and animate CLLD phrases) can be non-presupposed. To the extent that one assumes a uniform and strong analysis of PS-as-CLLD that includes the topic-like properties of CLLD phrases, these contrasts are problematic.

Arregi (2003) points out that in the context of a question like (38a), there are two possible answers, (38b) and (38c), but whereas the first answer is a complete answer to the question, the second one presupposes that the speaker gave things to other people.

(38)   a. ¿Qué le diste a Juan?   (Spanish)
what CL.3.SG gave to Juan
'What did you give to Juan?'

b. Le di un libro (a Juan).
CL.3.SG gave a book to Juan
'I gave Juan a book.'

c. A Juan, le di un libro.
to Juan CL.3.SG gave a book
'Juan, I gave him a book.'   (from Arregi, 2003, 33, ex. 6)

206   *The status of preverbal subjects in null subject languages*

On the other hand, PSs are not possible answers to a parallel type of question, as seen in (39). Thus, the answer to (39a) could be (39b) with a PS, but not (39c), with a postverbal subject (with regular, non-contrastive stress assigned to the subject). Note that (38c) contrasts with (39b) in that the first example has the presupposition just described, but the second one does not have anything similar.

(39)   a. ¿Qué le   dio Ana a Juan?   (Spanish)
          what CL.3.SG gave Ana to Juan
          'What did Ana give Juan?'

       b. Ana le   dio un libro (a Juan).
          Ana CL.3.SG gave the book to Juan
          'Ana gave him a book.'

       c. # Le   dio un libro Ana.
            CL.3.SG gave a   book Ana
          'Ana gave him a book.'

These contrasts suggest that the CLLD phrase in (38c) induces a contrastive reading (i.e. the presupposition is that no one but Juan was given a book, but the answer denies this presupposition), whereas the PS in (39b) does not induce such a reading. These differences, in turn, question whether PS and CLLD items have the same discourse properties.

8.2.3   Possible antecedents

Cardinaletti (1997, 44) notes a certain asymmetry between CLLD phrases and PSs with respect to what kind of antecedent they can pick out from the preceding clause. In (40a), the subject of the second clause (*il regista* 'the director') is left-dislocated, since it appears before a CLLD object *il premio* 'the award'. In this context, coreference with the object of the first clause *Wim Wenders* is not possible. In the second example, the subject of the second clause, *il regista* 'the director' is not dislocated, since it is adjacent to the verb, and coreference with the preceding object *Wim Wenders* is possible.

(40)   a. Ha-nno   premiato   un film su   Wim Wenders$_j$. Dopo la
          have-3.PL given a prize to a film about Wim Wenders   after the
          proiezione, il regista$_{*i/j}$, il premio, l'   ha ricevuto dal
          show   the director   the award   CL.3.SG has received from-the
          ministro.   (Italian)
          minister
          'A film about Wim Wenders$_j$ has been awarded a prize. After the show, the director$_{*i/j}$ received the prize from the Minister.'

b. Ho visto ieri alla Biennale un film su Wim Wenders$_i$.
have.1.SG seen yesterday at-the Biennale a film about Wim Wenders
Dopo la proiezione, il regista$_{i/j}$ ha ricevuto un premio alla carriera.
after the show the director has received an award to-the career
'I saw a film about Wim Wenders$_i$ yesterday at the Biennale. After the show, the director$_{i/j}$ received a prize celebrating his career.'

(from Cardinaletti, 1997, 44, exx. 42–43)

I believe the same contrast obtains in Spanish, as seen in a simplified version of (40) in (41).

(41) a. Ayer le dieron un premio a una película de Wim Wenders$_i$.
yesterday CL.3.DAT.SG gave a prize to a film of Wim Wenders.
Después de la proyección, el director$_{*i/j}$, el premio lo
After of the show, the director the award CL.3.ACC.SG
recibió del ministro. (Spanish)
received of-the minister.

'Yesterday, they awarded a prize to a film about Wim Wenders$_i$. After the show, the director$_{*i/j}$ received the award from the Minister.'

b. Ayer le dieron un premio a una película de Wim Wenders$_i$.
yesterday CL.3.DAT.SG gave a prize to a film of Wim Wenders.
Después de la proyección, el director$_{i/j}$ recibió el premio del
After of the show, the director received the award of-the
ministro.
minister.

'Yesterday, they awarded a prize to a film about Wim Wenders$_i$. After the show, the director$_{i/j}$ received the award from the Minister.'

We might try to relate this observation with Arregi's in the preceding section. In the question/answer pair, the question introduced the IO as presupposed, so dislocating the IO in the answer forced an additional interpretation where some other people were given books. Suppose that a similar situation takes place in (40a) and (41a), where by the second clause, Wim Wenders is now presuppposed. A dislocated subject that is coreferential with *Wim Wenders* would force a contrastive interpretation (i.e. something like "other directors were given other awards"), but given the definite determiners and the situation, this yields a contradictory reading ("the film's only director received the night's only award but there were other awards given to other directors"). If the subject is not dislocated, this interpretation is not forced.

8.2.4 Section summary

To summarize these sections, there seems to be clear evidence against the strong version of the PS-as-CLLD hypothesis. On the one hand, CLLD phrases show distinct properties that challenge a unified representation as dislocated topics. On the other hand, the distribution of subjects and CLLD phrases diverge in several ways that do not warrant grouping them together with CLLD phrases. The emerging picture is that PSs themselves cannot be said to occupy a single position.

8.3 The status of preverbal subjects

The discussion from preceding sections leads me to conclude that preverbal subjects are not necessarily or typically dislocated. The proposed analysis would lead us to expect just that, if as we have argued, Infl is not pronominal, and *pro* is available as a separate category. Given these results, an NSL like Italian or Spanish can have the following potential representations.

(42)   a. [*pro* Infl]
       b. [DP Infl]
       c. [DP [*pro* Infl]]

In the first one, *pro* is valued by Infl and subsequently discourse-linked by a topic. *Pro* fullfils the Subject Criterion. In (42b), on the other hand, the DP and Infl agree, but VALUATION is vacuous, because both Infl and the DP are specified, and the DP does not need a topic to link to in discourse. The data from subject NPIs in Section 8.1.4 would fall into this category: the NPI must be adjacent to Infl.[4] Finally, in (42c), *pro* is valued by Infl, discourse-linked by DP, which is dislocated.

8.4 Chapter summary

This chapter has presented the evidence for the analysis that treats subjects as CLLD phrases. We have shown that there is no conclusive evidence for a unified structural treatment of PSs either as topics, or as always occupying a dislocated position. We have reviewed evidence from the scope interactions between quantified subjects and other clausal items, and have concluded that this evidence does not support treating PSs like CLLD items. From the point

---

[4] For non-subject NPIs, I assume that they satisfy the Subject Criterion, but Infl will still license a postverbal *pro*.

of view of the discourse status, I have also suggested that PSs do not pattern like CLLD constituents, concluding that PSs may occupy different positions in the IP/CP area. This conclusion is consistent with the assumptions developed in the preceding sections, namely that the availability of *pro* and the agreement copying mechanism proposed yields two possible configurations: one where an overt DP is the true argument, and one where it acts as the antecedent for a null subject.

9 *Parametrization, learnability and acquisition*

The 1980s formulation of the NSP entailed not only a macro-parameter that divided languages into two large groups (those with and those without null subjects), but also the set of connected properties described in the preceding chapters. This formulation made clear predictions about acquisition and learnability in general. On the one hand, a macro-parameter will trigger 'cascade effects' that allow for learning multiple properties of a language when the relevant parameter is set. However, as noted in the previous chapters, the cluster of properties ascribed to the NSP does not seem to be a product of a macro-parametric setting. While this does not contradict the macro-parametric view in general, it does question whether the NSP exists as a macro-parameter.

On the other hand, the macro-parametric view leads one to expect a certain order of acquisition of the parametric properties depending on which one of them is considered more basic. If inflectional richness is the driving force for the parameter, then one would expect it to be a necessary property for the others to appear. Likewise, if the basic property is inversion, then one should find instances of it before any of the other properties are attested. Finally, if the NSP exists as a macro-parameter, what is its default, unmarked value? Will children start out assuming that languages have null subjects and then potentially reset the value depending on the input? Crucially, the default setting for the NSP interacts with general learnability principles, such as the Subset Principle (see Berwick, 1985; Manzini and Wexler, 1987; Wexler, 1994, among others), which can be informally stated as in (1). Put another way, the grammatical hypothesis a learner makes must fit the positive data in the input in the most conservative way possible.

(1)   The learner must guess the smallest possible language compatible with the input at each stage of the learning procedure (Clark and Roberts, 1993, 304–305).

Because an NSL like Quechua has both null and overt subjects, whereas English only has overt ones, the unmarked value would seem to be the overt subject grammar, because it is the minimal hypothesis compatible with the English data, and also a hypothesis that is easily falsifiable from the data a Quechua child hears. However, as we will see in the following sections, data from L1 acquisition show that children learning English systematically drop subjects.

9.1 L1 acquisition and the unmarked value of the Null Subject Parameter

Children learning English initially have null subjects, as illustrated in the following example from Bloom's (1973) CHILDES database (cf. Bloom, 1973; MacWhinney, 2000). Allison (age 2; 4) replies to her mother's question with the sentence with a null subject in (2b). During the null subject period, children also produce overt pronominal subjects.

(2)   a. Mother: What would you like to do?
       b. Allison: Want eat my snack.
        (childes.psy.cmu.edu/browser/index.php?url=Eng-USA/
        Bloom73/allison5.cha)

Null, non-target-like subjects have been reported in studies of other languages, as illustrated in (3)–(4) (cf. Pierce, 1992; Rasetti, 2000 for French; Hamann, 1996 for German; Hamann and Plunkett, 1998 for Danish, among others).

(3)   a. Ikke kore traktor.   (Danish)
        not drive tractor
        '(I, you, he) doesn't drive the tractor.'
       b. Se, blomster har.
        Look, flowers have.
        'Look, (I, you, he, she, etc.) have/s flowers.'
                    (from Hamann and Plunkett, 1998, quoted in Hyams, 2009, 16)

(4)   a. A tout tout tout mangé.   (French)
        has all all all eaten
        '(He) has eaten everything.'
       b. Oter tout ta.
        empty all that
        '(I) empty all that.'
                    (from Hamann and Plunkett, 1998, 16, quoted in Hyams, 2009, 16)

These data raise several questions: first, do children's null subjects have the same structural representation as those of adults in NSLs? If so, do they somehow represent the default or unmarked value of the parameter? If not, why do they arise and what are they? Hyams (Hyams, 1986, 1987; Jaeggli and Hyams, 1988, among others) proposed that the child's grammatical representation is adult-like (the so-called strong-continuity hypothesis) and that NSs reflect the unmarked option of the parameter. English-speaking children would subsequentlly reset the parameter after hearing overt expletives and unstressed subject pronouns in the input. Although this proposal seems counter-intuitive from the point of view of the Subset Principle (because Italian allows for more options than English), Hyams suggests that the distribution of overt expletives and modals makes the grammar of English and Italian intersecting sets, rather than subsets, therefore the principle does guide this portion of the acquisition process.

Subsequent work has suggested that the properties of child NSs (in non-NSLs) are not exactly the same as those of adult NSLs like Italian or Spanish. As Valian (1990, 115) points out, "a very young American child ... produces many more [overt, J.C.] subjects (69%) in non-imitative utterances containing verbs than Italian children of a comparable age do (30%)." Austin et al. (1996) have found similar percentages: young children (2;0.2–2;6.18) never produce more than 33% of NSs. As children grow older, overt subjects gradually increase. At the same time, children produce very few overt expletives, even when they produce overt subjects 90% of the time. In this sense, overt expletives do not seem to be a trigger to reset the NSP from the initial null-subject setting to the target overt-subject one. Furthermore, the higher frequency of overt subjects in English raises doubts about whether this reflects a true NSL language like Spanish or Quechua. Rather, Valian suggests that NSs in English are the result of processing constraints (see below).

On the other hand, it has been argued that the distribution of those NSs in child English (and other non-NSLs) is restricted to root-initial contexts: they do not appear in embedded contexts or after wh-words, suggesting that their structural representation is different from that of child and adult NSs in NSLs. In order to account for the root-initial nature of NSs, Rizzi (1993/4, 2005a, 2005c) combines the grammar-based explanations and the performance-based accounts. He proposes that "discrepancies between child and target systems are *grammar-based and performance-driven*. Certain parameters are initially set on values which facilitate the task of an immature production system" (Rizzi, 2005a, 22). In particular, Rizzi associates child NSs with 'root subject drop' (RSD), which allows a subject to be dropped in the specifier of the root. This formalizes the observation that most instances of dropped subjects in non-NSL child speech happen in clause-initial position of root clauses. Thus, they are not

9.1 L1 acquisition and the unmarked value of the Null Subject Parameter

found after clause-initial wh-words, as illustrated in (5). For example, Valian (1990, 39) only found nine NSs out of 552 non-subject wh-questions, and no NSs in early embedded clauses.

(5)   a. Where dis goes?
       b. *Where goes?   (Rizzi, 2005a)

The same observation holds for children learning other non-NSLs like early Dutch, German, Swedish and French (see Rizzi, 2005a). In French, moved wh-words contrast with in situ wh-questions, where NSs do appear (Hamman, 2000).

Root subject drop is observed in a variety of contexts in adult languages, as Rizzi (2005a) notes. For example subjects can be dropped in diary register (Haegeman, 1990) and in languages like Levantine Arabic (Kenstowicz, 1989), the Franco-Provençal patois from Gruyère (Crousaz and Shlonsky, 2003) and Corsican (Agostini, 1955). Each of those phenomena shares similar properties with subject drop in child acquisition. Some examples from Rizzi (2005a) are presented in (6)–(7). Diary register, illustrated in (6), shows dropped subjects that have been argued to be constrained to the root. In this sentence, for example, the root subject is dropped, whereas the embedded clause subject is overt (*je* 'I'). Example (7) illustrates the same root constraint in a different setting: NSs can be generally dropped root-initially in Levantine Arabic (cf. (7a)), but not in embedded contexts, as in (7b), where the overt subject (*ha* 'she') is required.

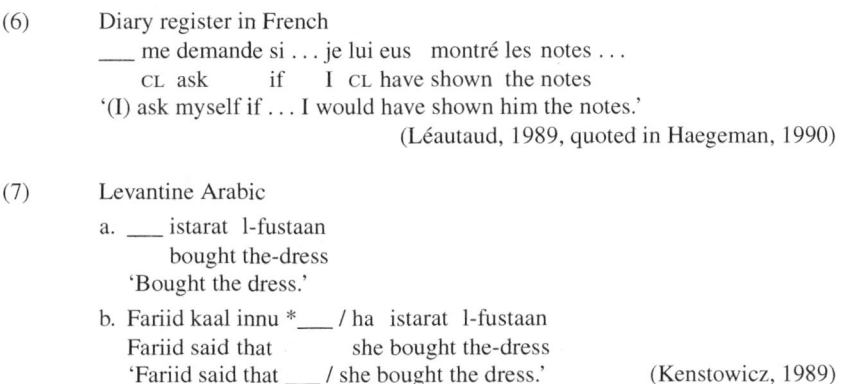

These examples show that RSD, as well as other phenomena that leave the specifier of the root projection null, are available as options in adult grammars. Rizzi argues that child acquisition may adopt these kinds of strategies to decrease processing load. In this view, RSD competes and initially supersedes the Subset Principle, allowing the child to temporarily adopt a grammar that is the superset of the target one. As the child matures, the Subset Principle gradually takes over, inducing a resetting of the inconsistent parameter.[1]

In Rizzi's analysis, RSD crucially depends on the notion of clausal truncation (Rizzi, 1993/4), a process by which part of the clausal structure may be missing. Assuming his own articulated representation of the left periphery from Rizzi (1997), Rizzi (2005a) proposes that clausal structure can be truncated at any of the different levels in (8), yielding a variety of root-drop phenomena such as the ones we have just described for both child and adult grammars.

(8)   [$_{ForceP}$ ... [$_{TopP}$ ... [$_{FocP}$ ... [$_{FinP}$ ... [$_{AgrSP}$ ... [$_{TP}$ ...]]]]]]

Clause truncation provides a template for where elision can take place. In the case of the RSD phenomena illustrated earlier, elision would result from truncating the clause at AgrSP. However, subject drop specifically results from a principle that targets the Spec of the highest available projection (the root) for deletion. In Rizzi's (2005a) analysis, this Spec can be targeted because roots are phases (in Chomsky's (2001) sense), and the edge of the phase is not spelled out when the rest of the phase is.[2]

Several researchers (Bloom, 1990, 1993; Valian, 1990; Aronoff, 2003, among others) have suggested that child NSs in non-NSLs are strictly the result of processing limitations. Bloom (1990) notes that VPs are significantly shorter for clauses with overt subjects than for clauses without them, suggesting that omission of subjects may be connected with overall processing complexity. However, Hyams and Wexler (1993) found that the same difference in VP length can be observed in adult Italian speakers, which points to the conclusion that VP length may be orthogonal to the child/adult difference. Bloom also points out that Hyams's (1987) observation that NSs are much more frequent than null objects in child English can be due to their different pragmatic value: if subjects tend to be old information, it makes more sense to omit them when processing limitations exist.

---

[1] As Hyams (2009) points out, this view raises the issue of how RSD reappears in adult grammars, if it is superseded by the Subset Principle.

[2] It isn't completely obvious from this proposal why only root structures are targeted, since embedded phases would display the same structural requirements that allow for deletion of the edge of the strong phase after spell-out of that strong phase. Clearly, RSD falls under a much larger set of root-embedded clause asymmetries that Ross (1973) has exquisitely named the Penthouse Principle.

9.1 L1 acquisition and the unmarked value of the Null Subject Parameter

In support of the processing account, Aronoff (2003) notes that the rate of subject and the rate of verb omissions are highly correlated both for children acquiring English and for the adult speakers in the same CHILDES corpora. This statistical correlation argues in favor of a processing account for two reasons. On the one hand, NSs and null verbs in adults cannot be the result of a representational deficit (in the sense that their 'parameters' are not set), on the other hand, the representational-deficit accounts of NSs do not usually explain why verbs would also be null. By contrast, if subjects and verbs are null for processing reasons in adults, it follows that this explanation may better fit the children data as well.

While these patterns are relevant and interesting, it would be useful to have a better idea about the distribution of null verbs in Aronoff's (2003) data. If Rizzi is correct in thinking that children display a non-target-like behavior in areas where adult grammars also allow for these options, one such area involves drop of copular verbs, which is cross-linguistically frequent, including in dialects of English. In this sense, the three examples of null verbs that the paper provides are given in (9), and they all involve copular verbs.[3] As Becker (2000, 2004) points out, English children drop the copula much more frequently when the predicate is a locative than when it is a nominal predicate.

(9)   a. You car.
         b. You having a hard time?
         c. Mommy happy.

These data would seem to strengthen the case for a combined processing + structural truncation proposal: processing constraints drive overall reduction of overt grammatical categories, but the location of the deletion target is highly constrained by grammatical representation, frequently mirrored in the grammar of adult speakers. In this sense, children acquiring Spanish have few instances of copula drop and they produce few non-target-like uses of the distinction between the two copulas *ser* and *estar* (see Liceras *et al.*, 2012, 92). If children are deleting material to decrease processing load, one would expect this type of strategy to be available across languages.

9.1.1   Morphological richness and null subject acquisition

Acquisition studies of Spanish, Italian or Catalan show that children master the distribution of NSs from early on, in what looks like an adult-like distribution.

---

[3] Other examples are present in the coding section, but it is not clear whether they represent attested data.

In Bel's (2003) study of the acquisition of Spanish and Catalan, she found NSs ranging from 58% to 72% of the time for four Spanish-speaking children and four Catalan-speaking children. As she notes, these percentages are comparable to the frequency for adult speakers of both languages.[4] However, children display certain uses that are not adult-like. On the one hand, they have root infinitives (RIs), and on the other, subjects with RIs are overwhelmingly null (see also Liceras *et al.*, 1999). Regarding the frequency of RIs, Bel (2003, 13) quotes 189 RIs in the files of six children from Bel (2001) out of 2018 constructions with finite or infinitival verbs (9.3%), and of the 189 RIs, 181 had NSs (95.7%).

Bel extends Rizzi's (1993/4) Truncation Hypothesis to Spanish and Catalan, assuming that RIs reflect a truncated structure at the level of TP. Because neither AgrP nor TP are projected, we should not expect overt subjects (since Agr/T are crucial in licensing overt subjects). However, given that inflection is missing, one would also not expect NS *pro*, so, consistent with Rizzi's initial analysis, these NSs are null constants ([-pronominal, -anaphoric, -variable]) similar to those of Chinese (cf. Li's 2007 Totally Empty Position, presented in Section 6.4.1).

The process of acquisition of NSs has also been analyzed in languages with a complex inflectional paradigm, such as Quechua. In this language, the verb potentially incorporates many suffixes, as seen in (10). Not only is this template highly variable (in terms of which suffixes appear with a root in any given instance), but the sequencing can be variable (cf. Courtney, 1998, 59 and Muysken, 1986).

(10) Yacha -chi -wa -sha -rqa -n -ku -pis. (Quechua)
learn -CAUS -1.OBJ -PROG -PAST -3.SUBJ -PL -ADD
'They were teaching it to me, too.' (from Courtney, 1998, 59)

Courtney (1998) recorded the acquisition of Quechua by six children starting at different points in time (2;0, 2;5, 2;10, 3;0, 3;2 and 3;7). Her report for three of these children (pp. 102–106) indicate that they produce all six possible word orders of subject, verb and different types of complements, suggesting that whatever drives word order (Courtney suggests it may be case-marking) is

---

[4] Bel notes that the longitudinal development for two of the girls show opposite patterns: María, who is acquiring Spanish, starts with only 26.1% of NSs at 1;7 and reaches 74% at 1;10, whereas Júlia, who is acquiring Catalan, starts with 92.8% of NSs at 1;11 and decreases to 73.5% at 2;2.11. Importantly, the development of NSs does not track length of the utterance (MLUw), arguing against a processing explanation that connects the availability of NSs to lack of segmental space for overt subjects.

9.1 L1 acquisition and the unmarked value of the Null Subject Parameter 217

present fairly early. However, overt subjects are initially much more frequent than those of adults. During the earliest sessions (2;5–2;6), JN produced 85% overt subjects, compared to 38% for adults. For the other two children, they are somewhat lower, but still higher than adults (BT, 3;10–3;11: 51% and FE, 3;2–3;5: 47%). In the case of JN, the percentage of overt subjects decreases to 50% by 2;9–2;10. Note that these percentages are much higher than the averages reported by Bel (2001) above; however, recall that one of her children initially had very high percentages of overt subjects.

Interestingly, the period of most intense production of overt subjects also coincides with non-target-like production of inflectional person morphology. In fact, JN produced 89 verbs at ages 2;5–2;6, out of which 24 were bare roots (37%), which are not possible in adult grammars. Of the 89 verb total, only 46 (52%) were marked for 3rd person singular inflection, whereas no verbs were inflected for 2nd person and only one for 1st person (see Courtney, 1998, 178).[5] Additionally, this child seems to be generalizing the 1st person future suffix /-saq/ as a 1st person marker. Person marking is obligatory in adult grammars, and plural marking is only optional for 3rd person plural.

During that same period, JN produced many more overt pronominal subjects than adults (see Courtney, 1998, 105–06). For example, out of JN's total 1st and 2nd person utterances (44), 38 had an overt pronoun (86%); 41% of those subjects coincided with incomplete person morphology on the verb, as illustrated in (11). In the adult grammar, the verb would appear as *muna-ni* want-1.SG 'I want', and an overt pronoun is usually left-peripheral and/or contrastive (thanks to Liliana Sánchez, p.c. for discussion). For adults, only 16% of utterances with 1st and 2nd person subjects involved overt pronouns in Courtney's data.

(11) Carru-ta muna noqa. (Quechua)
car-ACC want 1.SG
'I want the car.' (from Courtney, 1998, 105)

If we take absence of person morphology to reflect some kind of bare infinitival stage, this pattern seems to contradict what has been observed for non-NSLs like French, Dutch, English and German, where RIs tend to go with NSs (see Kramer, 1993; Rizzi, 1993/4; Hyams, 1996, among others), and challenges Wexler's (1994, 1998) implication that *pro*-drop entails non-optional infinitives, as others have also done (cf. Liceras *et al.*, 1999; Ezeizabarrena, 2003).

---

[5] Presumably, 18 verbs had some suffix (i.e. were not bare roots) but not person marking, if I am interpreting these percentages correctly.

At age 2;7–2;8, JN's overt 1st and 2nd person pronouns had been reduced to 23% of the 1st and 2nd person utterances (17/73), and by 2;9–2;10 they were down to 20% (14/69). Another one of the children, whose data ranges from 3;2 to 3;5, showed only 11% overt 1st and 2nd person pronouns.

During the initial recorded file, JN also showed large percentage of subject-final utterances (see Courtney, 1998, 103–104). Specifically, from 2;5 to 2;6 47 (34%) of the utterances were subject-final. If we only take into account those utterances with overt subjects, then the percentage is 42.3%. By age 2;9–2;10, utterance-final subjects were down to 15 (14%) of utterances, and to 28.8% of utterances with overt subjects. By contrast, adults only had 10% of subject-final utterances, or 26.4% of utterances with overt subjects. Final subjects represent a marked word order in Quechua, since SOV is the unmarked order.

To summarize, the acquisition of Quechua presents several interesting features. First, availability of NSs depends on the availability of inflectional morphology, more specifically, of person morphology. The same finding has been reported for the acquisition of Hebrew (Levy and Vainikka, 2000), where by age 2, children show both evidence of inflection and mastery of the mixed NS system. Second, absent inflectional morphology, many overt subjects are utterance-final.[6]

It is worth comparing the acquisition of Quechua with the acquisition of Basque, another language that has a fairly rich inflectional system, tracking all possible arguments on verbs. Like Quechua, Basque shows a fairly large percentage of root infinitives, which Ezeizabarrena (2003, 90–91) classifies either as RIs compatible with the adult grammar or as *RIs that are not possible in the adult grammar, as illustrated in (12). This *RI was produced in the absence of any discourse that would license it. In the first example, the future morpheme *ko* and the auxiliary *dut* are absent, and this example could only be interpreted as an imperative in the adult language. The corresponding adult example would be (12b).

(12)   a. Bota hemen   (Child Basque)
            throw here
            '(I will) throw (it) here'   (adapted from Ezeizabarrena, 2003, 92, ex. 8a)
       b. Bota-ko   dut   hemen   (Adult Basque)
            throw-FUT AUX.1SG here
            'I will throw it here.'   (from Estibaliz Amorrortu, p.c.)

---

[6] Déprez and Pierce (1993, 42) also observe postverbal lexical subjects in child French, a language that tends to be rigidly SV in adult speech. The four children acquiring French in their study produced anywhere from 65% to 85% of postverbal lexical subjects. In their analysis, this follows from the fact that S does not raise from the VP-internal position to Spec, IP.

9.1 L1 acquisition and the unmarked value of the Null Subject Parameter

The three children who she analyzes (two bilinguals and one monolingual) show between 20.5% and 38.6% of *RIs over total verbs in the first stage of acquisition (when the first verbs appear). These *RIs significantly decrease in stages II (evidence of subject verb agreement morphology) and III (evidence of verb agreement morphology with two arguments), ranging from 3.2% to 13.1% in stage III.

As Ezeizabarrena (2003, 95) points out, NSs are very frequent in Mikel's corpus (the bilingual child that she analyzes in detail), and they appear with finite and non-finite verbs, as well as with *RIs. Null subjects with finite verbs appear an average of 64.5% of the time (range 40–84%), NSs with infinitivals are more frequent (90.4%, range 50–100%) and NSs with *RIs appear on average 83.7% (range 33–100%). Because the frequency of overt subjects with *RIs is closer to that of overt subjects with finite verbs, Ezeizabarrena concludes that *RIs are finite verbs with null inflection that are subject to a processing deletion strategy.

It is unclear whether RIs in Quechua and Basque can be analyzed as a case of clausal truncation, as proposed by Rizzi and Bel among others. Recall that both of those proposals assume that most root infinitives involve NSs, which, according to Rizzi, are null constants. However, as we have just seen, both Basque and Quechua have overt subjects with RIs, suggesting that the relevant functional projections are present. Furthermore, the verbal root in Quechua can appear with other, lower suffixes, such as progressive aspect *sha* in (13b).

(13) a. Mankakuna ka-n-chu? (Quechua)
         pots   be-3.SG-Q
         'Are there pots?'
      b. ka-sha   ma(n)kakuna.
         be-PROG pots
         'There are pots.' (from Courtney, 1998, 265)

One possibility is that Quechua and Basque have different analyses. In Quechua, children do seem to be acquiring the inflectional paradigm, since they have frequent agreement mismatches and extensions of 1st person future inflectional morphology beyond future contexts. Furthermore, Quechua children have a preference for utterance-final subjects. Sánchez (2010) has proposed that the right periphery in Quechua is where ambiguous discourse-referents are disambiguated. Thus, a child learning Quechua would initially lack a fully developed representation for inflectional features, and only in those cases where inflection is available would NSs be properly identified. In other cases where inflection is missing, she could resort to an overt pronoun instead of the NS, since overt pronouns seem initially to be in complementary distribution with NSs. Finally, utterance-final lexical subjects may be a strategy independently available in the adult grammar to identify NSs whenever the NS is not properly identified by inflection. In this sense, the overt subject would serve as the discourse antecedent for the referent of the NS, as illustrated in the following exchange, where the child's answer lacks the proper inflectional morphology on the verb and therefore resorts to an overt, utterance-final pronoun.

(14)   a. Mana-chu ati-nki? (Quechua)
           NEG-Q   can-2.SG
           'Can't you (go)?'

       b. Mana ati noqa.
           NEG can 1.SG
           'I can't.' (from Courtney, 1998, 265)

What unifies the development paths of these languages is the idea that processing builds on top of existing representations that are available in the adult grammar. In the case of English, if Rizzi is right, these strategies are connected to adult diary-drop; in the case of Basque, to RIs consistent with the adult grammar, and in the case of Quechua, to the productive use of the right periphery to disambiguate discourse referents.

From a wider perspective, Quechua shows a clear instance in which inflection licenses NSs in a very direct way: if inflection is present, *pro* is possible, if it is absent, then *pro* can be licensed discoursively through the right-dislocated lexical subject.

9.2   Null subjects in early bilinguals and in L2 acquisition

Bilingual and L2 acquisition of NSs provide us with interesting perspectives not only on overall aspects of the NSP but also on the issue of learnability. For example, Liceras *et al.*'s (2012) study of two bilingual (English–Spanish) twins has shown that they have very different development trajectories for NSs in each language. On the one hand, these children have null subjects in both languages, illustrated in (15)–(16), just like their monolingual counterparts.

(15)   a. No puedo subir (Leo, 2;05, Spanish)
           not can.1.SG go-up
           '(I) cannot go upstairs.'

	b.	Ahora hacemos esto	(Simon, 3;00, Spanish)
		now do.3.SG this	
		'Now (we) do that.'	
(16)	a.	Roars	(Simon, 2;05)
		'It roars.'	
	b.	Falled	(Simon, 2;06)
		'I fell.'	
	c.	Chased	(Leo, 2;06)
		'He chased.'	

However, whereas Spanish overt subject production goes from 16% to 26.4% to 27.1% in the three stages the authors have identified according to their MLU, English overt subjects go from 32% to 95.5% and remain at 95%. In other words, the production of English overt subjects is initially much more frequent than that of NSL acquirers and shifts very quickly and drastically. This development path mirrors that of English monolingual children. The Spanish development, on the other hand, mirrors that of Spanish monolinguals: a large percentage of NSs that only decreases slightly. Furthermore, for English, the decrease in NSs correlates with the increase in overt pronominals, whereas in Spanish, the ratio of NSs to overt pronominals remains fairly stable across the three stages, like for corresponding monolinguals (cf. Liceras *et al.*, 2012 and Bel, 2001). Both twins acquire inflection early in Spanish, so that the rate of omission of the inflectional information on the verb at stage I is only 4.28% (Liceras *et al.*, 2008).

As Liceras *et al.* (2008) point out, the fact that the development of subjects in the two languages follows distinct paths and shows different distribution patterns does not seem consistent with an explanation based on processing, since processing loads should uniformly decrease across the two grammars, but the rates at which NSs change are not comparable. Furthermore, the fact that overt pronouns increase as NSs decrease only in English also seems to favor a competence account. In fact, if both grammars were constrained by processing in the same way, we would expect a substantial increase in overt subjects in Spanish, since they are subject to pragmatic constraints, which are acquired later.

Liceras *et al.* (2008, 2012) account for the difference in early target convergence for Spanish vs. English by assuming Alexiadou and Anagnostopoulou's (1998) account that inflection satisfies the EPP in Spanish by head movement, whereas English requires movement of an overt DP to the specifier of IP. Furthermore, they argue that head movement is a less costly operation, hence the default or unmarked option, whereas movement to the specifier is a marked option.

Turning now to research on the acquisition of NSs in L2, there have been many studies with different pairs of languages (see White, 1985; Liceras, 1989; Al-Kasey and Perez-Leroux, 1998; Perez-Leroux and Glass, 1999; Park, 2004, among others, and LaFond, 2001 for an overview). Much of this research has attempted to apply the theoretical frameworks proposed for monolingual syntax, or to extend the L1 acquisition work to L2. From the point of view of the contribution to the general debate on the status of NSs, the most interesting results are the following (see LaFond, 2001, 115, among others):

(17)   a. Null subjects are acquired early by L2 speakers of a non-NSL L1 (Phinney, 1987; Liceras and Diaz, 1999).

         b. Learners initially overgenerate overt pronouns, although they may be able to detect the ungrammaticality of the overgenerated pronouns (Fleming, 1977; Liceras, 1988; Al-Kasey and Perez-Leroux, 1998).

         c. Not all of the alleged properties of the NSP are acquired at the same time. NS > inversion > *that*-trace (Liceras, 1989; Belletti and Leonini, 2004).

         d. Mastery of the discourse constraints for L2 NSs appears late and is gradual (Perez-Leroux and Glass, 1999; Sánchez *et al.*, 2010; Zhao, 2011).

         e. Patterns of acquisition are systematic and related to the influence of the L1.

Properties (17c–d) are particularly relevant for the overall conception of the NSP. Property (17c) suggests that the different properties associated with the NSP do not appear simultaneously in the process of acquisition. Liceras (1988), for example, notes that French and English learners of L2 Spanish show no correlation between acquiring the inflectional properties of Spanish and other NSP properties like inversion, *that*-trace effects or optional/obligatory subjects. Even advanced learners do not seem to have a clear mastery of the conventions related to stylistic inversion. In fact, according to Liceras (1989), some postverbal subjects seem to be interpreted as objects, which may suggest that the acquisition of inversion is linked to the acquisition of the differential object marker *a*.

Belletti and Leonini (2004) have found converging results, noting that L2 learners of Italian do not properly acquire VS word order. In this case, the participants had German as L1 and produced VS word orders 27% of the time, vs. 98% for monolingual controls (in the relevant contexts). By contrast, the German L1 group produced NSs 55% of the time (vs. 95% for monolinguals). If the primary property of the NSP is the availability of inversion, these speakers seem to be able to recognize NSs much more frequently than their ability to produce VS orders.[7]

For Spanish L2 learners (with English as L1), LaFond (2001, 162–166) reports that inversion was very low in contexts without focus on any particular item, so beginners inverted 16% of the time, intermediates 10%, advanced 14%, near-natives 22% and natives 5%. In items with contrastive focus, on the other hand, inversion was higher across the board (24%, 15%, 28%, 53% and 36% respectively), but low enough to argue that contrastive focus does not trigger obligatory inversion in Spanish (unlike in Italian).[8]

LaFond (2001, 158–172) also found that learners accept NSs early (58% of the time for beginners), a result that is partially consistent with the pattern observed for L1 acquisition. However, unlike natives, L2 learners did not choose NSs as often as previous research has found. Additionally, only when they achieve advanced level do they drop topic-connected subjects like natives, a result that mirrors what others have found for Italian L2 (see Sorace, 2005) and Italian early bilinguals (see Serratrice, 2005). Early learners and intermediates also drop non-topic subjects, in a way that does not resemble the monolingual English or Spanish pattern (unlike results for other languages like Italian; see Sorace, 2005).

Regarding *that*-trace effects, LaFond (2001, 167–172) found that native Spanish speakers and near-native Spanish L2 learners overwhelmingly preferred overt *que* 'that' (91% and 86% of the time respectively), in contexts of an embedded NS. In that same context, beginners included the complementizer only 46% of the time, intermediates 56% and advanced speakers 70%.

---

[7] I am assuming that L2 acquisition is constrained by the same principles as L1 acquisition. If that is not the case, then L2 can contribute very little to the overall discussion about parameters. However, the fact that L2 research has repeatedly shown results that are consistent with parameters of variation within natural languages suggests similar constraints between L1 and L2 acquisition, even if modulated by the fact that adult L2 learners already have an L1, and other potential differences.

[8] There are some questions about the methodology of this study, however. For example, one of the items quoted (LaFond, 2001, 165, no. 4) presents a choice between (i) with inversion and a stressed overt pronoun and (ii) with an NS. However (ii) is not a possible choice regardless of inversion, because the contrastive nature of that example requires stress on the subject, so a NS would be ungrammatical for indepedent reasons.

(i) ¡No! tienes que limpiarla tú, no yo.
    no have to clean.CL you, not I

(ii) ¡No! tienes que limpiarla, no yo.
    no, have to clean.CL, not I
    'No, you have to clean it, not me.'

Statistically, L2 learners achieve monolingual-like results only when they are near-natives.[9]

All of these results seem to suggest that L2 learners have more difficulty with properties that relate syntactic operations to discourse-related information. Sorace (2005) suggests that this "residual transfer" is connected to the additional processing cost of linking two separate modules of the linguistic faculty, as opposed to the lower cost of applying only core-syntactic principles. If this view is correct, acquisition of discourse-pragmatic properties may crucially differentiate L1 and L2 acquisition, since as we have seen, L1 learners seem to acquire the pragmatic contrasts associated with the null/overt distinction in Spanish and Italian, whereas in English, null and overt pronouns are in complementary distribution throughout development. In the L2, on the other hand, pragmatic constraints are subject to residual transfer. Recall, however, that the L1 results are somewhat tempered by the acquisition patterns observed for Quechua children, who do not seem to be sensitive to the pragmatic correlates of overt pronominals in the initial stages of their acquisition.

In any case, the fact that L2 acquisition is sensitive pragmatic distinctions suggests that the original conception of parametric variation as clustering of properties may have conflated two or perhaps more different parametric settings, some of them may be related to syntactic properties (identification of NSs by inflection, criterial freezing, etc.), whereas others may be connected to interfaces between syntax and other components, such as the lexicon, discourse processing, etc.

To summarize, the L1, bilingual and L2 acquisition research on NSs leads to the following conclusions:

(18)   a. NSs are developmentally related to inflection in inflection-identified NSLs.
       b. Children acquiring an NSL tend to acquire it early.
       c. Children learning non-NSLs have NSLs with a different distribution than that seen in NSL acquisition.
       d. Acquisition of NSs in some NSLs as well as in non-NSLs suggests that representations are constrained by processing, with deletion of overt forms wherever possible.
       e. L1 and L2 acquisition patterns do not support clustering of properties around the NSP.

---

[9] Some of the examples of *that*-trace sentences involve wh-questions and others simple embedded declaratives with or without *que* 'that', but it is not clear from the text whether they were mixed in the same tasks or whether they were differentiated by tasks, so it is possible that these results are not conclusive.

9.3 Development of null subjects

Levy and Vainikka (2000, 381) observe that "[t]he apparent ease with which the complex mixed system is acquired suggests that the mechanisms involved are very basic," a conclusion also supported by the Quechua data, and by the acquisition of other NSL systems licensed by inflection. Thus, children learning Catalan, European Portuguese, Italian and Spanish have been reported to show a similar distribution and frequency of NSs as adult speakers of those languages, as do children acquiring discourse-identified NSLs such as Chinese or Korean (Hyams, 2009). On the other hand, certain studies have reported higher rates of NSs for children acquiring Italian (70% vs. 50%; see Valian, 1990) and European Portuguese (see Valian and Eisenberg, 1996) than the adult speakers of those languages. Likewise, Cabré Sans and Gavarró (2006) quoted similar patterns for Catalan-speaking children and adults, but Grinstead (2004) found much larger proportions of NSs for children.

These diverging results could be the product of different methodologies, or different stages in the acquisition process, but another possibility would be that they reflect different acquisition strategies. Pursuing the analysis I have advanced, the acquisition paths are the following: children must first acquire the inflectional paradigm, which entails mastering the hierarchical properties described in Section 5.2 (see below). Additionally, children must determine the Minimal Morphological Threshold (MMT) for the input they receive, and establish when NSs are possible in that grammar. This process is guided by the general principle that NSs must be identified (i.e. their ϕ-features must be valued), as described in Section 5.4, and it is constrained by the Subset Principle.

The acquisition of the grammar of NSs interacts with a separate acquisition strategy, namely reducing processing load, a process that dovetails existing grammatical options in the adult language. As a result, children learning English or French will truncate syntactic structure and delete the specifier of the root taking advantage of existing grammatical options instantiated in diary-drop, for example. Quechua children will have NSs not identified by inflection in contexts where they are identified by an overt DP in the right periphery, an independently available option in the adult grammar, used to disambiguate discourse referents. Basque children, on the other hand, seem to delete inflectional material in PF, in what looks like a RI, but through a strategy that is also available in the adult grammar.

Why do different studies report different frequencies of NSs in languages like Italian or Catalan? As mentioned above, it could be a consequence of different methodologies. However, it is also possible that children apply different strategies. We should note that, as Hyams (2009) points out, children show awareness of the principles that regulate information structure, in particular, that they are more likely to drop arguments that are more prominent in discourse (see Clancy, 1993, 1997 for Korean children; Allen, 2000 for Inuktitut children; Serratrice and Sorace, 2003 for Italian). On the other hand, this sensitivity to discourse prominence interacts with how each language divides labor between overt and null subjects. Thus, although Caribbean varieties of Spanish are NSLs, they have a higher frequency of overt subject pronouns than other varieties. Likewise, the discourse distributions of NSs in Italian and Spanish are not identical. This means that input frequencies, discourse roles of overt and null subjects and processing strategies may be weighed differently by individual children, resulting in slightly distinct paths to acquisition. The fact that interface constraints may be a source of individual variation in L1 should not be a surprise, since they seem to be a systematic source of variation and transfer in L2 acquisition, as mentioned earlier.

9.3.1 Learnability of ϕ-features

The proposed analysis of NSs relies on the notion of MMT, which operates on a scale of ϕ-features (see (11) in Section 5.1). I have also argued that this scale reflects regularities that are best treated as the result of a hierarchical structure of ϕ-features. As a result, each grammar sets the complexity of the feature structure to a different level (the MMT). This level, in turn, is indirectly reflected in the morphology. Thus, inflection (and possibly pronominal forms) will mark at least those nodes in the ϕ-feature hierarchy that the MMT includes, but it is certainly possible that ϕ-feature hierarchies specify more nodes than the MMT, as we saw for gender in Arabic, Hindi and Spanish adjectives in Section 5.4.

This situation raises the issue of how these aspects of the grammar are acquired, specifically does a child learning an L1 have enough evidence in the input to determine the MMT, and, does she have enough evidence to acquire the specific ϕ-feature hierarchy for that language.

The evidence for fixing the MMT seems to be transparent in most cases. Assuming that the acquisition process is guided by the Subset Principle and possibly additional acquisition strategies connected to processing (truncation, etc.), as discussed in Section 9.1, a learner would assume the lowest MMT by default, and adjust the hypothesis when they process data that are not compatible with the hypothesis. Specifically, if the learner encounters an NS in a sentence whose verb has inflection specified for PERSON, the learner will assume that the MMT for that language is at least PERSON. In the case of a language like English, no positive evidence changes the initial setting of the MMT, hence the result is a non-NS grammar. As we have already discussed, NSs in child English seem to be the result of structural truncation.

Regarding the second question, namely whether there is positive evidence to acquire ϕ-feature hierarchies specific to a given grammar, since ϕ-feature hierarchies are reflected in the morphology of the language, those morphemes provide positive evidence. In effect, acquisition becomes a matter of mapping structural hierarchies to specific morphemes. A more complicated issue relates to whether the actual ϕ-feature hierarchy must be postulated as a universal, innate template, or whether it is learnable from positive input. On the one hand, researchers like Baker (1985) have suggested a correspondence between morpheme order and hierarchical structure (the Mirror Principle). To the extent that this kind of principle is available, the child could draw overt evidence from morpheme orders to establish ϕ-feature hierarchies. On the other hand, some of these morpheme orderings are also manifested in typological tendencies, which would suggest a common template for both.

9.4 General conclusions

This book started out by looking at the cluster of properties associated with the NSP, namely having null subjects and null expletives, having free inversion in simple sentences, availability of 'long wh-movement' of subjects, availability of empty resumptive pronouns in embedded clauses, presence of overt complementizers in *that*-trace contexts and interpretive differences between null and overt pronouns. Additionally, I considered whether and how rich inflection can be formalized as a basic property of NS languages. In the background of this discussion lies the question of whether the NSP is a macro-parameter or a set of micro-parameters (or a combination of both). After reviewing evidence from several languages, I concluded that none of the correlations initially thought to cluster around the NSP are direct. Essentially, the NSP should be seen as a constellation of several micro-parameters: availability of ϕ-feature geometries that satisfy a language-particular Minimal Morphological Threshold for identifying NSs, locality constraints to assess the MMT, AGREE as an operation that values unvalued matrices, the Subject Criterion, criterial freezing and a series of alignment constraints for the EPP.

ϕ-feature geometries in conjunction with the MMT determine whether NSs will be possible or not, distinguishing languages that require more or less morphological information to allow for NSs. Formally, the ϕ-feature values of inflection will be copied onto an NS, and if the information complies with the MMT, NSs will be locally identified. Otherwise, they must be identified by an antecedent in discourse. The Subject Criterion requires a certain category to appear in the Spec of IP or a CP-related projection, depending on the language. Once that category moves to Spec, IP, it is frozen, giving rise to several types of subject–object asymmetries (so-called *that*-trace effects). However, these asymmetries can be bypassed in different ways depending on the language; for example, agreement on C is one available strategy, having a null expletive to satisfy the Subject Criterion is another way to bypass the freezing effect.

Finally, the Subject Criterion is best viewed as a conspiracy of two microparameters that are ranked constraints, namely one that requires a DP to be aligned with the edge of the Subject projection, and another that requires any XP to be aligned with the edge of the Topic projection. In some cases, these two constraints may be satisfied by the same item (namely, a subject DP), but in other cases, complying with Topic alignment is ranked higher (topic-prominent languages) and in others complying with Subject alignment is ranked higher (subject-prominent languages).

References

Abney, S., 1987. The English Noun Phrase in its Sentential Aspect. Ph.D. thesis. MIT.
Agostini, P.M., 1955. *L'usu di a nostra lingua*. Edizioni Scola Corsa, Bastia.
Al-Kasey, T., Perez-Leroux, A.T., 1998. Second language acquisition of Spanish null subjects, in: Flynn, S., Martohardjono, G., O'Neil, W. (eds.), *The Generative Study of Second Language Acquisition*. Lawrence Erlbaum, Mahwah, NJ, pp. 161–185. Database Name: CSA Linguistics and Language Behavior Abstracts.
Alexiadou, A., Anagnostopoulou, E., 1998. Parametrizing AGR: word order, v-movement and EPP-checking. *Natural Language and Linguistic Theory* **16**, 491–539.
Allen, S., 2000. A discourse-pragmatic explanation for argument representation in child Inuktitut. *Linguistics* **38**, 483–521.
Altmann, H., 1984. Das System der enklitischen Personalpronomina in einer mittelbairischen Mundart. *Zeitschrift für Dialektologie und Linguistik* **51**, 191–211.
Aronoff, J., 2003. Null subjects in child language: evidence for a performance account, in: Garding, G., Tsujimura, M. (eds.), *Proceedings of the 22nd West Coast Conference on Formal Linguistics*. Cascadilla Press, Somerville, MA, pp. 43–55.
Arregi, K., 2003. Clitic left dislocation is contrastive topicalization. *Penn Working Papers in Linguistics* **9**, 31–44.
Austin, J., Blume, M., Lust, B., Núñez del Prado, Z., Parkinson, D., Proman, R., 1996. Current challenges to the parameter-setting paradigm: the pro-drop parameter, in: Koster, C., Wijnen, F. (eds.), *Proceedings of the Groningen Assembly on Language Acquisition*, held at the University of Groningen, 7–9 September 1995. Centre for Language and Cognition, Groningen, pp. 87–96.
Baker, M., 1985. The Mirror Principle and morphosyntactic explanation. *Linguistic Inquiry* **16**, 373–416.
2008a. The macroparameter in a microparametric world, in: Biberauer, T. (ed.), *The Limits of Syntactic Variation*. Benjamins, Amsterdam, pp. 351–374.
2008b. *The Syntax of Agreement and Concord*. Cambridge University Press, Cambridge, UK.
Barbosa, P., 1995. Null Subjects. Ph.D. thesis. MIT.
2009. Two kinds of subject pro. *Studia Linguistica* **63**, 2–58.
2010. Partial *pro*-drop as null NP-anaphora. Presented at *NELS 41*, UPenn, 2010 and Romania Nova, Campos do Jordão, 2011.
Barbosa, P., Kato, M., Duarte, M.E., 2005. Null subjects in European and Brasilian Portuguese. *Journal of Portuguese Linguistics* **4**, 11–52.

Bayer, J., 1984. Comp in Bavarian syntax. *The Linguistic Review* **3**, 209–274.
   1999. Comments on Cardinaletti and Starke "The typology of structural deficiency", in: van Riemsdijk, H. (ed.), *Clitics in the Languages of Europe*. Mouton de Gruyter, Berlin, pp. 235–242.
Becker, M., 2000. The Development of Copula in Child English: The Lightness of Be. Ph.D. thesis. University of California, Los Angeles.
   2004. Copula omission is a grammatical reflex. *Language Acquisition* **12**, 157–167.
Béjar, S., 2003. Phi-Syntax: A Theory of Agreement. Ph.D. thesis. University of Toronto.
Béjar, S., Rezac, M., 2009. Cyclic agree. *Linguistic Inquiry* **40**, 35–73.
Bel, A., 2001. *Teoria lingüística i adquisició del llenguatge. Anàlisi comparada dels trets morfològics em català i en castellà*. Institut d'Estudis Catalans, Barcelona.
   2003. The syntax of subjects in the acquisition of Spanish and Catalan. *Probus* **15**, 1–26.
Belletti, A., 1990. *Generalized Verb Movement*. Rosenberg and Sellier, Turin.
Belletti, A., Leonini, C., 2004. Subject inversion in L2 Italian, in *EUROSLA Yearbook 4*, pp. 95–118. Database Name: CSA Linguistics and Language Behavior Abstracts.
Berwick, R., 1985. *The Acquisition of Syntactic Knowledge*. MIT Press, Cambridge, MA.
Biberauer, T., Holmberg, A., Roberts, I., Sheehan, M., 2010. *Parametric Variation: Null Subjects in Minimalist Theory*. Cambridge University Press, Cambridge, UK.
Bloom, L., 1973. *One Word at a Time: The Use of Single-Word Utterances before Syntax*. Mouton, The Hague.
Bloom, P., 1990. Subjectless sentences in child language. *Linguistic Inquiry* **21**, 491–504.
   1993. Grammatical continuity in language development: the case of subjectless sentences. *Linguistic Inquiry* **24**, 721–734.
Borer, H., 1986. I-subjects. *Linguistic Inquiry* **17**, 375–416.
   1989. Anaphoric agr, in: Jaeggli, O., Safir, K. (eds.), *The Null Subject Parameter*. Kluwer, Dordrecht, pp. 69–110.
Bosque, I., 1980. *Sobre la negación*. Cátedra, Madrid.
   1987. Construcciones morfológicas sobre la coordinación. *Lingüística española actual* **9**, 83–100.
Brandi, L., Cordin, P., 1989. Two Italian dialects and the Null Subject Parameter, in: Jaeggli, O., Safir, K. (eds.), *The Null Subject Parameter*. Kluwer, Dordrecht, pp. 111–142.
Bullock, B.E., Toribio, A.J., 2009. Reconsidering Dominican Spanish: data from the rural Cibao. *Revista Internacional de Linguistica Iberoamericana* **14**, 49–73.
Burzio, L., 1986. *Italian Syntax*. Riedel, Dordrecht.
Cabré Sans, Y., Gavarró, A., 2006. Subject distribution and verb classes in child Catalan, in: Belikova, A., Meroni, L., Umeda, M. (eds.), *Proceedings of the 2nd Conference on Generative Approaches to Language Acquisition in North America (GALANA)*. Cascadilla Press, Somerville, MA, pp. 51–60.
Cabrera, M.J., 2007. Null Subject Patterns in Language Contact: The Case of Dominican Spanish. Ph.D. thesis. Rutgers University.

Camacho, J., 2001. On the interpretation of focus features, in: Herschenson, J., Mallén, E., Zagona, K. (eds.), *Features and Interfaces*. Benjamins, Philadelphia, PA, pp. 39–48.
  2003. *The Structure of Coordination*. Kluwer, Dordrecht.
  2006. Do subjects have a place in Spanish?, in: Montreuil, J.P., Nishida, C. (eds.), *New Perspectives in Romance Linguistics*. Benjamins, Philadelphia, PA, pp. 51–66.
  2008. Variation in generative grammar: state of the art. *Studies in Hispanic and Lusophone Linguistics* **1**, 415–434.
  2010a. The null subject parameter revisited: Spanish and Portuguese in discourse. Paper presented at the IVth Romania Nova Workshop. Campos do Jordão, Brazil.
  2010b. On case concord: the syntax of switch-reference clauses in Shipibo. *Natural Language and Linguistic Theory* **28**, 239–274.
  2011. Chinese-type pro in a romance-type null-subject language. *Lingua* **121**, 987–1008.
Camacho, J., Elías-Ulloa, J., 2010. Null subject systems in Shipibo switch-reference, in: Camacho, J., Guitérrez-Bravo, R., Sánchez, L. (eds.), *Information Structure in Languages of the Americas*. Mouton de Gruyter, Berlin, pp. 65–85.
Cardinaletti, A., 1997. Subjects and clause structure, in: Haegeman, L. (ed.), *The New Comparative Syntax*. Longman, Harlow, UK, pp. 33–63.
  2004. Towards a cartography of subject positions, in: Rizzi, L. (ed.), *The Cartography of Syntactic Structures*, vol. 2. Oxford University Press, Oxford, UK, pp. 115–165.
Cardinaletti, A., Starke, M., 1999. The typology of structural deficiency, in: Riemsdijk, H.V. (ed.), *Clitics in the Languages of Europe* Mouton de Gruyter, Berlin, pp. 145–233.
Chierchia, G., 1998. Reference to kinds across language. *Natural Language Semantics* **6**, 339–405. 10.1023/A:1008324218506.
Chomsky, N., 1975. *Reflections on Language*. Pantheon Books, New York.
  1981. *Lectures on Government and Binding*. Foris, Dordrecht.
  1986. *Knowledge of Language: Its Nature, Origins, and Use*. Praeger, New York.
  1988. *Language and Problems of Knowledge: The Managua Lectures*. MIT Press, Cambridge, MA.
  1993. A minimalist program for linguistic theory, in: Hale, K., Keyser, S. (eds.), *The View from Building 20*. MIT Press, Cambridge, MA, pp. 1–52.
  1995. *The Minimalist Program*. MIT Press, Cambridge, MA.
  2000. Minimalist inquiries: the framework, in: Martin, R., Michaels, D., Uriagereka, J. (eds.), *Step by Step: Essays on Minimalist Syntax in Honor of Howard Lasnik*. MIT Press, Cambridge, MA, pp. 89–156.
  2001. Derivation by phase, in: Kenstowicz, M., Keyser, S. (eds.), *Ken Hale: A Life in Language*. MIT Press, Cambridge, MA, pp. 1–52.
Chomsky, N., Lasnik, H., 1977. Filters and control. *Linguistic Inquiry* **8**, 425–504.
Chung, S., 1998. *The Design of Agreement: Evidence from Chamorro*. University of Chicago Press, Chicago, IL.
Cinque, G., 1990. *Types of A-bar Dependencies*. MIT Press, Cambridge, MA.

Clamons, R., Mulkern, A.E., Sanders, G., Stenson, N., 1999. The limits of formal analysis: pragmatic motivation in Oromo grammar, in: Darnell, M., Moravcsik, E.A., Newmeyer, F., Noonan, M., Wheatley, K.M. (eds.), *Functionalism and Formalism in Linguistics Case Studies*. Benjamins, Philadelphia, PA, vol. 2, pp. 59–76.

Clancy, P., 1993. Preferred argument structure in Korean acquisition, in: Clark, E. (ed.), *Proceedings of the 25th Annual Child Language Research Forum*. CSLI, Stanford, CA, pp. 307–314.

1997. Discourse motivations of referential choice in Korean acquisition, in: Sohn, H.M., Haig, J. (eds.), *Japanese/Korean Linguistics*. CSLI, Stanford, CA, pp. 639–659.

Clark, R., Roberts, I., 1993. A computational approach to language learnability and language change. *Linguistic Inquiry* **24**, 299–345.

Cole, M., 2000. The Syntax, Morphology, and Semantics of Null Subjects. Ph.D. thesis. University of Manchester, Manchester, UK.

2009. Null subjects: a reanalysis of the data. *Linguistics* **47**, 559–587.

Comínguez, J.P., 2011. Occurrence and interpretation of subject pronouns in temporal embedded clauses in L1 English near-native speakers of L2 Spanish. Rutgers University, New Brunswick, NJ.

2012. Interrogative wh-movement in Puerto Rican Spanish: preverbal subjects, t-to-c movement and phase parameterization. Rutgers University, New Brunswick, NJ.

Contreras, H., 1991. On the position of subjects, in: Rothstein, S. (ed.), *Perspectives on Phrase Structure: Heads and Licensing*. Academic Press, San Diego, CA, pp. 63–79.

Costa, J.A., 2001. Marked versus unmarked inversion and optimality theory, in: Hulk, A., Pollock, J.Y. (eds.), *Subject Inversion and the Theory of Universal Grammar*. Oxford University Press, Oxford, UK, pp. 91–106.

Courtney, E.H., 1998. Child Acquisition of Quechua Morphosyntax. Ph.D. thesis. University of Arizona, Tucson, AZ.

Cowart, W., 1997. *Experimental Syntax*. Sage, Thousand Oaks, CA.

Cowper, E., Hall, W.D.C., 2002. The syntactic manifestation of nominal feature geometry, in: Burelle, S., Somesfalean, S. (eds.), *Proceedings of the 2002 Annual Conference of the Canadian Linguistic Association*. Cahiers Linguistiques de l'UQAM, pp. 55–66.

Croft, W., 1988. Agreement vs. case marking and direct objects, in: Barlow, M., Ferguson, C.A. (eds.), *Agreement in Natural Language*. CSLI, Stanford, CA, pp. 159–179.

Crousaz, I.D., Shlonsky, U., 2003. The distribution of a subject clitic pronoun in a Franco-Provençal dialect and the licensing of pro. *Linguistic Inquiry* **34**, 413–442.

Crowley, T., Rigsby, B., 1979. Cape York creole, in: Shopen, T. (ed.), *Languages and Their Status*. Winthrop Publishers, Cambridge, MA, pp. 153–207.

Dasgupta, P., 2003. Bangla, in: Cardona, G., Jain, D. (eds.), *The Indo-Aryan Languages*. Routledge, London, pp. 386–428.

Déchaine, R.M., Wiltschko, M., 2002. Decomposing pronouns. *Linguistic Inquiry* **33**, 409–442.

Déprez, V., Pierce, A., 1993. Negation and functional projections in early grammar. *Linguistic Inquiry* **24**, 25–67.
Diercks, M., 2009. Subject extraction and (so-called) anti-agreement effects in Lubukusu: a criterial freezing approach. *Proceedings of the Annual Meeting of the Chicago Linguistic Society* **45**, 55–69.
2010. Agreement with Subjects in Lubukusu. Ph.D. thesis. Georgetown University, Washington, DC.
Duarte, M.E., 1993. Do pronome nulo ao pronome pleno: a trajetória do sujeito no português do Brasil, in: Roberts, I., Kato, M. (eds.), *Do pronome nulo ao pronome pleno: a trajetória do sujeito no português do Brasil*. Editora da UNICAMP, pp. 107–128.
1995. A Perda do Princípio "Evite pronome" no Português Brasileiro. Ph.D. thesis. UNICAMP.
2000. The loss of the avoid pronoun principle in Brazilian Portuguese, in: Kato, M.A., Negrão, E. (eds.), *Brazilian Portuguese and the Null Subject Parameter*. Vervuert-Iberoamericana, Frankfurt, pp. 17–36.
Elías-Ulloa, J., 2002. Subject doubling in Capanahua. Paper presented at *HUMDRUM 2002*, University of Massachusetts, Amherst, MA.
Ezeizabarrena, M.J., 2003. Null subjects and optional infinitives in Basque, in: Müller, N. (ed.), *(In)vulnerable Domains in Multilingualism*. Benjamins, Philadelphia, PA, pp. 83–106.
Fassi Fehri, A., 1993. *Issues in the Structure of Arabic Clauses and Words*. Kluwer, Dordrecht.
Figueiredo Silva, M.C., 1994. La posicition sujet en Portugais Brésilien. Ph.D. thesis. Université de Genève, Geneva.
Finer, D., 1985. *The Formal Grammar of Switch-Reference*. Garland Publishing, New York.
Fleming, D., 1977. A Study of the Interlanguage of English Speaking Learners of Spanish. Ph.D. thesis. University of Massachusetts, Amherst, MA.
Frascarelli, M., 2007. Subjects, topics and the interpretation of referential pro: an interface approach to the linking of (null) pronouns. *Natural Language and Linguistic Theory* **25**, 691–734.
Frascarelli, M., Hinterhölzl, R., 2007. Types of topics in German and Italian, in: Winkler, S., Schwabe, K. (eds.), *On Information Structure, Meaning and Form*. Benjamins, Philadelphia, PA, pp. 87–116.
Fukui, N., 1988. Deriving the difference between English and Japanese: a case study in parametric syntax. *English Linguistics* **5**, 249–270.
Fuß, E., 2005. *The Rise of Agreement*. Benjamins, Philadelphia, PA.
Gilligan, G., 1987. A Cross-linguistic Approach to the Pro-drop Parameter. Ph.D. thesis. University of Southern California, Los Angeles, CA.
Giupponi, E., 1988. Pro Drop Parameter und Restrukturierung im Trentino. Ph.D. thesis. University of Vienna.
Givón, T., 1983. Topic continuity in discourse: an introduction, in: Givón, T. (ed.), *Topic Continuity in Discourse*. Benjamins, Philadelphia, PA, pp. 1–42.

Goodall, G., 1999. On preverbal subjects in Spanish, in: Satterfield, T., Christina, T., Cresti, D. (eds.), *Current Issues in Romance Languages*. Benjamins, Philadelphia, PA, pp. 95–110.

Grimshaw, J., Samek-Lodovici, V., 1998. Optimal subjects and subject universals, in: Barbosa, P., Fox, D., Hagstrom, P., Pesetsky, D. (eds.), *Is the Best Good Enough? Optimality and Competition in Syntax*. MIT Press, Cambridge, MA, pp. 193–219.

Grinstead, J., 2004. Subjects and interface delay in child Spanish and Catalan. *Language* **80**, 40–72.

Gutman, E., 2004. Third person null subjects in Hebrew, Finnish and Rumanian: an accessibility-theoretic account. *Journal of Linguistics* **40**, 463–490.

Haegeman, L., 1990. Non overt subjects in diary contexts, in: Mascaró, J., Nespor, M. (eds.), *Grammar in Progress*. Foris, Dordrecht, pp. 167–179.

Hale, K., 1983. Papago (k)c. *International Journal of American Linguistics* **49**, 299–327.

Hamann, C., 1996. Null arguments in German child language. *Language Acquisition* **5**, 155–208.

2000. The acquisition of constituent questions and the requirements of interpretation, in: Friedemann, M.A., Rizzi, L. (eds.), *The Acquisition of Syntax: Studies in Comparative Developmental Linguistics*. Longman, Havlin, UK, pp. 170–201.

Hamann, C., Plunkett, K., 1998. Subjectless sentences in child Danish. *Cognition* **69**, 35–72.

Harbour, D., Adger, D., Béjar, S., 2008. *Phi Theory: Phi-Features across Modules and Interfaces*. Oxford University Press, Oxford, UK.

Harley, H., Ritter, E., 2002. A feature-geometric analysis of person and number. *Language* **78**, 482–526.

Henríquez Ureña, P., 1939. Ello. *Revista de Filología Hispánica* **1**, 209–229.

1940/1975. *El español en Santo Domingo*. El Taller, Santo Domingo.

Hernanz, M.L., 1990. En torno a los sujetos arbitrarios: la segunda persona del singular, in: Violeta, D., Garza Cuarón, B. (eds.), *Estudios de lingüística de España y México*. Colegio de México, México, pp. 151–178.

Hinzelin, M.O., Kaiser, G.A., 2006. *Das neutrale Pronomen ello im dominikanischen Spanisch und die Nullsubjekteigenschaft anhang: Korpus und Bibliographie zu "ello" und unpersönlichen Konstruktionen (mit Subjekt) im Spanischen*. Fachbereich Sprachwissenschaft der Universität Konstanz, Konstanz, Germany.

2007. El pronombre ello en el léxico del español dominicano, in: Mihatsch, W., Sokol, M. (eds.), *Language Contact and Language Change in the Caribbean and Beyond*. Peter Lang, Frankfurt, pp. 171–188.

Hoekstra, T., 1983. The distribution of sentential complements, in: Bennis, H., van Lessen Kloeke, W. (eds.), *Linguistics in the Netherlands 1983*. Foris, Dordrecht, pp. 93–103.

Hoji, H., 1998. Null object and sloppy identity in Japanese. *Linguistic Inquiry* **29**, 127–152.

Holmberg, A., 2005. Is there a little pro? evidence from Finnish. *Linguistic Inquiry* **36**, 533–564.

Holmberg, A., Nikkane, U., 2002. Expletives, subjects and topics in Finnish, in: Svenonius, P. (ed.), *Subjects, Expletives and the EPP*. Oxford University Press, Oxford, UK, pp. 71–106.
Holmberg, A., Sheehan, M., 2010. Control into finite clauses in partial null-subject languages, in: Biberauer, T., Holmberg, A., Roberts, I., Sheehan, M. (eds.), *Parametric Variation: Null Subjects in Minimalist Theory*. Cambridge University Press, Cambridge, UK, pp. 125–152.
Holmberg, A., Nayudu, A., Sheehan, M., 2009. Three partial null-subject languages: a comparison of Brazilian Portuguese, Finnish and Marathi. *Studia Linguistica* **63**, 59–97.
Hornstein, N., 2000. Control in GB and minimalism, in: Cheng, L., Sybesma, R. (eds.), *The First GLOT International State-of-the-Art Book: The Latest in Linguistics*. Walter de Gruyter, Berlin, pp. 27–46.
  2003. On control, in: Hendrick, R. (ed.), *Minimalist Syntax*. Blackwell, Oxford, UK, pp. 6–81.
  2009. *A Theory of Syntax: Minimal Operations and Universal Grammar*. Cambridge University Press, Cambridge, UK.
Huang, C.J., 1982. Move wh in a language without wh movement. *The Linguistic Review* **1**, 369–416.
  1984. On the distribution and reference of empty pronouns. *Linguistic Inquiry* **15**, 531–574.
  1989. Pro-drop in Chinese: a generalized control theory, in: Jaeggli, O., Safir, K. (eds.), *The Null Subject Parameter*. Kluwer, Dordrecht, pp. 185–214.
Huang, Y., 1992. Against Chomsky's typology of empty categories. *Journal of Pragmatics* **17**, 1–29.
  2000. *Anaphora: A Cross-Linguistic Study*. Oxford University Press, Oxford, UK.
Huidobro, S., 2005. Phonological constraints on verum focus in Argentinian Spanish. SUNY, Stony Brook, NY.
Hyams, N., 1986. *Language Acqusition and the Theory of Parameters*. Reidel, Dordrecht.
  1987. The theory of parameters and syntactic development, in: Roeper, T., Williams, E. (eds.), *Parameter Setting*. Reidel, Dordrecht, pp. 1–18.
  1992. A reanalysis of null subjects in child language, in: Weissenborn, J., Goodluck, H., Roeper, T. (eds.), *Theoretical Issues in Language Acqusition*. Lawrence Erlbaum, Hillsdale, NJ, pp. 249–268.
  1996. The underspecification of functional categories in early grammar, in: Clahsen, H. (ed.), *Generative Perspectives on Language Acquisition*. Benjamins, Philadelphia, PA, pp. 91–128.
  2009. Missing subjects in early child language, in: De Villiers, J., Roeper, T. (eds.), *Handbook of Language Acquisition Theory in Generative Grammar*. Kluwer, Dordrecht, pp. 13–52.
Hyams, N., Wexler, K., 1993. On the grammatical basis of null subjects in child language. *Linguistic Inquiry* **24**, 421–459.
Iatridou, S., Embick, D., 1997. Apropos pro. *Language* **73**, 58–78.

Jaeggli, O., 1980. On Some Phonologically-Null Elements in Syntax. Ph.D. thesis. MIT.
  1982. *Topics in Romance Syntax*. Foris, Dordrecht.
  1986. Arbitrary plural pronouns. *Natural Language and Linguistic Theory* 4, 43–76.
  1987. ECP effects at lf in Spanish, in: Birdsong, D., Montreuil, J.P. (eds.), *Advances in Romance Linguistics*. Foris, Dordrecht, pp. 113–151.
Jaeggli, O., Hyams, N., 1988. Morphological uniformity and the setting of the null subject parameter. *Proceedings of the North Eastern Linguistic Society* 17, 239–253.
Jaeggli, O., Safir, K.J., 1989. The null subject parameter and parametric theory, in: Jaeggli, O., Safir, K.J. (eds.), *The Null Subject Parameter*. Reidel, Dordrecht, pp. 1–44.
Jelinek, E., 1984. Emtpy categories, case and configurationality. *Natural Language and Linguistic Theory* 2, 39–76.
Johns, C., 2007. Interpreting Agreement. Ph.D. thesis. University of Durham, UK.
Kanno, K., 1997. The acquisition of null and overt pronominals in Japanese by English speakers. *Second Language Research* 13, 265–287.
Kato, M., 1999. Strong pronouns and weak pronominals in the null subject parameter. *Probus* 11, 1–37.
  2000. The partial pro-drop nature and the restricted VS order in Brazilian Portuguese, in: Kato, M.A., Negrão, E. (eds.), *Brazilian Portuguese and the Null Subject Parameter*. Vervuert, Madrid, pp. 223–255.
Kato, M.A., Negrão, E., 2000. *Brazilian Portuguese and the Null Subject Parameter*. Vervuert, Madrid.
Kayne, R., 1980. Extensions of binding and case-marking. *Linguistic Inquiry* 11, 75–96.
  2005. Some notes on comparative syntax, with special reference to English and French, in: Cinque, G., Kayne, R. (eds.), *The Oxford Handbook of Comparative Syntax*. Oxford University Press, Oxford, UK, pp. 3–69.
Kempchinsky, P., 1987. The subjunctive disjoint reference effect, in: Neidle, C., Núñez-Cedeño, R. (eds.), *Studies in Romance Languages*. Foris, Dordrecht, pp. 123–140.
Kenstowicz, M., 1989. The null subject parameter in modern Arabic dialects, in: Jaeggli, O., Safir, K.J. (eds.) *The Null Subject Parameter*. Reidel, Dordrecht, pp. 263–275.
Kiss, K., 2002. The EPP in a topic-prominent language, in: Svenonius, P. (ed.), *Subjects, Expletives, and the EPP*. Oxford University Press, Oxford, UK, pp. 107–124.
Koopman, H., Sportiche, D., 1991. The position of subjects. *Lingua* 85, 211–258.
Kramer, I., 1993. The licensing of subjects in early child language, in: Phillips, C. (ed.), *Papers on Case and Agreement*, vol. 2. Cambridge, MA, MIT Press, pp. 197–212.
LaFond, L., 2001. The Pro-drop Parameter in Second Language Acquisition Revisited: A Developmental Account. Ph.D. thesis. University of South Carolina, Columbia, SC.
Laka, I., 1990. Negation in Syntax: On the Nature of Functional Categories and Projections. Ph.D. thesis. MIT.

Larson, R., Luján, M., 1989. Emphatic Pronouns. Ms. SUNY, Stony Brook, NY.

Léautaud, P., 1989. *Le Fléau: journal particulier*, 1917–1930. Mercure de France, Paris.

Levy, Y., Vainikka, A., 2000. The development of a mixed null subject system: a crosslinguistic perspective with data on the acquisition of hebrew. *Language Acquisition* **8**, 363–384.

Li, C.N., Thompson, S.A., 1976. Subject and topic: a new typology of language, in: Li, C.N. (ed.), *Subject and Topic*. Academic Press, New York, pp. 458–489.

Li, Y.H.A., 1999. Form and function correspondence: structures and interpretations of nominal expressions in Mandarin Chinese, in: Takubo, Y. (ed.), *Comparative Syntax of Japanese, Korean, Chinese and English*, Report of the International Scientific Research Program. Ministry of Education, Science and Culture, Japan, pp. 147–186.

2007. Beyond empty categories. *Bulletin of the Chinese Linguistic Society of Japan* **254**, 74–106.

Liceras, J., 1988. Syntax and stylistics: more on the pro-drop parameter, in: Pankhurst, J., Sharwood, M., Van Buren, P. (eds.), *Learnability and Second Languages*. Foris, Dordrecht, pp. 71–93.

1989. On some properties of the pro-drop parameter: looking for missing subjects in non-native Spanish, in: Gass, S., Schacter, J. (ed.), *Linguistic Perspectives on Second Language Acquisition*. Foris, Dordrecht, pp. 109–133.

Liceras, J.M., Diaz, L., 1999. Topic-drop versus pro-drop: null subjects and pronominal subjects in the Spanish L2 of Chinese, English, French, German and Japanese speakers. *Second Language Research* **15**, 1–40. Database Name: CSA Linguistics and Language Behavior Abstracts.

Liceras, J.M., Valenzuela, E., Diaz, L., 1999. L1/L2 Spanish grammars and the pragmatic deficit hypothesis. *Second Language Research* **15**, 161–190. Database Name: CSA Linguistics and Language Behavior Abstracts.

Liceras, J.M., Fernández Fuertes, R., Pérez-Tattam, R., 2008. Null and overt subjects in the developing grammars (L1 English/L1 Spanish) of two bilingual twins, in: Pérez-Vidal, C., Juan-Garau, M., Bel, A. (eds.), *A Portrait of the Young in the New Multilingual Spain*. Multilingual Matters, Clevendon, pp. 111–134.

Liceras, J.M., Fernández Fuertes, R., Alba de la Fuente, A., 2012. Subject and copula omission in the English grammar of English–Spanish bilinguals: on the issue of directionality of interlinguistic influence. *First Language* **32**, 88–115.

Lima, A., 2005. Predicate inversion, person asymmetries and agreement alternations in Brazilian Portuguese. www.linguistics.ucla.edu/people/grads/lima/LASSOHandout.pdf.

Linares, C., 2012. The Dependency Axiom and the Relation between Agreement and Movement. Ph.D. thesis. Rutgers University, New Brunswick, NJ.

Longobardi, G., 1994. Reference and proper names. *Linguistic Inquiry* **25**, 609–666.

Loriot, J., Lauriault, E., Day, D., 1993. *Diccionario Shipibo-Castellano*. Ministerio de Educación-Instituto Lingüístico de Verano, Lima.

Lozano, C., 2002. Universal Grammar and Focus Constraints: Focus, Pronouns and Word Order in the acquisition of L2 and L3 Spanish. Ph.D. thesis. University of Essex, UK.

Luján, M., 1987. Los pronombres implícitos y explícitos del español. *Revista Argentina de Lingüística* **3**, 19–54.

MacWhinney, B., 2000. *The CHILDES Project: Tools for Analyzing Talk*. Lawrence Erlbaum, Mahwah, NJ.

Manzini, M.R., Savoia, L.M., 2002. Parameters of subject inflection in Italian dialects, in: Svenonius, P. (ed.), *Subjects, Expletives, and the EPP*. Oxford University Press, Oxford, UK, pp. 157–200.

Manzini, R., Wexler, K., 1987. Parameters, binding theory, and learnability. *Linguistic Inquiry* **18**, 413–444.

McClelland, C.W., 1996. Interrelations of Prosody, Clause Structure and Discourse Pragmatics in Tarifit Berber. Ph.D. thesis. University of Texas, Arlington, TX.

McCloskey, J., 1991. Clause structure, ellipsis and proper government in Irish. *Lingua* **85**, 259–302.

1996. Subjects and subject positions in Irish, in: Borsley, R., Roberts, I. (eds.), *Celtic and Beyond: Papers on Celtic Syntax*. Cambridge University Press, Cambridge, UK, pp. 241–283.

1997. Subjecthood and subject positions, in: Haegeman, L. (ed.), *Elements of Grammar*. Kluwer, Dordrecht, pp. 197–235.

McCloskey, J., Hale, K., 1984. On the syntax of person–number inflection in modern Irish. *Natural Language and Linguistic Theory* **1**, 487–533.

Menuzzi, S.D.M., 2000. That-trace effects in Portuguese. *Fórum Lingüístico* **2**, 13–39.

Modesto, M., 2000. Null subject without 'rich' agreement, in: Kato, M.A., Negrão, E. (eds.), *The Null Subject Parameter in Brazilian Portuguese*. Verveurt-Iberoamericana, Frankfurt/Madrid, pp. 147–174.

2008. Topic prominence and null subjects, in: Biberauer, T. (ed.), *The Limits of Syntactic Variation*. Benjamins, Philadelphia, PA, pp. 375–409.

Montalbetti, M., 1984. After Binding. Ph.D. thesis. MIT.

Moro, A., 1993. *I predicati nominali e la struttura della frase*. Unipress, Padua.

Muysken, P., 1986. Approaches to affix order. *Linguistics* **24**, 629–643.

Neeleman, A., Szendroi, K., 2005. Pro drop and pronouns. *West Coast Conference on Formal Linguistics* **24**, 299–307.

2007. Radical pro drop and the morphology of pronouns. *Linguistic Inquiry* **38**, 671–714.

2008. Case morphology and radical pro-drop, in: Biberauer, T. (ed.), *The Limits of Syntactic Variation*. Benjamins, Philadelphia, PA, pp. 331–348.

Nicolis, M., 2005. On pro–drop. Ph.D. thesis. Università degli Studi di Siena, Italy.

2008. The null subject parameter and correlating properties: the case of Creole languages, in: Biberauer, T. (ed.), *The Limits of Syntactic Variation*. Benjamins, Philadelphia, PA, pp. 271–294.

Noguchi, T., 1997. Two types of pronouns and variable binding. *Language* **73**, 770–797.

Ordóñez, F., 1997. Word Order and Clause Structure in Spanish and Other Romance Languages. Ph.D. thesis. CUNY, New York.

Ordóñez, F., Olarrea, A., 2006. Microvariation in Caribbean/non Caribbean Spanish interrogatives. *Probus* **18**, 59–96.

Ordóñez, F., Treviño, E., 1999. Left dislocated subjects and the pro-drop parameter: a case study of Spanish. *Lingua* **107**, 39–68.

Ortiz López, L.A., 2009. El español del caribe: orden de palabras a la luz de la interfaz léxico-sintaxis y sintaxis-pragmática. *Revista Internacional de Lingüística Iberoamericana* **7**, 75–94.

Otheguy, R., Zentella, A.C., Livert, D., 2007. Language and diaelct contact in Spanish in New York: towards the formation of a speech community. *Language* **83**, 770–802.

Ouhalla, J., 1988. A note on bound pronouns. *Linguistic Inquiry* **19**, 485–494.

Park, H., 2004. A minimalist approach to null subjects and objects in second language acquisition. *Second Language Research* **20**, 1–32. Database Name: CSA Linguistics and Language Behavior Abstracts.

Pérez Jiménez, I., 2007. *Las cláusulas absolutas*. Visor Libros, Madrid.

Perez-Leroux, A.T., Glass, W.R., 1999. Null anaphora in Spanish second language acquisition: probabilistic versus generative approaches. *Second Language Research* **15**, 220–249. Database Name: CSA Linguistics and Language Behavior Abstracts.

Perlmutter, D., 1971. *Deep and Surface Structure Constraints in Syntax*. Holt, Rinehard and Winston, New York.

Perrott, D.V., 1972. *Teach Yourself Swahili*. David McKay, New York.

Pesetsky, D., Torrego, E., 2001. T-to-C movement: causes and consequences, in: Kenstowicz, M., Keyser, S. (eds.), *Ken Hale: A Life in Language*. MIT Press, Cambridge, MA, pp. 355–426.

2004. Tense, case and the nature of syntactic categories, in: Guéron, J., Lecarme, J. (eds.), *The Syntax of Time*. MIT Press, Cambridge, MA, pp. 495–538.

2006. Probes, goals and syntactic categories, in: Otsu, Y. (ed.), *Proceedings of the 7th Tokyo Conference on Psycholinguistics*. Hituzi Syobo Publishing Company, Tokyo, pp. 25–60.

2007. The syntax of valuation and the interpretability of features, in: Karimi, S., Samiian, V., Wilkins, W. (eds.), *Phrasal and Clausal Architecture: Syntactic Derivation and Interpretation*. Benjamins, Philadelphia, PA, pp. 262–294.

Phinney, M., 1987. The pro-drop parameter in second language acquisition, in: Roeper, T., Edwin Williams, E. (eds.), *Parameter Setting*. Reidel, Dordrecht, pp. 221–238.

Pica, P., 2001. Introduction. *Linguistic Variation Yearbook* **1**, v–xii.

Pierce, A., 1992. *Language Acquisition and Syntactic Theory: A Comparative Analysis of French and English Child Grammars*. Kluwer, Dordrecht.

Platzack, C., 1987. The Scandinavian languages and the null-subject parameter. *Natural Language and Linguistic Theory* **5**, 377–401.

2003. Agreement and null subjects. *Nordlyd* **31**, 326–355.

Poletto, C., 1993. *La sintassi del soggetto nei dialetti dell' Italia settentrionale*. Unipress, Padua.

2000. *The Higher Functional Field: Evidence from Northern Italian Dialects*. Oxford University Press, Oxford, UK.

Postal, P., 1966. On so-called 'pronouns' in English, in: Dinneen, F. (ed.), *19th Monograph on Languages and Linguistics*. Georgetown University Press, Washington, DC, pp. 177–206.

Rasetti, L., 2000. Null subjects and root infinitives in child grammar of French, in: Friedemann, M., Rizzi, L. (eds.), *The Acquisition of Syntax*. Longman, Harlow, UK, pp. 236–268.

Rice, K., 1989. *A Grammar of Slave*. Mouton de Gruyter, Berlin.
Riemsdijk, H. van, Williams, E., 1986. *Introduction to the Theory of Grammar*. MIT Press, Cambridge, MA.
Rigau, G., 1988. Strong pronouns. *Linguistic Inquiry* **19**, 503–511.
Rizzi, L., 1982. *Issues in Italian Syntax*. Foris, Dordrecht.
  1986a. Null objects in Italian and the theory of pro. *Linguistic Inquiry* **17**, 501–557.
  1986b. On the status of subjects clitics in Romance, in: Jaeggli, O., Silva-Corvalán, C. (eds.), *Studies in Romance Syntax*. Foris, Dordrecht, pp. 391–419.
  1987. Three remarks on null subjects. Talk given at the Workshop on Dialectology, GLOW X, University of Venice.
  1993/4. Some notes on linguistic theory and language development: the case of root infinitives. *Language Acquisition* **3**, 371–393.
  1996. Residual verb second and the wh-criterion, in: Belletti, A., Rizzi, L. (eds.), *Parameters and Functional Heads*. Oxford University Press, Oxford, UK, vol. 2, pp. 63–90.
  1997. The fine structure of the left periphery, in: Haegeman, L. (ed.), *Elements of Grammar*. Kluwer, Dordrecht, pp. 281–337.
  2005a. Grammatically-based target-inconsistencies in child language, in: Deen, K.U., Nomura, J., Schulz, B., Schwartz, B.D. (eds.), *Proceedings of the Inaugural Conference of GALANA*. UCONN/MIT Working Papers in Linguistics, Cambridge, MA, pp. 19–49.
  2005b. On some properties of subjects and topics, in: Brugè, L., Giusti, G., Munaro, N., Schweikert, W., Turano, G. (eds.), *Proceedings of the 30th Incontro di Grammatica Generativa*. Cafoscarina, Venice, pp. 203–224.
  2005c. On the grammatical basis of language development: a case study, in: Cinque, G., Kayne, R. (eds.), *The Oxford Handbook of Comparative Syntax*. Oxford University Press, Oxford, UK, pp. 70–109.
  2006. On the form of chains: criterial positions and ECP effects, in: Cheng, L., Corver, N. (eds.), *Wh Movement: Moving On*. MIT Press, Cambridge, MA, pp. 97–133.
Rizzi, L., Shlonsky, U., 2007. Strategies of subject extraction, in: Sauerland, U., Gärtner, H.M. (eds.), *Interfaces + Recursion = Language? Chomsky's Minimalism and the View from Syntax-Semantics*. Mouton de Gruyter, Berlin, pp. 115–160.
Roberts, I., 2010a. A deletion analysis of null subject, in: Biberauer, T., Holmberg, A., Roberts, I., Sheehan, M. (eds.), *Parametric Variation: Null Subjects in Minimalist Theory*. Cambridge University Press, Cambridge, UK, pp. 58–87.
  2010b. Varieties of French and the Null Subject Parameter, in: Biberauer, T., Holmberg, A., Roberts, I., Sheehan, M. (eds.), *Parametric Variation: Null Subjects in Minimalist Theory*. Cambridge University Press, Cambridge, UK, pp. 303–327.
Roberts, I., Holmberg, A., 2010. Introduction: parameters in minimalist theory, in: Biberauer, T., Holmberg, A., Roberts, I., Sheehan, M. (eds.), *Parametric Variation: Null Subjects in Minimalist Theory*. Cambridge University Press, Cambridge, UK, pp. 1–57.

Rodríguez-Mondoñedo, M., 2006. Spanish existentials and other accusative constructions, in: Boeckx, C. (ed.), *Minimalist Essays*. Benjamins, Philadelphia, PA, pp. 326–394.

Rosenkvist, H., 2009. Null referential subjects in Germanic languages: an overview. *Working Papers in Scandinavian Syntax* **84**, 151–180.

2010a. Null referential subjects in Germanic languages: an overview. Subjects in Diachrony Conference.

2010b. Null referential subjects in Övdalian. *Nordic Journal of Linguistics* **33**, 231–267. 10.1017/S033258651000020X.

Ross, J.R., 1973. The Penthouse Principle and the order of constituents, in: Corum, C.T., Smith-Stark, T., Weiser, A. (eds.), *You Take the High Node and I'll Take the Low Node*. Chicago Linguistic Society, Chicago, IL, pp. 397–422.

Saab, A., 2009. Hacia una teoría de la identidad parcial en la elipsis. Ph.D. thesis. Universidad de Buenos Aires.

2010. Null subjects at the syntax–morphology connection. Paper presented at *Romania Nova IV*, Brazil.

2012. On the notion of partial (non-) pro-drop in romance. Universidad Nacional del Coahue/Leiden University.

Safir, K., 1985. Missing subjects in German, in: Toman, J. (ed.), *Studies in German Grammar*. Foris, Dordrecht, pp. 193–230.

2004. Person, context and perspective. *Italian Journal of Linguistics (Rivista di Linguistica)* **16**, 107–153.

Samek-Lodovici, V., 1996. Structural contrastive focus in Italian with and without emphatic stress. Universität Konstanz, Germany.

Sánchez, L., 1994. On the interpretation of intensified DPs and emphatic pronouns, in: Mazzola, M.L. (ed.), *Issues and Theory in Romance Linguistics: Selected Papers from the Linguistic Symposium on Romance Languages 23*. Georgetown University Press, Georgetown, Washington, DC, pp. 479–491.

2010. *The Morphology and Syntax of Focus and Topic: Minimalist Inquiries in the Quechua Periphery*. Benjamins, Philadelphia, PA.

Sánchez, L., Camacho, J., Elías-Ulloa, J., 2010. Shipibo–Spanish: differences in residual transfer at the syntax–morphology and the syntax–pragmatics interfaces. *Second Language Research* **26**, 329–354. Database Name: CSA Linguistics and Language Behavior Abstracts.

Schlenker, P., 2003. A plea for monsters. *Linguistics and Philosophy* **26**, 29–120.

Sengupta, G., 1999. Lexical anaphors and pronouns in Bangla, in: Lust, B., Wali, K., Gair, J., Subbarao, K. (eds.), *Lexical Anaphors and Pronouns in Selected South Asian Languages: A Principled Typology*. Mouton de Gruyter, Berlin, pp. 277–332.

Serratrice, L., 2005. The role of discourse pragmatics in the acquisition of subjects in Italian. *Applied Psycholinguistics* **26**, 437–462.

Serratrice, L., Sorace, A., 2003. Overt and null subjects in monolingual and bilingual Italian acquisition, in: Beachley, B., Brown, A., Conlin, F. (eds.), *Proceedings of the 27th Annual BUCLD*. Cascadilla Press, Somerville, MA, vol. 2, pp. 739–750.

Sheehan, M., 2007. The EPP and Null Subjects in Romance. Ph.D. thesis. Newcastle University, UK.

Shlonsky, U., 1997. *Clause Structure and Word Order in Hebrew and Arabic*. Oxford University Press, Oxford, UK.

2009. Hebrew as a partial null-subject language. *Studia Linguistica* **63**, 133–157.

Sigurðsson, H.A., 2004. The syntax of person, tense, and speech features. *Italian Journal of Linguistics* **16**, 219–251.

2010. On EPP effects. *Studia Linguistica* **64**, 159–189.

2011. Conditions on argument drop. *Linguistic Inquiry* **42**, 267–304.

Sigurðsson, H.A., Holmberg, A., 2008. Icelandic dative intervention: person and number are separate probes, in: D'Alessandro, R., Fischer, S., Hrafnbjargarson, G.H. (eds.), *Agreement Restrictions*. Mouton de Gruyter, Berlin, pp. 251–279.

Silva-Villar, L., 1998. Subject positions and the roles of CP, in: Schwegler, A., Tranel, B., Uribe-Etxebarria, M. (eds.), *Romance Linguistics: Theoretical Perspectives*. Benjamins, Philadelphia, PA, pp. 247–270.

Smith, N., Law, A., 2007. Twangling instruments: is parametric variation definitional of human language? *UCL Working Papers in Linguistics* **19**, 1–28.

Solà, J., 1992. Agreement and Subjects. Ph.D. thesis. Universitat Autònoma de Barcelona, Spain.

Sommerstein, A., 1972. On the so-called 'definite article' in English. *Linguistic Inquiry* **3**, 197–205.

Sorace, A., 2005. Syntactic optionality at interfaces, in: Cornips, L., Corrigan, K. (eds.), *Syntax and Variation: Reconciling the Biological and the Social*. Benjamins, Philadelphia, PA, pp. 46–111.

Speas, M., 1995. Economy, agreement and the representation of null arguments. University of Massachusetts Amherst, MA.

2004. Evidentiality, logophoricity and the syntactic representation of pragmatic features. *Lingua* **114**, 255–276.

Sportiche, D., 1988. A theory of floating quantifiers and its corollaries for constituent structure. *Linguistic Inquiry* **19**, 425–449.

Stirling, L., 1993. *Switch-Reference and Discourse Representation*. Cambridge University Press, Cambridge, UK.

Stowell, T., 1993. Syntax of tense. University of California, Los Angeles, CA.

1996. The phrase structure of tense, in: Zaring, L., Rooryck, J. (eds.), *Phrase Structure and the Lexicon*. Kluwer, Dordrecht, pp. 277–291.

Suñer, M., 1983. Pro$_{arb}$. *Linguistic Inquiry* **14**, 188–191.

1994. V-movement and the licensing of argumental wh-phrases in Spanish. *Natural Language and Linguistic Theory* **12**, 335–372.

2003. The lexical preverbal subject in a Romance null subject language: where are thou?, in: Núñez-Cedeño, R., López, L., Cameron, R. (eds.), *A Romance Perspective on Language Knowledge and Use, Selected Papers from the 31st Linguistic Symposium on Romance Languages*. Benjamins, Philadelphia, PA, pp. 341–358.

Svenonius, P., 2002. Subjects, expletives, and the EPP, in: Svenonius, P. (ed.), *Subjects, Expletives, and the EPP*. Oxford University Press, Oxford, UK, pp. 3–28.

Szczegielniak, A., 1999. 'That-t effects' crosslinguistically and successive cyclic movement. *Papers on Morphology and Syntax, Cycle One* **33**, 369–393.

Taraldsen, T., 1980. On the nic, vacuous application and the *that-trace* filter. MIT and Indiana Linguistics Club.

Tomioka, S., 1999. A sloppy identity puzzle. *Natural Language Semantics* **7**, 217–241.

2003. The semantics of Japanese null pronouns and its cross-linguistic implications, in: Schwabe, K., Winkler, S. (eds.), *The Interfaces: Deriving and Interpreting Omitted Structures*. Benjamins, Philadelphia, PA, pp. 321–340.

Toribio, A.J., 1993. Lexical subjects in finite and non-finite clauses. *Cornell Working Papers in Linguistics* **11**, 149–178.

Trutkowski, E., 2011. Referential null subjects in German, in: Cummins, C., Eldder, C.H., Godard, T., Macleod, M., Schmidt, E., Walkden, G. (eds.), *Proceedings of the 6th Cambridge Postgraduate Conference in Language Research*. Cambridge Institute of Language Research, Cambridge, UK, pp. 206–217.

Vainikka, A., Levy, Y., 1999. Empty subjects in Finnish and Hebrew. *Natural Language and Linguistic Theory* **17**, 613–671.

Valenzuela, P., 2003a. Evidentiality in Shipibo-Konibo, with a comparative overview of the category in Panoan, in: Aikhenvald, A., Dixon, R. (eds.), *Studies in Evidentiality*. Benjamins, Philadelphia, PA, pp. 33–62.

Valenzuela, P., 2003b. Transitivity in Shipibo-Konibo Grammar. Ph.D. thesis. University of Oregon, Eugene, OR.

Valian, V., 1990. Null subjects: a problem for parameter setting models of language acquisition. *Cognition* **35**, 105–122.

Valian, V., Eisenberg, Z., 1996. Syntactic subjects in the spontaneous speech of Portuguese-speaking children. *Journal of Child Language* **23**, 103–128.

Vergnaud, J.R., Zubizarreta, M.L., 1992. The definite determiner and the inalienable constructions in French and English. *Linguistic Inquiry* **23**, 595–652.

Wasike, A., 2007. The Left Periphery, wh-in-situ and A-bar Movement in Lubukusu and other Bantu languages. Ph.D. thesis. Cornell University, Ithaca, NY.

Wexler, K., 1994. Optional infinitives, head movement and the economy of derivations, in: Lightfoot, D., Hornstein, N. (eds.), *Verb Movement*. Cambridge University Press, Cambridge, UK, pp. 305–350.

1998. Very early parameter setting and the unique checking constraint: a new explanation of the optional infinitive stage. *Lingua* **106**, 23–79.

White, L., 1985. The pro-drop parameter in adult second language learning. *Language Learning* **35**, 47–62.

Yamada, K., 2005. The status of the overt pronoun constraint in grammatical theory and SLA of Japanese. *Essex Graduate Student Papers in Language and Linguistics* **7**, 180–201.

Zagona, K., 1982. Government and Proper Government of Verbal Projections. Ph.D. thesis. University of Washington, Seattle, WA.

1990. Times as temporal argument structure. University of Washington, Seattle, WA.

Zhao, L.X., 2011. The syntax and interpretation of embedded null subjects in Chinese, and their acquisition by English-speaking learners. *EUROSLA Yearbook* **11**, 191–217.

Zubizarreta, M.L., 1994. The grammatical representation of topic and focus: implications for the structure of the clause. *University of Venice Working Papers in Linguistics* **4**, 97–126.

1998. *Prosody, Focus, and Word Order*. MIT Press, Cambridge, MA.

Zushi, M., 2003. Null arguments: the case of Japanese and romance. *Lingua* **113**, 559–604.

Index

aboutness, 98
acquisition
  bilingual and L2, 220
  ease of, for L1 null subjects, 225
  of Basque vs. Quechua null subjects, 219
  of L1 vs. L2, 224
  of the minimal morphological threshold (MMT), 226
  of null subjects in L2, 222
  of overt subject languages by children, 211
  of Spanish and Catalan as L1, 216
  omission rate of subjects and verbs in, 215
  order of, 210
  performance-based accounts of null-subject, 212
  positive evidence for, 227
  strategies, 225
  trajectories of, for bilinguals, 220
AGREE, 120, 122, 144
agreement, 5, *see also* variation in agreement
  arguments against the pronominal properties of, 83
  asymmetries in Italian dialects, 75
  binding by, 39
  blocked by intervention effects, 123
  in complementizers, 98
  default, in Northern Italian dialects, 23
  in Germanic, 141
  in Northern Italian dialects, 23
  in Oromo, 102
  pronominal properties of, 76
    and 3rd person, 80
    and DPs, 80
    in infinitivals, 80
  referential properties of, 78, 79
    in Spanish, 78
  rich, 32, 39, 67
  topic, 103

Alexiadou, Artemis, 67, 191, 192
  and the pronominal agreement hypothesis, 77
alignment, 102
Anagnostopoulou, Elena, 67, 191, 192
  and the pronominal agreement hypothesis, 77
analysis, pronominal agreement, 70,
  see also pronominal agreement hypothesis
anaphora, backwards, 180
antecedent, topic, 182
Arabic
  gender and person, 131
  Levantene
    diary register, 213
    null subjects, 55
Arregi, Karlos, 205
asymmetries
  in agreement, *see* agreement
  in person, *see* person
  subject–object extraction, *see* extaction
  with topicalizations in Chinese, 165

Baker, Mark, 6, 7, 123, 143, 144
Barbosa, Pilar, 24, 34, 57, 89, 193
Basque
  acquisition, as L1, 218–219
  root infinitives, 218
    compatible with adult grammars, 218
    and null subjects, 219
Bayer, Joseph, 140
Béjar, Susana, 115, 116
Bel, Aurora, 216
Bengali
  inflectional probe in, 130
  null subject identification by person, 129
Bloom, Paul, 214

245

Borer, Hagit, 34, 76
Borer–Chomsky conjecture, 7,
    see also parameters
Bullock, Barbara, 56
Burzio, Luigi, 69

C
  domain, 150
  inflected, 140
Cabrera, María, 51
Camacho, José, 65, 152
Cape York Creole, 15
Cardinaletti, Anna, 71, 73, 91, 175, 177
categories
  C/edge linked, 159
  conditions on referential, 149
  null, in Japanese and Chinese, 168
  principled distinction between null, 168
Chamorro, null subjects in, 13, 15
Chierchia, Genaro, 117, 171
Chinese, see null categories
Chomsky, Noam, 13, 21, 120
Chung, Sandra, 13
Clamons, Robbin, 103, 104
clauses
  absolute, in Spanish, see Spanish absolute clauses
  adjunct, in Hebrew, see Hebrew adjunct clauses
  conditional
    in Italian, see Italian conditional clauses
    in Spanish, see Spanish conditional clauses
  impersonal, 176
  with impoverished structure, 162
  reference to, see reference to clauses with null or overt pronouns
  structure of conditional, 185–186
  subjunctive, 162
  and structural truncation, 214
clitic
  left-dislocated phrase (CLLD), 190
    animate, 205
    contrastive reading for, 206
    inanimate, 205
    quantified preverbal subjects, 202
    preverbal subjects as, 190, 191
    relative scopes of dative vs. accusative, 194
  overt partitive, 201

Cole, Melvyn, 112
control
  movement account of obligatory, 163
  null pronominal, 164
Constraint
  Avoid Pronoun, 27
    in Brazilian Portuguese, 28
    in Shipibo, see Shipibo, Avoid Pronoun Constraint
  Overt Pronoun, 30
Contreras, Heles, 78
context, root-initial, 212
Corsican, diary register, 213
Courtney, Helen, 216
Cowart, Wayne, 22
criterial freezing, strategy for by-passing, 98
Criterion
  Subject, 98, 102, 104, see also Brazilian, Central Colombian Spanish, Dominican Spanish (El Cibao), Iceland, Lubukusu, Övdalian, Portuguese and Northwestern Iberian languages, 102

D, non-referential interpretation of, 180
Danish
  acquisition of, as L1, 211
  expletives, 50
Diercks, Michael, 59, 99
drop
  discourse pro-, generalization, 33
  root subject (RSD), 212–214
  topic, see topic drop in German, Icelandic, Swedish
Duarte, Maria E., 57

edge, of phase, 214
effect
  Filled Left Edge (FLEE), 61
  person, 62, see also logophoricity, variation in
Elías-Ulloa, José, 65
ellipsis, see also pro, and ellipsis
  interpretability requirements under, 81
  sloppy interpretations in, 169
Embick, David, 28
English, expletives, 102
expletives, 186, see also null subjects
  according to Chomsky, 17

classification, 18
  by construction, 18
  depending on referential content, 17–18
clause-initial, 48
CP-related
  in Central Colombian Spanish, 47, 102
  in European Portuguese, 47
  in Galician, 47
  in Leonese, 47
  in Romance varieties, 46
extraposition of, 186
  as quasi-referential, 17
evidence against null, 95–97
focused, 187
  in Danish, *see* Danish, expletives
  in Dominican Spanish, *see* Dominican Spanish, expletives
  in English, *see* English, expletives
  in Finnish, *see* Finnish, expletives
  in German, *see* German, expletives
  in Haitian Creole, *see* Haitian Creole, expletives
  in Hungarian, *see* Hungarian, expletives
  in Icelandic, *see* Icelandic, expletives
  in Irish, *see* Irish, expletives
  in Norwegian, *see* Norwegian, expletives
  in Romance-based Creoles, 18
  in Swedish, *see* Swedish, expletives
null, 105
pure null, 93
quasi-referential, 17
referentially empty, 17
semantic content of, 186
with weather-verbs
  and control, 17, 186
  as quasi-referential, 17
Extended Projection Principle (EPP), 4, 67, 87, *see also* Extended Projection Principle; features
  checking of, 77
  as a D feature, 77
  parametrized, 77
  satisfaction of
    in null subject languages, 68
    through a DP, 77
    through an overt expletive, 77, 88
    through rich inflection, 84
  universality of, 93, 105

extraction
  asymmetries
    in Brazilian Portuguese, *see* Brazilian Portuguese, extraction
    in conditional clauses, 184
    in Lubukusu, *see* Lubukusu, extraction
    in preverbal vs. postverbal subjects, 196
  long wh-, 25
Ezeizabarrena, María José, 218

features
  absence in feature hierarchy, 119
  D, 117
    in IP as EPP features, 67
  definite, 117
  deictic, 117
  EPP, 6, 19
  +human, 176
  interpretable, 81
  person (π), 116
  phi-, 115
    Zurich German, Schwabian and Övdalian and phi-, *see* German
  R, 118
  root, 118
  specific, 117
  strong D, as an EPP feature in IP, 67
  uninterpretable, 81
  weak D, as an EPP feature in IP, 67
Figueiredo Silva, Maria Cristina, 57
Finnish, 87
  expletives
    optional, 42
    overt, 84
    null thematic subjects and overt expletives in, 41
  partial null subject, 34
  person asymmetries, 88
  subjects, 16
focus, cleft, in Spanish, 63
Franco-Provençal, diary register, 213
Frascarelli, Mara, 149
freezing, 98
  positional, 97
  of quantified subjects, 197
French
  acquisition of, as L1, 211
  subjects, 16
frequency, in input, 226
Fuß, Eric, 140

Galician, CP-related expletives, *see* expletives
gender, 114
   and person in Arabic, *see* Arabic, gender
   and secondary predicates in Spanish, *see* Spanish, secondary predicates
   in Hindi auxiliaries, 129
Generalized Control Rule (GCR), 166
geometry, *see also* hierarchy
   phi-feature and infl, 120
   phi-feature, in Spanish, 127
German
   acquisition of, as L1, 211
   agreement
      in Bavarian, 141
      in Frisian, 141
      in Lower Bavarian, 141
      in Schwabian, 141
      in Standard, 141
      in Zurich, 141
   Bavarian, partial null subjects, 53, 139
   expletives in, 19
   Frisian, 139
   Lower Bavarian, 139
   Schwabian, phi-features, 135, 137
   topic drop, 158
   vernaculars, 135
   Zurich, phi-features, 135, 137
Gilligan, Gary, 39, 50
goal, 120

Haitian Creole, expletives, 18
Hale, Ken, 76, 78
Harley, Heidi, 115
Hebrew
   adjunct clauses, 153
   as a partial null subject, 34
   person asymmetries, 109, 132
hierarchy
   phi-feature, 115, 116
   as universal, 227
Holmberg, Anders, 19, 26, 41, 52, 67, 76, 84, 86
Hornstein, Norbert, 5
Huang, James, 32, 164
Hungarian, expletives, 17
hypothesis, strong-continuity, 212

Iatridou, Sabine, 28

Icelandic
   overt expletives, 50
   Subject Criterion, 102
   topic drop, 158
Identification, *see* morphology; pro; subject; threshold
identity, strict, 82
index, referential, 177
infinitives
   child root, in Basque, *see* Basque root-infinitives
   root, 216, 218
      as truncated structure, 216
inflection, *see also* agreement
   rich, as neither necessary nor sufficient for null subjects, 111
   uninterpretable D/π feature for, 177
inversion, *see also* order
   as a basic property of the null subject parameter, 210
   free, 20
      in European Portuguese, *see* European Portuguese, free inversion
   that-trace violations and, *see that*-trace
Irish
   analytic verbal forms, 84
   lack of expletives, 93–94
   null subjects, 3
   pro and coordination, 92
   putative unaccusatives, 83
   salient unaccusatives, 83
   synthetic verbal forms, 84
Italian
   Ancona dialect, 74, 85
   conditional clauses, 182
   Fiorentino, 22
   Identification of null subjects, 126
   Northern dialects, 22, 85
      null subject position, 22–24
   preverbal position of pro, 71
   subjunctive, identification of null subjects, 148, 156
   Trentino, 22
   word order, 74

Jaeggli, Osvaldo, 13, 32
Japanese, *see also* noun phrases
   licensing of pro, 170
   verbal paradigm, 31
Jelinek, Eloise, 76, 78

Kato, Mary, 57
Kayne, Richard, 13
Kenstowicz, Michael, 54

language
  null subject
    consistent, 31, 36
    discourse-related, 32, 36
    have a specifier of AGRSP, 78
  partial null subject, 34, 36
Larson, Richard, 180
Lasnik, Howard, 13, 21
learnability, 135
Leonese, CP-related expletives, *see* expletives
Levy, Yonata, 34
Li, Audrey, 166
Liceras, Juana, 220
Lima, Ananda, 62
limitations, processing, 214
Linares, Carlo, 6, 123
linking, to discourse, 160
locality
  in embedded subjunctive clauses, 162
  mid-range, 160
  in Shipibo, 161
logophoricity, variation in, 62, *see also* person
Lubukusu
  extraction asymmetries, 59, 99
  and the Subject Criterion, 102
Luján, Marta, 180

Manzini, Rita, 67
Marathi, as a partial null subject, 36
MATCH, 120
maximality, morphological, 113
McCloskey, James, 83, 93
Menuzzi, Sergio de Moura, 58, 99
Montalbetti, Mario, 13, 30
Moro, Andrea, 63
morphology
  and identification, *see* identification
  and recoverability of subject reference, 109,
    see also threshold
  in Spanish and Italian, 110
  verbal paradigm, null subjects and, 31

Neeleman, Ad, 168
Nikkane, Urpo, 19, 67
Norwegian, overt expletives, 50
noun phrases, bare, in Japanese and pro, 33

Null Subject Parameter, 8, 32, 105
  agreement, 105
  free inversion, *see also* inversion, free
  long wh-movement, 13
  property cluster of, 13, 40, 106
  resumptive pronouns, *see also* pronouns,
    null resumptive
  that-trace contexts, *see that*-trace filter

order, word, *see* Italian; Portuguese, European;
  Spanish
Ordóñez, Francisco, 78
Oromo, *see* agreement
Ortiz López, Luis, 56
ostention, 176
Övdalian, 135
  agreement, 141
  as a partial null subject language, 53
  phi-features, 137

paradigm, morphologically derived, 32
parameters, 1, 7, *see also* Baker, Mark;
  Borer–Chomsky conjecture; language
  variation
  cascade effect of, 6
  macro, 6, 7, 210
  macro vs. micro, 7
  micro, 7
  unmarked value for, 210
participant
  clitics in speech act, 134
  missing node for, in phi-feature hierarchy,
    134
  speech act, phrase, 134
Pashto, person asymmetries, 109
Pérez Jiménez, Isabel, 151
Perlmutter, David, 13, 22
person, *see also* logophoricity
  1st and 2nd, 155
  asymmetries
    in Finnish, *see* Finnish, person
      asymmetries
    in Hebrew, *see* Hebrew, person
      asymmetries
    in Pashto, *see* Pashto, person asymmetries
    in Shipibo, *see* Shipibo, person
      asymmetries
  morphological underspecification of, 155

person (cont.)
    null subject identification by, in Bengali,
        see Bengali, null subject identification
        by person
    number encoding, 31, 109
    representation of 1st, as a constant function,
        155
phi-feature, *see also* agreement
    arguments against interpretable inflectional,
        82
    strict identity of, under ellipsis, 82
Portuguese
    Brazilian
        extraction asymmetries, 99–102
        and the Subject Criterion, 102
    European
        CP-related expletives, *see* expletives
        free inversion, 57
        topicalized subjects, 203
        word order, 56
poverty of stimulus, 1
Principle
    C, violation of, 181
    Independence, 123
    Projection, 3
    subset, 210
pro, 68, *see also* subjects
    and coordination, 92
        in Irish, *see* Irish, pro and coordination
    and ellipsis, 81, 82
    and identification, 148, 153
    as adjacent to Spec, IP, 74
    as bound by a topic, 149
    as deleted version of an overt pronoun, 68,
        86
    as independent category, 68, 69, 76
    as weak pronoun, 90, 175
    in Shipibo, *see* Shipibo, pro
    licensing and identification of, 68
        in Japanese, *see* Japanese, licensing
        of pro
    position of, 73
    preverbal, 71
        in Italian, *see* Italian, preverbal position
        of pro
    prosodic constraints against conjoinability
        of, 92
    satisfies the EPP, 68
    topic orientation of, 146
    vs. pronominal agreement, 105

probe, 120
    functional, 122
    inflectional, in Bengali, *see* Bengali,
        inflectional probe in
    location of agreeing, in Standard vs.
        vernacular German, 138
    outcomes of, match with goal, 121
processing
    arguments against, explanations in
        acquisition, 221
    constraining existing structural
        representations, 220
    structural truncation, 215
projection, logophoric, 63
pronominal agreement hypothesis, 76,
    see also agreement
    and word order, 85
pronouns
    generic interpretation of overt, 179
    null resumptive, 20
    quantifier binding, 178
    reference to clauses, 28, 29, 188
    stressed, 181
    strong, structure of, 177
    weak, structure of, 177

quantifiers
    floated, 72
    negative, 198
    phrase blocked by an intervening preverbal
        subject, 199
    scope interactions with, 192
Quechua
    acquisition of, as L1, 216–218
    inflectional person, 217, 218
    null subjects, 13
    verbal paradigm, 31

reading
    lack of contrastive for preverbal subject, 206
    shifted
        in Slave and Amharic, 143, 144
        local, 160
register, diary, 213
    in Corsican, *see* Corsican, diary register
    in Franco-Provençal, *see* Franco-Provençal,
        diary register
    in Levantene Arabic, *see* Arabic, Levantene,
        diary register
    restricted to root contexts, 213

richness
  of agreement, *see* agreement, rich
  of inflection, 8, 68
Ritter, Elizabeth, 115
Rizzi, Luigi, 13, 22, 39, 68, 72, 76, 98, 212
Roberts, Ian, 41, 52
Rosenkvist, Henrik, 53

Saab, Andrés, 68, 81, 86, 89
Safir, Ken, 13, 32, 155
Samek-Lodovici, Vieri, 146
Savoia, Leonardo, 67
scale, recoverability, 113
scope
  dative vs. accusative clitic left-dislocated
    phrase, *see* clitic left-dislocated phrase
  indefinite subjects with wide, 193
  interactions, *see* quantifier
  modal, 194
  preverbal subjects with narrow, 192
sentences
  copular, 70
  presentational, 69
    in Italian, 69
    in Spanish, 69
Sheehan, Michelle, 26
Shipibo
  as a partial null subject, 35
  Avoid Pronoun Constraint in, 27
  person asymmetries in, 64, 65
  pro, 171
Shlonsky, Ur, 98, 133, 153
Silva-Villar, Luis, 48
Solà, Jaume, 71
Sorace, Antonella, 224
space, extending the search, 163
Spanish, 9, *see also* acquisition; agreement;
    constraint; expletive; focus; identifica-
    tion; order; person; sentence; stress;
    subject; *that*-trace
  absolute clauses, 151
  acquisition, as L2, 223
  Caribbean
    word order, 56
  Central Colombian
    CP-related expletives, *see* expletives
    Subject Criterion in, 102
  Conditional clauses, 183
  Dominican
    ello as a discourse marker, 44
    expletives, *see* expletives
    expletives, in El Cibao, 43, 44
    null thematic subjects and overt
      expletives, 42
    optional overt subjects, 43
    preverbal subjects, 45
    Subject Criterion, in El Cibao Dominican
      Spanish, 102
    word order, 56
  null subjects in, 13
    identification of, 126
  Porteño, 181
  secondary predicates and gender, 128
  subjunctive
    subject identification, 157
Speas, Margaret, 112
Sportiche, Dominique, 72
Starke, Michal, 91, 175, 177
stress
  nuclear, 71
  subject position in Spanish, 72
structure
  DP, in Chinese vs. Japanese, 169
  Information, 226
subjects
  adverbs and preverbal, 197
  antecedent of preverbal, vs. clitic left-
    dislocated (CLLD) constituents,
    206
  arbitrary or indefinite interpretations of null,
    26, 37
  bare NP as preverbal, 200
  dislocated of A', 190
  expletive, 17, *see also* expletives
  extraction position of, in wh-questions, 24
  generic interpretation of 2nd person, 26
  identification of
    by discourse antecedent, 115
    by morphology, 115
    by rich agreement, 178, *see also* pro
    by topic, 178
    in Italian, *see* Italian, null subject
      identification
    in Spanish, *see* Spanish, null subject
      identification
    in subjunctive in Italian, *see* Italian,
      subjunctive
    in subjunctive in Spanish, *see* Spanish,
      subjunctive

subjects (cont.)
  in Tarifit, see Tarifit, null subject identification
  of pro by a topic as a sufficient condition, 149
  in Cape York Creole, see Cape York Creole, subjects
  in Finnish, see Finnish, subjects
  in French, see French, subjects
  null, 13, see also pro
    acceptability of, in Spanish L2 acquisition, 223
    distribution of, in early acquisition, 215
    generic interpretation of, 26
    in Chamorro, see Chamorro, null subjects
    in child language, 212
    in Irish, see Irish, null subjects
    in Levantine Arabic, see Arabic, null subjects in main clauses
    in Quechua, see Quechua, null subjects
    in Spanish, see Spanish, null subjects
    in subjunctive clauses, 154
    indefiniteness restrictions of, 36
    licensed by topic antecedents, 146
    long-distance antecedents of, 153
    null constants, 216
    person restrictions of, 34, 35, 36
    properties of null, in Brazilian Portuguese, 57
    root infinitives in Basque, see Basque, root infinitives and null subjects
    structure of, 167
    typology of, 86
  overt
    frequency of, 217
    status of, in null subject languages, 174
    vs. expletive, 15, 16
    vs. null subjects in Hebrew and Chinese, 147
    vs. null subjects with generic interpretations, 26, 28
  Phrase, 98
  position, in Northern Italian dialects, see Italian, subject position in Northern dialects
  preverbal
    blocking a quantified phrase, see quantifier
    clitic left-dislocated constituents, see clitic left-dislocated phrase
    clitic left-dislocated constituents and informational status, 203
    in Dominican Spanish, see Dominican Spanish, preverbal subjects
    quantified, and clitic left-dislocated constituents (CLLD), see clitic left-dislocated phrase
    status of, 208
    vs. clitic left-dislocated (CLLD) constituent, see clitic left-dislocated phrase
    vs. postverbal, see agreement, extraction
  scope of, see quantifiers, scope
  thematic vs. expletive, 14, 16
  topicalized, in European Portuguese, see European Portugese, topicalized subjects
  wide focus of topicalized, vs. clitic left-dislocated phrases, 204
subjunctive, identification of null subjects in, see Italian, subjunctive; Spanish, subjunctive
Suñer, Margarita, 25, 192
Svenonius. Peter, 17
Swedish
  overt expletives, 50
  topic drop, 158
switch-reference, 64
Szendroi, Kriszta, 168

Taraldsen, Knut, 13, 39
Tarifit, null subject identification in, 124
that-trace
  asymmetries and null subject languages, 22
  effects
    in Bavarian, 142
    in Brazilian Portuguese, 58
    in Dominican Spanish, 56
    in L2 Spanish, 223
    in Levantine Arabic, 54
    in Lubukusu, 59
    in Övdalian, 54
  filter, 21
  free inversion and, 52
  overt complementizers
    in Bavarian German, 52
    in Dominican Spanish, 51
    in Lubukusu, 52
    in Övdalian, 52
  violations, 41

theta-theory, 69
threshold, minimal morphological (MMT), 112, 114, 226
Tomioka, Satoshi, 33, 36, 86, 89, 117, 168
topic
    aboutness shift, 149
    as a discourse-related property, 191
    continuity, and subjects, 147
    contrastive, 150
    familiar, 150
Toribio, A. Jacqueline, 56
Treviño, Esthela, 78

unaccusatives
    putative, in Irish, *see* Irish, putative unaccusatives
    salient, in Irish, *see* Irish, salient unaccusatives

uniformity, morphological, 32

Vainikka, Anne, 34
VALUATION, 122, *see also* VALUE
    by agreement, 160
    of pro's referential value by a quantifier, 179
    outcomes, 122
    output of, as terminal node sharing, 174
VALUE, 120
variation, 1, *see also* parameters
    in agreement, 5
    in surface movement, 5
    in the Minimalist Program, 5
    in wh-question word order, 2, 5

widest possible, 194

Zubizarreta, María Luisa, 71, 194